The Vega Adventures

SHANE GRANGER

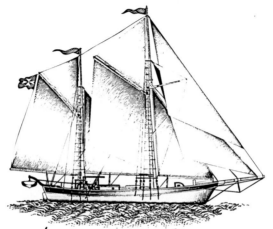

The Vega Adventures

EQUINOX
PUBLISHING
JAKARTA   KUALA LUMPUR

Equinox Publishing (Asia) Pte. Ltd.

www.EquinoxPublishing.com

The Vega Adventures
by Shane Granger

ISBN 978-602-8397-46-9

Contents

Prelude 9

1. The Mother of All Storms...........................12
2. Birth of a Legend 16
3. Battered, not Beaten 27
4. The Master's Touch....................................30
5. Of Tillers and Davey Jones.........................34
6. A Devious Change of Flags 37
7. Sun, Stars, and Hope 43
8. The Fine Art of Naviguessing.......................50
9. Calm Before the Tsunami...........................52
10. The Great Tsunami 55
11. Loading the Beast 59
12. A Mission of Mercy....................................63
13. Into the Jaws of Hell 67
14. Of Standing Waves and Whirl Pools...........71
15. The Art of Making a Difference..................75
16. Life on the Bounding Main 77
17. Jakarta 81
18. Rough, Wet, and Wild...............................84
19. Her First Day on the Job 87
20. Befriending Paradise..................................92
21. Who Wants an Adventure 96
22. Welcome to Medang...................................98
23. A Miracle for Mitha................................102
24. Hot Air, Nails, and Noise.........................104
25. A Great Day for Sailing............................108
26. An Arrow Through Time 111
27. The Finger of Fate....................................116
28. A Cargo of Hope......................................119
29. A Trail of Tears..123
30. Another Island, Another World 127
31. A Star to Steer By.....................................131
32. With a Razor Blade and a Prayer..............133
33. The Wind of Change................................136
34. Welcome to Paradise.................................142
35. The Wonders of Coffee.............................146
36. The Sighting of Komba 151
37. Why Dolphins Are so Playful 156
38. A Successful Failure...................................160
39. A Change of Heart....................................162

40. A Stroll Through the Jungle 164
41. Transforming a Dream 169
42. Treasure in a Backpack 171
43. The Great Fuel Drama.. 175
44. Of Charts and Counter Jumpers............................ 178
45. Goat tracks and Leaky Roofs 181
46. Noodles for Fuel 188
47. The Doctor Dances a Jig 191
48. A Rocky Row Home 194
49. Back to the Mountains 198
50. On the Sea Again 204
51. The Castaways 208
52. The Island of Teun 213
53. The Castaways Tale 219
54. Nila's Great Sewing Machine Drama.................... 225
55. Without a Paddle 230
56. The Original Spice Islands.................................... 233
57. The Heart of History 236
58. Pirates, Patrons, and Thieves................................ 240
59. What is it Like Out There 243
60. Thousands of Miles From Home 246
61. Lost but not Forgotten 250
62. The Hatta Break 264
63. The Mystery of the Missing Forts......................... 266
64. Old Stones and Older Boats 268
65. The Lost Forts of Gunung Api 271
66. Of Broken Bottles and a Sunken Ship.................. 277
67. Meggi Discovers a Treasure.................................. 280
68. Goodwill for All... 284
69. Good bye Banda 286
70. That Magic Hour 289
71. A Promise Made Good 292
72. The Skipper Gets Worried 297
73. The Cat and the Milk Sea...................................... 300
74. Pilot Whales and Sunsets...................................... 303

Epilogue 305

Preview: *The Windsong Adventures*.............................. 309

About the Author 316

To Meggi who kept it all together and working,
while I disappeared into a world of words.
To Palgunadi T. Setyawan
one of the finest gentlemen I have ever met.
And to Mark who inspired me to reach "the end".

Prelude

It would be easy enough for me to blame it all on "The Book". It was an innocent little book. There was not a sinister image in it, unless you consider the page with the shark on it. In all honesty, even that fishy mouth full of teeth still managed to grin at you in a friendly sort of way. Auntie gave me that book for Christmas when I was seven years old, and it changed my life forever.

Without "The Book", I might have become a doctor, an architect, or maybe even a used car salesman. With my musical aptitude, I could have found my place playing piano in a house of negotiable repute, or become a politician, or even a tent preacher. Mind you, I cannot see a whole lot of difference between the last two other than the product. In fact, if you ask me playing piano for hard working girls, boys, sheep, and chickens during their idle hours would have been more reputable.

The book that changed my life was filled with images of old sailing ships. You know, those romantic pictures of old ships reaching across golden seas with the sailors all dancing a hornpipe, or scanning the horizon in search of a new adventure. From the first page I was captivated, hopelessly enthralled, by a world long past and a fantasy that eventually became who I am today.

Long into the night, I huddled under my blankets, clandestine lamp in hand, carefully studying those pictures until I knew the minutest detail each image had to offer. I even gave those old sailors names and ranks. The shark, by the way, I named after Mrs. Clark, a schoolteacher I had at the time.

You know the type, severe little glasses perched on one of those long noses a hawk would be proud of, with her hair pulled up in a bun so tight her eyes looked oriental. I can still see her standing by the blackboard, dressed like an undertaker's wife come to haunt the front of our classroom. She would stand there, lips pursed so tightly you could have used them for a ruler, arms crossed, foot tapping the drum roll of doom, and give me a look from over those glasses so old fashioned a Neanderthal's grandmother would have been proud of it. It was enough to freeze the blood of an Eskimo.

To my young mind, if that woman fell in the water with the shark it would be even odds which one would take the first bite. More than likely, they would have circled each other a few times, before going their own way – a sort of professional courtesy between evil-minded equals.

By the time I reached eleven or twelve, I could draw a full clipper ship in all her glory with every rigging detail exactly and precisely rendered. I knew the names of every piece of rigging, and could bore my friends for hours with trivia about sailing ships. While other kids dreamed of being football heroes, I dreamed of commanding a sailing ship off to the ends of the world in search of adventure. The televised adventures of Capt. Irving Johnson, Thor Heyerdahl, and others of that ilk only served to heighten my resolve.

The fact is, we all dream of a romantic escape from the hectic rat race of today's highly accelerated world. A retreat into the leisurely ways of those glorious days long ago sacrificed to the twin gods of efficiency and profit. Back to a time when elegant travel was an art form in its self, a time of discovery, adventure, exotic island destinations, and of course romance. The romance of bark-tanned sails and wooden ships reaching out to far horizons in search of the mysterious unknown and the great contrast of cultures that made travel so stimulating.

Red sails in the sunset, set flying from the tall masts of a traditional ship, never fail to invoke those magical memories still echoing down through the ages – all that remains from the great golden age of sail. Vivid images of freely roaming the world and a carefree lifestyle inspired my fantasies, even as a youngster. Not so much from the military aspect, mind you. My admiration was strictly reserved for small and medium sized cargo boats and the amazing voyages they made with their modest crews of hardy sailors, the winds of fate providing their only source of power.

There was a time when boats like *Vega*, one of the heroes in this story, could be found trading for cargo in almost every port. After all, at one time Norway had the largest fleet of merchant sailing vessels in the world. North America, the Caribbean, and Africa, were common voyages for those hardy sailors of iron who crewed their sturdy ships of wood. Some of Norway's small trading boats even sailed around Cape Horn where they loaded cargos of nitrate-rich *guano* in Chile. Others may have ventured as far as India and Indonesia.

I can easily imagine when faced with the choice between another freezing cold Scandinavian winter, cooped up with some badgering Valkyrie and a brood of screaming urchins, or a long profitable trading voyage, most of it in the tropics, those old sailors didn't have to think very long, or even very hard, before making their choice.

Of course, every sailor worth his salt knew that friendly girls populated those lush tropical islands, congenial raven-haired beauties whose total wardrobe consisted of a grass skirt and a complete ignorance of knickers. That common knowledge may have had some slight influence on their ultimate decision to cast off the lines. Those old boys may have been mostly illiterate, but they were far from stupid. To this day, I am convinced it was a Norwegian sailor, on a long voyage to the tropics, who invented the first fully automated grass-trimming device.

Vega was carefully designed and built for some of the worst sailing conditions in the world. Therefore, for those old sailors rounding Cape Horn or Cape of Good Hope in a weatherly boat like *Vega* would not have been as drastic an endeavor as it seems today. Having done tens of thousands of miles on the old girl I can assure you that properly maintained she would have had little problem with the average trade routes of the day.

Chapter 1

The Mother of All Storms

Ripping through an ominous sky blacker than the inside of the devil's back pocket, a searing billion volts of lightning illuminated ragged clouds scudding along not much higher than the ship's mast. An explosive crash of thunder, so close it was painful, set my ears to ringing. Through half-closed eyes, burning from the constant onslaught of wind-driven salt water, I struggled to maintain our heading on the ancient dimly lit compass.

This was not your common garden-variety storm. The kind that blows a little, rains a lot, and then slinks off to do whatever storms do in their off hours. This was a sailor's worst nightmare: a full-blown rip roaring Indian Ocean cyclone fully intent on claiming our small wooden vessel and its occupants as sacrifices.

All that stood between us and the depths of eternity were the skill of *Vega*'s long-departed Norwegian builders and the flagging abilities of one exhausted man.

After seven straight hours of fighting that hell-spawned storm, I was cold, wet, and completely exhausted.

Using both hands, I turned the wheel to meet the next onslaught from a world where chaos and madness ruled. Should I miscalculate, or suffer a single moment of lost concentration, within seconds the boat might whip broadside to those enormous thundering waves. The next breaking wave would overwhelm her in a catastrophic avalanche of white foam, rolling her repeatedly like a rubber ducky trapped in someone's washing machine, shattering her stout timbers, violently dooming us all to a watery grave.

The rigging howled like a band of banshees chasing the souls of a thousand tormented sailors. Souls long ago lost in the sheer brutality of winds like these.

It was almost impossible to breathe the air that was filled with torrential rain and seawater blown from the tops of passing waves.

The raging wind seemed fully intent on ripping the air from my lungs. Fighting for every gasping water logged breath, no matter which way I turned my head there was flying water. Only 20 meters away, the bow of our 120-year-old vessel was completely lost in a swirling mass of wind, rain, and wildly foaming sea.

With monotonous regularity, precipitous walls of tortured water loomed out of the darkness rushing toward the unprotected stern of the *Vega*. Yet as a seemingly vertical wall of water raced toward her, its top curling over in a seething welter of foam, our brave vessel would lift her stern allowing another raging monster to pass harmlessly beneath her keel.

With each wave, the long anchor warps trailing in a loop from our stern screamed against the mooring bits as they took the full strain. Fighting desperately those thick ropes were all we had to reduce *Vega's* mad rush into the next valley of tormented water. Their paltry resistance was all that stood between us and 42 tons of boat surfing madly out of control down the near-vertical waves.

As the boat fought valiantly, lifting her stern to meet each successive wave, she would dig in her forefoot; a motion that unchecked might quickly swing her broadside to the violent seas. Should that happen, the end would be quick and brutal. Once turned broadside, the next breaking wave would roll the boat 360 degrees, an action that would repeat until nothing remained afloat.

With helm and wind creating a precarious balance, our future was at the mercy of one small scrap of storm canvas. Without that sail to provide forward thrust, the boat would quickly become impossible to steer. It can be rather nerve-racking when your entire future depends upon a single scrap of cloth stretched as taut as a plate of steel, its heavy sheet straining rigid as an iron bar against the brutal forces of an Indian Ocean Cyclone.

While out on deck all hell was breaking loose, down below the off watch were all squirreled away in their bunks warm and more or less dry. To avoid being hurled from their bunks, each of the crew was tightly wedged between the hull and the weatherboards. Little did they realize that at least once every 8-10 seconds I was fighting another giant wave intent on our destruction. Squinting and blinking, I tried to read the wind speed gauge, but the numbers were only a blur.

Glancing astern, I could dimly make out one wave much larger than the rest. It reared out of the darkness like some harbinger of doom, its curling vertical face rushing towards us like an unstoppable watery cliff, growing in height and apparent malice as it came.

It was then I noticed a second rogue wave rushing out of the night. A wave that sent shivers racing up and down my spine. Nothing in my years at sea had prepared me for a giant whitecap raging across that storm-ravaged sea at 90 degrees to the prevailing waves.

Frozen in horror, I watched that watery monster rip its way toward where I sat. As it collided with the first giant wave, roaring along its length like a head on collision between two out of control avalanches determined to destroy all in their path, the interaction was explosive. Towering eruptions of white water rocketed skyward; the unbridled violence was beyond imagination.

Converging from completely different directions, those twin monsters were like a manifest curse from the darkest depths of a nightmare. Water tortured beyond endurance exploded upwards, as the sea forced even higher in a frenzy of tormented white water, loomed over our frail wooden boat. Clearly, those two waves would arrive at the same time, the one slamming into us like a huge bloody-minded mallet, while the other played the part of a watery anvil, and not a damned thing in the world I could do about it.

For a split second that seemed like eternity, a gut wrenching fear paralyzed me. No matter which way I turned, one of those monsters would slam directly into the side of our boat rolling her onto her beam-ends and certain destruction. It all happened so fast there was no time to take action.

There was just enough time for me to take a deep breath, before the combined explosive power of those tormented seas erupted from every direction, transforming my world into a swirling white maelstrom of destruction. My hands were numb, trembling from cold and fatigue as I gripped the wheel in desperation. Struggling against impossible forces, I fought to escape being swept overboard.

Something swirling in the water struck me a fierce blow to the head. Slammed hard against the wheel, I felt a sharp stab of pain in my ribs. As I began to lose consciousness, my only thought was, *so this is the end.* I gripped the wheel as hard as I could, attempting to turn it against the sideways slide I could feel building. Then my world turned black.

Chapter 2
Birth of a Legend

With a whip-like crack, a shower of sparks exploded from a log as it collapsed into the heart of the fire. A fire that crackled invitingly in the ancient stone fireplace, casting its warm glow across the faces of two men comfortably sipping on small glasses of fiery Norwegian aquavit. The year was 1890.

There was a companionable silence between them, broken only by the stately ticking of a grandfather clock standing in the hallway and the crackling of the fire. A cat sleeping beside the fireplace stirred long enough to arch its back in a languorous stretch before resuming its former position as a snug ball of gently purring fur. Somewhere a floorboard creaked. Although separated by their difference in age the two men were old friends who respected each other professionally and liked each other on a personal level.

Oil lamps illuminated the comfortable room where they sat. The Nerhus family farmhouse was ancient, constructed over many generations from native stone and aromatic Norwegian pine. Over the years, that wood had aged to a deep golden brown luster.

Captain Nils Vagan, a native of Herøysund, was a big man with the broad shoulders of a professional seaman. His muscular body tapered to a narrow waist. A strong nose, twice broken in sailing accidents, was set in a wide face weathered by the harsh conditions of his profession. He wore his dark brown hair long, as was the fashion of the day. That night he had it tightly clasped behind his head in a ponytail tied back with a piece of lightly tanned leather.

What most people noticed first about the captain were his razor sharp dark brown eyes. When he was irritated, something that happened rarely, those diamond hard orbs seemed to bore mercilessly into the object of his anger. Most of the time, they gave the impression of focusing somewhere just over the nearest horizon.

His full mouth always seemed to curl slightly at the corners, as if inwardly smiling at some private joke. His powerful voice befitted a man accustomed to making himself heard above the howling winds and raging seas of a North Sea gale. That night, in the warmth of such a cozy room, he wore an expression of comfortable contentment.

A true man of the sea, at 27 years of age Vagan was already one of the most sought after and highly respected sailing captains on Hardanger fiord. Tracing his linage directly back to fearsome Viking raiders who originated along Norway's bitter west coast, had he been born in an earlier age Captain Nils Vagan would have made a fearsome seagoing adversary and a master pirate.

Born in 1840, Ola H. Nerhus was a completely different sort of man. Here was a man with a quick highly observant mind who designed and built sailing ships. His hands were large and callused, his reputation for creating strong swift sailing cargo ships unrivaled.

Age had brought a slight squint to the eyes of Ola Nerhus; eyes that arched down ever so slightly as they branched out into a modest collection of crow's feet. His nose was somewhat wider than normal. It suggested a distant Asiatic ancestry; a trait enhanced by his short stocky stature. One could easily imagine hordes of men like Nerhus pouring out of Mongolia, raging across the great steeps of Asia on their sturdy little ponies, hell bent on conquest and adventure.

As was his style, Ola Nerhus wore a neatly trimmed mustache above the expressive curve of his lip. A slight dimple creased his strong chin. He had not shaved for several days. This gave his normally agreeable countenance a somewhat sinister appearance.

His once intense sapphire blue eyes had grown lighter over the years, but could still flash lightning bolts of displeasure at any worker who dared give less than his very best in the building of those fast sailing little cargo ships he was famous for designing and building.

To quote Ola's great grandson, himself a boat builder:

> By 1891 Ola Nerhus had an unrivaled reputation for strong well-formed ships, and high quality workmanship. His designs were so successful that he became a demanded shipbuilder and was the responsible model builder (the naval architect of the day) and surveyor for many of the most prominent 'yard locations' in this region of Norway.

> In 1876 Ola had seven vessels under construction: three at his Nerhuson yard in Ølve, one at Onarheim in Tysnes, one at Malkenes, one in Strandebarm Kvam, and one in Varaldsøy. From historic documents, we find "There is reason to believe that most of the famous Hardanger jachts sailed by the men of Tysnes were designed and built by Ola H. Nerhus". This is a pretty impressive statement, considering Tysnes had quite a large fleet at that time.

Raising from his comfortable leather armchair, Captain Vagan moved over to a window. With one hand, he pushed aside the thick curtain that helped keep the fire's heat in and the intense Nordic cold out. His other hand came to rest on the polished wooden window frame. The scene that met his eyes was a glistening world of snow and ice. Even the great fiords restless water stood frozen for as far as the eye could see.

Through the window, he could hear the relentless Artic wind as it roared around the stout stone and wood farmhouse. As he gazed into the dim whiteness beyond the glass he mentally reviewed his mission and how best to accomplish it. Ola Nerhus was a busy man, with quite a few ships already under construction. Convincing him to take on another project might not be an easy task.

Turning away from the window, he allowed the curtain to fall back into position. Taking a deep breath, he resumed his place by the fire. Both men knew that Captain Vagan's visit was more than just a casual social call. What they could not know was that over 100 years later, decisions taken on that winter night in Norway would directly affect the lives of over 250,000 people living half a world away in the tropics of South East Asia.

Taking a small sip from his glass of aquavit, Captain Vagan slowly began to explain the motive for his visit. Over the next few minutes, Ola Nerhus listened closely. In his mind, an image began to form. Various well-known shapes merged then diverged only to merge once again into something entirely different.

By the time Captain Vagan finished his proposal, Ola Nerhus knew he could not pass over this strange request, the way he did so many others that simply did not interest or challenge him.

A small cough broke the spell, reminding both men that Ola's oldest son, Jens Nerhus, was sitting quietly at the room's large wooden table reading from a book he had found in the village. Having heard the entire presentation, Jens was not to know the deep and lasting impact this meeting would have on his own life.

Ola rose from his chair and refilled both of their glasses. Returning to his seat the two men soon immersed themselves in the details of this new and exciting project. When Captain Vagan finally left for his own home it was early morning, but deep inside he felt the warm glow of a mission well accomplished. The result of that night's work would be nothing short of revolutionary.

* * *

Several months before that auspicious meeting between Captain Nils Vagan and Ola Nerhus, Mr. Johan Carlsson, the successful owner of a cement factory in Degerhamn, Sweden waddled into his study. He wore only a bathrobe and his well-worn rabbit fur slippers. It was clearly a man's room. The centerpiece was a massive wooden desk made from the deck planks of a trading ship cast ashore during his great grand fathers' time. The remains of that ship were still visible, on the coast close to where Mr. Carlsson's new cement factory now stood.

A portly man whose nose was tainted red from many a cheerful tankard, he dearly loved his food and drink. That night, unable to sleep, Mr. Carlsson was not exactly the spitting image of a successful merchant as he lit the whale oil lamp on his desk and settled back into his leather-covered chair.

Replacing the lamp's glass chimney, he leaned on his desk supporting his head in one-hand. Fingers splayed across his forehead accentuated the fact he was slowly going bald. His other hand carefully adjusted the lamp wick until it stopped smoking. Only then did he reach into the top right hand drawer of his desk for the bottle of light brown liquid he knew from long experience was safely ensconced there. On the corner of his desk, a small crystal glass stood covered with a hand embroidered linen napkin.

Johan Carlsson had a problem, one that was starting to effect his profits. His new state-of-the-art cement factory was producing more, and better quality, cement than the old factory had. Of course, that was exactly why he had built the new factory in the first place, but it was also the root of his problem.

Although he currently owned several sturdy little sailing cargo boats his factory was making cement, and his agents were selling it faster than he could deliver. He was even starting to get orders from far away England and more surprisingly Imperial Germany. Business was looking up, if he could only find a way to make his deliveries.

Most of his new clients were located in the small harbor towns and villages spread along Sweden's long convoluted coast. Many of those ports were closed to his larger cargo boats due to their shallow water and their small or non-existent pier facilities. The stopgap solution of chartering boats to make those deliveries was currently cutting deeply into his profits. After all, cement is something sold in tons on tight margins.

Pouring a glass of his special Scotch whisky, smuggled on his own boats from England, he took a leisurely sip while staring distractedly off into space. As much as he hated the idea (Johan Carlsson dearly hated spending money on things other than himself and his family), he needed a new boat to deliver his cement. The question was where to build the best boat at the lowest cost.

As Carlsson sat deeply immersed in thought you could have waved a hand in front of his face. He would not have noticed. Myriad facts were racing through his mind, as he rapidly made and discarded calculations then reviewed the various options at his disposal. As his thoughts became more complex, he unconsciously twirled the almost empty glass between his hands. Quite well informed, for his day, Johan Carlsson may have been fat and flabby, but he was far from being stupid.

This happened at a time when Sweden and Norway united, to form "The Union", a time when many Swedish owners were building ships in Norway where labor was cheaper. Therefore, after exhausting all other possibilities, it seemed only natural that Mr. Carlsson should look to the famous, and more economical, ship builders of Norway for his newest *jacht. Jacht*, or *jagkt*, are generic Scandinavian names for small sailing cargo boats, and the original source of the word *yacht*.

Taking a sheet of paper from his desk drawer, he carefully positioned it then picked up an elegant silver pen, dipped it in ink, and began to write out instructions for his agent in Norway. He also sent a short note to an old Swedish friend and associate in Oslo asking for his advice. With the decision taken, and his letters written, he drained his glass, snuffed out the lamp, then shuffled back up the stairs to his bedroom. Soon, happily dreaming of massive profits and huge meals, his deep snores, the reason his wife insisted on her own bedroom, were rattling the windowpanes.

Within a few short weeks, Carlsson had answers from both of his correspondents. For once, his sources agreed completely with each other. Outstanding among Norwegian *jachts* of the time were those designed and built on Hardanger fiord. A place where the tradition of building strong swift sailing cargo boats was already well established since the late 1400s. At the time Carlsson needed his new boat, the finest Hardanger *jachts* were designed and built by Ola H. Nerhus in his Nerhuson boat yard at Ølve.

Carlsson's Oslo associate went so far as to suggest that a certain Captain Nils Vagan, as a man of impeccable reputation, act as Carlsson's representative on the project. In late autumn of 1890, Carlsson contacted Captain Nils Vagan of Herøysund to act as his intermediary, with special instructions stating Ola Nerhus should design and build the vessel to the highest specifications.

Carlsson wanted the new vessel designed specifically for heavy concentrated weights, such as cement, bricks, building stone, and even pig iron – cargos most wooden vessels avoided like the plague in the North Sea. He also specified certification for trade in the Artic, a classification few wooden boats of the day rated. In a burst of fatherly pride, he decided to name his latest boat *Vega*, after his youngest daughter.

As autumn advanced into another freezing cold Nordic winter, Carlsson impatiently anticipated word from Captain Vagan. It was not until late November that a letter arrived from Norway. His hands shaking with excitement, Carlsson slit open the envelope with a solid silver letter opener. Unfolding the single sheet, he spread it out on his desk and began to read.

Almost at once, he found the news he had been anxiously awaiting for the past several months. Ola Nerhus had agreed to take on the project to design and build the boat, although he stipulated white oak, a wood not normally used in Norwegian boat building, for the keel and frames. That white oak wood was not available in Norway. Ship building grade oak, for use as frames and keel, would need to be carefully selected locally, then shipped from Sweden to Hardanger Fiord by sea.

Although he could understand the logic behind this stipulation, procuring and transporting the wood was going to be a costly exercise. On the other hand, what was a son-in-law good for, if not to help in times of need? With a curt nod of his head, he grudgingly agreed.

Shaking his head at the additional cost, Johann did what ship owners throughout the ages have done when faced with similar circumstances: he pulled open the drawer to his desk and retrieved his bottle of fine Scotch. Perhaps a drink would take some of the sting out of the extra cost. At least he could use one of his own ships to transport the wood.

* * *

At the same moment Johann Carlsson was pouring himself a double tot of Scotch, Ola Nerhus felt as if not even a stiff drink would solve his problems. Tucked away in a corner of his boatyard's main building shed was his private workbench, well stocked with the precision wood working tools he employed to make half models.

Many of those tools he had made himself over the years. Each of them was like an old cherished friend. A rare sliver of golden sunlight filtered down through dancing dust motes onto the workbench. It came from a skylight he himself had installed 35 years before. In his work hardened, yet highly sensitive, hands he held the freshly carved model of a ship's hull. That model was about 50 centimeters long and only 10 or so centimeters wide.

Ola Nerhus worked in the old traditional manner by first making a half model as a miniature version of what the real ship's body would look like. Once approved by the owner, he would cut the model into slices perpendicular to the centerline. Those sections were then reproduced full size on the lofting floor. There the ship's frames would be laid out and formed before being transported, using a small hand operated overhead crane, to where the keel awaited them. The true art of ship design was in the making of perfect half models, an art at which Ola Nerhus was considered a grand master.

Slowly rotating the latest model he carefully studied each compound curve of its graceful underwater body, first from the stern, then from the bow. His practiced eye picked out tiny faults in the lines, but nothing a scraper or fine wood rasp could not redress. From long years of experience, he was imagining that model as a full size ship. A ship tortured by some merciless North Sea storm, while fully loaded. What he saw was a lovely design, one that would sail admirably, yet it still did not please him.

This boat was destined to carry heavy concentrated weight, a wooden boat builder's nightmare. With all of her load right in the center, if the boat hung between two waves it might literally break in half, sinking without a trace in only seconds. Ola Nerhus was an intuitive boat designer, backed up by the wisdom he had earned so long ago during his years as an apprentice in Hardanger's finest boat yards. His empathy with the sea made him a good designer, one whose boats were famous for being fast and safe.

With a tiny shake of his head, Ola slowly got to his feet brushing aside a loose strand of hair that had fallen across his face. With a sigh, he carried the latest model a few meters to the end of his workbench. There he gently placed it alongside a growing mountain of similar models. Giving it a gentle pat, he turned to retrieve another piece of wood from his special store.

With no further sign of emotion, he made his way back to a well-worn wooden stool. What he needed was a different approach from the standard Hardanger *jacht* with her fine entry and smooth exit runs. The problem he faced was not one of size it was one of carrying capacity. Shifting his position on the stool, he ran a hand over his chin. The rasping sound of a two-day beard greeted the gesture. How to make a little 60-foot boat carry 55 tons of concentrated cargo and still be safe at sea in the worst of storms?

Placing his new piece of wood off to one side, he meticulously cleaned up his workbench. Then he carefully put away his tools. Ola was so deeply engrossed in the problem of this new design he hardly noticed pushing his stool into its place under the workbench or taking his trademark black hat from its peg on the wall. Perhaps a walk along the shore would help.

He did some of his best problem solving while walking.

If you had ask Ola Nerhus, one of the finest small cargo boat designers alive, he would have been the first to admit that this project had him baffled and intrigued.

Vega's intended cargo demanded a strong full-bodied vessel with a high displacement to length / beam ratio. Due to tax and harbor pilot regulations, she needed to be a bit short of 60 feet between perpendiculars. Mr. Carlsson was quite insistent his new boat be rated at 55 tones. This capacity was meant to satisfy the demands of his cement, brick, and building stone trade. Additional regulations meant the boat be rigged as a traditional cutter. Although an effective rig, the cutter rig demanded a much larger crew than the well-proven two masted galleass, with its greater sail area and smaller crew.

With all of these disparate elements, spinning around in his head Ola let himself out through a small wooden door set into the northern side of his boat building shed. As he opened it, the old bronze hinges on that sturdy wooden door gave out their usual mournful squeak. For the thousandth time, he swore he would give them a squirt of oil as soon as he returned from his walk.

Stepping into the bright sunlight, he pulled his hat a little lower to better shade his eyes. Threading his way across the busy boat yard, Ola followed a well-worn path that led to the shore. He paused only to answer a question from one of his workers.

Ola had not gone far before a small raft of wild ducks swimming in the clear water of the fiord shortly distracted him. Their bright plumage glistened in the afternoon sunlight as they went about the serious business of feeding themselves. Ola stopped to watch how effortlessly they moved through the water, their wide breasts precisely supporting and balancing the weight of their long necks.

Perhaps it was something in the clear clean air of Hardanger Fiord, or perhaps it was the constant onslaught of a powerful master artisan's mind on the problem, but suddenly Ola had a flash of inspiration. Turning on his heels, he raced back toward the building shed waving his trademark black hat in his hand as he went.

Workers in the boat yard stopped what they were doing to watch in amazement as he rushed bye. The master never ran anywhere, nor could even the longest serving carpenter remember ever seeing him do so.

Back at his workbench, he took up the piece of wood selected for his next model. In a flurry of creative energy and began to carve. This new model would be radically different from the average Hardanger *jacht*. In a frenzy of intense concentration, the skilled hands and keen eye of master boat builder Ola Nerhus translated his newly inspired vision into a wooden hull model – one that was destined to win him an award for design innovations at the great Oslo exhibition of 1898.

Faced with the age-old conundrum of how to make a small boat carry the same amount of cargo as a much larger one, Ola Nerhus did a splendid job of designing *Vega*.

To gain more weight carrying capacity he would employ an old fashion buff bow combined with a stern much wider than his traditional heart shaped Hardanger *jacht* designs. In fact, *Vega's* stern seems to have been copied directly from the famous Danish "Marstall Jachts", then slightly modified into a wider version of the heart shaped stern that was a Nerhus trademark.

As the latest model took shape, a full deep body with a graceful tumblehome and sweeping compound curve along her sheer line began to emerge.

Three hours later Ola held in his hands the master model for a new type of small cargo boat. Carefully placing it on his workbench and covering it with a piece of cloth he blew out the oil lamp and made his way toward the building shed door. Once again, it squealed as he opened it, but this time he was too engrossed in his thoughts to even notice. Now that he had the hull shape, he could concentrate on how to build that hull strong enough to do the job properly.

As he walked along the well-worn path between the boat yard and his family's farmhouse, mentally Ola began to assemble the elements that would become *Vega*. His concept of a strong boat built for heavy concentrated loads and service in the Arctic was perhaps a bit different from what the Swedish considered sufficient at the time. Then again, the seas around Norway are some of the most vicious in the world.

Vega's all white oak frames would be more reminiscent of a naval man of war from the early 1800s than a merchant ship. Those frame sets would consist of between four and six grown oak frames tightly trunneled and bolted together with only enough room between each set for ventilation. Nowhere on *Vega* would there be more than 30 cm (12") between a frame set and that would be at the bow and stern. To insure rigidly and strength *Vega* would have a double hull with inter-liners even thicker than her 3" outer planking. The result would not be the fastest sailing boat he ever built, but without any doubt, it would be the strongest.

Pushing open the door to his family home, Ola Nerhus radiated his sense of achievement. That night he would enjoy a peaceful undisturbed sleep for the first time in weeks. In the morning, he would send a message to his friend Nils Vagan to come and examine the new half model.

Chapter 3
Battered, not Beaten

I have woken up in some of the strangest places in my life, everywhere from the boudoir of a countess to a small town jail in Louisiana. Mind you, I have also been awakened in some interesting ways, like the time I came round to find a lovely damsel dressed in only a feather boa sitting astride me going at it like a winning jockey in the final stretch. Although, none of them compare to being slammed back into consciousness by a few tons of cold seawater while lying totally stunned in the scuppers of a half foundered sailing ship. Give me my choice and I will happily take the feather boa clad nymph any day. Right little stunner she was, amazingly well versed in the equestrian arts.

Battling up from the depths of unconsciousness is a bit like rebooting a computer; everything starts over again from the here and now, not from there and then. With my senses slowly coming back on line, I had no idea where I was, or even who I was, as awareness clawed itself up from the blackness of oblivion into the raging violence of the presence. The boat rolled hard to port. From out of nowhere, another wave cascaded over the rail brutally slamming me back down onto the deck like a giant watery fist. Like some half-drowned animal, I fought my way through what seemed like a thick vortex of impenetrable black sludge back into reality.

Struggling onto my hands and knees, grasping a pin rail for support, I shook my head, desperately trying to clear away the fog of semi-coherence. Before I could, another wave flooded over the rail like an avalanche smashing me violently into the deck. Helpless to resist its overwhelming power, the torrent spun me around, washing me back into the lee scuppers.

Then in a sudden rush of sensations, it all came hurtling back to me. I was at sea in a vicious storm battling for my life and the lives of my shipmates. Shaking my head in an effort to clear my thoughts I pulled myself up on all fours. Scurrying like some bizarre crab-like creature, I clawed my way back to the wheel, coughing up seawater and struggling to breathe in that waterlogged atmosphere of savage wind-driven rage.

An intense pain shot through me like a bolt of lightning. A sharp stabbing agony from cracked ribs caused me to cry out as I pulled myself upright. I hung there clutching the wheel for support. Desperately I tried to blink the salty water from my eyes.

Squinting through salt-encrusted eyes that must have been redder than the devil's business card, I could just make out the compass and our present heading. Through the fog of my daze, I realized the heading was only a few degrees off our safest course.

Taking a firm grip on the wheel I turned it three spokes to port. The wheel's resistance to my effort felt strangely light. As I waited for the ship to respond the compass remained obstinately fixed on the same heading. When another two spokes to port also brought no result, I began to worry.

Just then, Meggi, who had been safely ensconced in our aft cabin bunk, stuck her head out of the aft hatch and screaming to be heard over the raging wind told me of an ungodly great rending crack that had come from where the steering ram is located just behind our aft cabin bunk.

Leaving the helm to Meggi I made my way into our aft cabin and opened the locker where the steering ram and rudder arm are located. Salt water and blood from a deep cut on my forehead dripped onto the cabin sole as I lifted the steering box cover. What I found inside was enough to freeze my blood with Icy despair. It was a sight straight from a nightmare. Our hydraulic steering ram shaft, made from one solid inch in diameter of high tensile machine steel, had shattered like a cheap plastic toy in the hands of an enraged mountain gorilla. The tiller arm was freely thrashing back and forth in the savage seas.

Vega was completely out of control. The only thing holding her in front of the waves was the drag generated by those long mooring ropes tightly attached to the stern bits in great loops and the thrust of the small storm jib set so far forward. I had few problems visualizing the probabilities presented by this new nightmare.

Without steering, there was nothing to stop *Vega* from broaching sideways across the waves and being rolled mercilessly into oblivion. The screaming of tortured wood coming from over my head where I knew the aft mooring cleats were located did nothing to relieve my worries. Should one of those cleats give way…well that was a thought simply not worth thinking about.

It was then that the real horror of our situation dawned on me, the rudder was not only swinging from port to starboard, fully at the mercy of the seas, it was also rocking from side to side, a horrifying indication that at least one of the rudder pintals had broken.

If you are not up to date on ship design, rudder pintals are like hinges that attach the rudder to the ship and allow it to rotate when the wheel is turned. *Vega* has two on her rudder and a stout bearing under the rudderstock. Should both the pintals break there would be nothing to stop our violently gyrating rudder from detaching itself from the boat and disappearing into the depths below us.

Just then, a sopping wet Meggi came down the aft hatch, followed by a great splash of seawater, telling me that the boat would not steer. The look of near panic on her face suddenly changed when she saw me full on in the light of the aft cabin.

I must have looked like a macabre escapee from the haunted house of horrors. I was soaking wet and had not shaved in days. Blood was trickling from my nose and a nasty cut over my forehead. My squinting eyes were a deep tortured red. My skin was shriveled like a prune from hours of emersion in salt water. There was a look of pure horror etched on my face. At that moment, I was feeling truly helpless, in the middle of a raging Indian Ocean Cyclone, on a sailing ship with no rudder.

Chapter 4

The Master's Touch

Soft golden light from a flaming Norwegian sunset exploded across the sky as master boat builder Ola Nerhus walked around the new ship hull that was slowly taking form. His keen eye perceived every detail. Like the skeleton of a beached whale, the half-finished boat stood proudly on her building cradle. All that was missing now were her hull planking and thick pitch pine decks. It was late October, already he could see the days getting shorter. Reaching out he ran a large calloused hand along the curve of a cant frame. Finding it smooth and well turned; he nodded to himself with approval.

His highly-trained artisans, and their apprentices, had worked wonders over the past few months skillfully shaping and fitting the many disparate elements that went into creating this lovely frame. The long days of a Nordic summer, often provided them with over eighteen hours of daylight for their work. It was hard work and the hours were grueling, but he knew that soon the cold hard Norwegian winter would return and the men would then have several months to relax by the fireside, enjoying the well-earned fruit of their labor.

Far from being the largest, or the fastest, boat he had ever designed and built, somehow this chubby cheeked little boat had found its way into his heart. So many things about her differed from the usual boats he built. Even her smell, a tangy tartness typical of oak rather than the rich resin-scented aroma of the local Norwegian pitch pine he had always employed was different.

* * *

Several months before, the long Norwegian winter had at last given way to the spring of 1891. Flowers bloomed, the fiords thawed. Slowly shipping began to reappear. Not surprisingly, one of the first foreign vessels to arrive came from Sweden. It carried in its hold a consignment of carefully selected and cured white oak. Ola had been pleasantly surprised at the quality of that wood.

From long experience, he knew that most ship owners were constantly trying to cut corners and save a few coins. Although he had suspected this would apply to his current Swedish client, he now grudgingly admitted that Mr. Carlsson had unstintingly provided first class, carefully selected, wood for the building of his new boat.

Little did Ola Nerhus know of the time Mr. Carlsson had spent harassing his son-in-law Alfred Olsen, himself the owner of a small boat yard in Bergkarva, Sweden, to procure the finest boat building wood possible. Nor did he know of Alfred's scouring of the best wood yards in Sweden to locate the wood Ola was now forming, and to gain a little relief from his father in laws constant badgering.

As his sharp eye caressed her smooth lines, Ola knew this little boat would never be a fast sailor, although he felt she would certainly be a dependable sailor, and a very stable, sea kindly, boat in bad weather. He was more than a little proud she was to be registered at an unprecedented 55 tons, something no Hardanger *jacht* of her size had ever achieved. Overall, he was rather satisfied with his work.

Looking around his busy boat yard Ola noted the other boats being built, or repaired. Off to one side his crew of serious looking craftsmen, dressed in their traditional coveralls, were busy repairing the stem of a boat he had built 30 years before. They were fine boats he had to admit; yet from his point of view they all had one common problem. Their owners all wanted racehorses to haul cargo. This little boat was different, from the very beginning she was designed as a workhorse, one that could carry a big load for her size, and do it in most weather without complaining.

Out of the corner of his eye, he noticed someone approaching. Shifting his gaze, he saw it was that man from Oslo, the one selling machinery and those newfangled boat engines. He did not really blame the man for his constant visits, each with a new approach to the same question. After all, his products were heavy and they needed delivering, often to small islands inside the Arctic Circle. Nor was this man the only one to have approached Ola over the past few months with the same proposition. They all wanted to employ *Vega*, with her special capacity for heavy concentrated cargo to deliver their products.

In many ways, Ola Nerhus was a very typical Norwegian. He was honest, hardworking, and above all a shrewd businessman, always on the lookout for a profitable opportunity. This little boat was not even launched and already people were begging him to carry their cargo with it.

Looking up at the growing boat in front of him Ola unconsciously took off his trademark black hat. Slowly waving it in front of his face to chase off an annoying fly, his thoughts were miles away on board a little boat carrying heavy cargo to isolated Arctic islands. Maybe tonight he would talk with his son Jens about an idea that had been taking shape over the past few weeks. If Jens was agreeable, Ola would sit down and write a letter that might just make them both a bit of extra money. Besides, Jens could use the experience, and of course the money.

* * *

Several weeks later Johan Carlsson sat at his massive wooden desk reading a letter from the man in Norway that was building his new boat. That letter from Ola Nerhus was short and to the point.

There were many businessmen in Norway with heavy cargos that needed delivering to out of the way places, many of those places within the Arctic Circle. Few if any boats were available that could make those deliveries, and the few available boats were booked up far in advance. The rates they charged were more than double the normal price for cargo. Carlsson's new boat *Vega* would be perfect for those jobs, and could turn a handy profit carrying those cargos. If Mr. Carlsson were agreeable,

Jens Nerhus would skipper the boat and Ola Nerhus would undertake to manage their little joint venture.

The letter then went on to propose various share options and other details of the proposed enterprise. In essence, all Johan Carlsson needed to do was agree. Then he could sit back contentedly collecting his annual share of the profits.

Carlsson needed few of his shrewd business skills to realize this was a very handy way to turn a profit, at almost no cost to himself. Twirling a silver writing pen between the palms of his chubby hands Johan turned to gaze out of the window behind his desk, while he carefully considered this latest business offer. For several long minutes, the only sound in the room was the stately tick-tock of a grandfather clock and the click-clack of the pen against his finger rings.

Times had changed since he had commissioned the building of *Vega*. These days most of the cement from his new factory went to Stockholm, or to his fast growing export trade. Almost all of the export trade went in larger ships. Those he chartered as needed. His existing small fleet of sailing cargo boats could easily manage the local deliveries. Johan was so engrossed in thought he hardly noticed when a small bird landed on his windowsill and began to sing.

Turning back from the window, Carlsson reached down and opened the upper left hand drawer of his desk noting as he did that the brass pull handle was working its way loose again. Taking out a piece of notepaper, he carefully placed it on the faded green leather pad in the center of his desk.

Moments later, he dipped his pen in a filigreed silver ink well and began to write. His response to Ola Nerhus was also short and to the point stating that in principal he agreed with Ola's proposal and thanked him for offering it. Being a good businessman, Johan could not resist adding that they would need to discuss the share options in closer detail. He was certain he could get at least another eight percent out of the deal if he negotiated properly with the crafty Old Norwegian.

Happily chortling to himself at the thought of getting the best of another deal, he sealed the letter then called for one of his house servants. Moments later he heard a door close and looking out of his window saw the son of his cook racing away down the road into the center of town the letter held tightly in his hand.

Chapter 5
Of Tillers and Davey Jones

They say time flies when you are having fun. What they all fail to mention are the moments when time simply shrugs its shoulders and wonders off looking for a cold beer, leaving you in a timeless limbo to get on with whatever you are doing, as best you can. Mind you, that is an attitude I can fully understand. At that moment, if it meant being somewhere else, I would gladly have paid the first round, and maybe even the second – with peanuts.

An insane roll threw me across the aft cabin where I fetched up with a painful thump against the side. Dancing around on the madly rolling deck I yelled for Meggi to get out the emergency tiller, while I fought my way back up on deck and retrieved two pieces of stout braided line. Being extremely strong and highly resistant to abrasion that line was perfect for what I had in mind for an emergency rudder repair.

As my head emerged from below, the wind almost blew my hair off. While rigging screamed in torment, raging winds shattered the wave crests into a froth of driven spray before hurling foaming white horses from the wave peaks into the troughs. Struggling to breathe, and reflecting on how Dante would have loved this place, I fought my way forward to the line locker.

Having a bright idea and making it work can be two very different propositions, especially when they involve a wildly gyrating boat and a rudder that violently swings from side to side every few seconds. What in port, on a calm day, would have taken me only minutes accomplish became an endless eternity of individual seconds, each accented with its own specific dangers and the constant fear of sudden death looming over it all.

Before the emergency tiller could be put in place, I first had to dismount the remains of the shattered steering ram. That involved removing a tight fitting stainless steel pin locked in place by a very reticent locking pin. Just getting the locking pin out was a major effort, involving pliers and hammers, lots of bashed fingers, and some very creative cursing. Then the big pin had to be pulled, a normally very easy job that turned into a marathon of horrors. Through all of this, a wildly flailing rudder and its heavy iron steering arm were constantly attacking me.

Of course, my being in a constant state of near panic was not helping. The strange thing about these life or death situations is that they focus your mind quite clearly in two completely separate directions. One instinct is to widdle your knickers then hide under the bed with your bum in the air and a pillow over your head, while another little voice in your head is screaming to get on with it before you find out if there really is a man with a scythe on the other side.

With the remains of the steering ram out of the way, yet another interesting little quandary presented itself, how to firmly reattach the rudder head to the boat so that when the emergency steering tiller was in place the rudder would actually pivot and not simply flop from side to side. That is where my two pieces of braded yacht line would come into play, if I could manage getting them into place.

Fortunately, there was a space between the steering arm and the rudder head. That space was critical to my plan of salvation. If I could get the two pieces of line through that space, and bouse them up tight to the sides of the boat, together they would hold the rudder head to the boat, and more or less on the center line so that the rudder could then be turned.

The problem was in getting the lines through that small space while retaining all of my fingers and avoiding a short sharp smack on the head from the flailing rudder arm. On shore, it would have taken only a minute or so to accomplish, at sea in a storm it took ages, each minute filled with anxiety and the stress of impending dissolution as my imagination vividly pictured the boat swinging wildly out of control. How long it really took, I will never know.

Once threaded into the space between the rudder head and the steering arm I anchored the lines firmly by passing them behind the beam shelf both port and starboard wedging them against a stout frame. That done, and after some anxious moments trying to get the close fitting emergency rudder over the steering arm, we could attempt to steer again. How we were still alive and not on our way to Davey Jones' locker is still a mystery to me, for all that effort seemed to have taken forever.

While I had been occupied cursing lines and rudders in general, along with all their inventors and ancestors through the ages, and having my fingers mashed with a disconcerting regularity, Meggi had been busy duct taping our hand bearing compass to a deck pillar so we would have something to steer by, when the steering was restored.

With the emergency steering tiller in place and a compass to steer by, I sat down on the bench in front of where the steering ram is located. I was amazed that we were still alive, but now at least we could regain some semblance of control over our destiny. Taking a deep breath, I gave the tiller an almighty shove. Nothing happened. Leaning into it with all my strength, I just managed to turn the rudder a few degrees. Clearly, our tribulations were not over yet.

Calling the two young men that were our crew for the voyage, I put one on each side of the tiller and gave them a course to steer. Then I set off in search of a few pulleys and some line to rig up relieving tackles for our reticent emergency steering tiller.

Little wonder that tiller was hard to budge. The original tiller on a boat like this would have been between 4 and 5 meters long and required a standing man to push it from one side to the other. The emergency tiller our lives now depended on was a little over one meter long, and could only be operated from a sitting position.

It is amazing what fear can do for your strength. Considering the wild gyrations of our boat at the time, just staying in one place was a major effort much less applying force to steer. Yet somehow, our two intrepid young lads managed it and actually got us back on course. Even so, I knew they would not be able to maintain that enormous effort for long.

Chapter 6
A Devious Change of Flags

The scene might have inspired a rural painting by one of the great masters. Seated on a stiff backed wooden chair was a tall man wearing only black trousers and a plain woolen shirt with the sleeves rolled back almost to his elbows. His hands were large with long expressive fingers. In his right hand, he held an artist's paintbrush, the wooden end of which he was unconsciously tapping against his front teeth. In his left hand was a palette displaying a rainbow of colored paint.

Clear azure blue eyes gazed intently at the small oil painting propped against a heavy candleholder on the table in front of him. The painting he had diligently spent the past few weeks working on portrayed a scene he never tired of seeing. The light from another short winter's day was fading quickly. He heard the voice of his wife coming from the kitchen. She would be busy helping his mother prepare the family dinner.

Soon the failing light would force Jens Nerhus, the oldest son of Ola Nerhus, to stop for the day. Reaching over he placed the paintbrush in a small jar of turpentine. Swishing the brush around until he was satisfied it was clean, he then wiped it on an old piece of cloth. Tomorrow he would paint a flag at the top of the little ships mast. That flag would proudly announce her name as *Vega*.

The winter of 1898 was a harsh one, even by Norwegian standards. To help pass the long winter hours Jens had decided to paint a portrait of the small cargo boat he skippered. It was a boat his father had designed and built, a hard working little boat he dearly loved and took immense pride in commanding. After all, her design had recently won an award for technical innovations at the great exhibition in Oslo, something his father was extremely proud of, even if he tried, unsuccessfully in most cases, to conceal the fact.

Jens had been captain of the *Vega* from the day she was launched in the spring of 1892. Under his command she had become one of the most successful little cargo boats on Hardanger Fiord. From the moment the winter ice first thawed until the winter storms returned, he and his little boat were constantly on the move, carrying heavy cargos from one port to another.

Although Jens Nerhus would follow in the footsteps of his father to become one of Norway's finest boat builders – designing and building over 75 small ships during his long life – he never forgot his days sailing the North Sea on his beloved *Vega*.

To quote Lars Nerhus, the grandson of Jens Nerhus: "When I was very young my grandfather would tell me wonderful tales of his sailing days. The boat he loved to remember most was always the *Vega*. He would tell me stories of her famous voyages, wonderful adventures of sailing her deep into the Arctic to remote islands and even further around the top of Norway loaded with heavy machines the other bigger *jachts* could never dream to carry. Many of the very first generators and engines to reach the northern islands, and engines for much bigger ships, were delivered by *Vega*."

This happy state of affairs continued until 1904-5 when the political Union of Sweden and Norway vanished. Each country once again became independent. Overnight, boats built in Norway could no longer be exported to Sweden or have Swedish owners.

* * *

Being in the difficult position of owning a cargo boat in Norway he could not legally bring back to Sweden, Johan Carlsson was not a happy man. Over the past 12 years, that little boat had paid for itself several times over. It was one of the best investments he ever made. Now, what with the Norwegians calling it a Swedish boat and the Swedish officials calling it Norwegian, the little dear was sitting idle, costing him money, while there was honest work it could be doing in Sweden.

Just after breakfast, in his frustration and general state of anger at the world, Johan even tried to kick the cook's rangy old tomcat, but the retched creature moved too fast for him. Not only that, but it fetched him such a swat on the ankle he had to go bandage his foot and change his stockings.

Now several hours later, Johann was busily damning all meddlesome politicians, and their ancestors, to the deepest pits of hell as he waddled across his son in laws bustling boat yard. The fact it had rained the night before, and the yard was still muddy, only served to fuel his anger at the whole world. By the time he reached the office door, Johann was actually looking forward to venting a bit of frustration on young Alfred.

As he watched his father in law approaching the office door, Alfred Olsen was also not a happy man. The way the old lick penny was wobbling along his face looked more like a fat constipated gorilla than a successful merchant. Alfred allowed himself a modest laugh at the thought. After all, it was not Alfred's fault Norway and Sweden had split apart again, in fact, he was rather pleased they had. Of course, the new shipping rules were nothing short of pure madness, everyone knew that. But, as with most silly laws, there were ways to get around them.

Alfred Olson was a big easygoing mountain of a man with broad shoulders and a bushy blonde mustache that only a walrus could love. Alfred was a boat builder, a man content with his place in life who dearly loved his wife and was as proud as any man could be of their two lovely children. On the other hand, his father in law was a tightfisted old curmudgeon without whom he could easily live a long and happy life.

Putting on his best face while making a rude gesture behind his back, Alfred politely opened the door for his guest. A tray stood on the corner of the main desk with a decanter of whisky and two glasses prominently on display. Perhaps the idea he had worked out with the local harbormaster and the ship surveyor would work after all. He dearly hoped so; it would make his life a lot more peaceful if it did.

Roughly one hour, and two stiff tots of whisky later, Johan Carlson left his son-in-law's office. Chortling away happily to himself, he could not help thinking maybe young Alfred was not so useless after all. If this scheme worked, Johan might just give him the cement he had been asking for to pave over the boat yard. There was always the batch from last month that was a bit off; after all, he would never be able to sell it to any of his customers, yet it should still be good enough for paving.

Fortunately, for Alfred, human ingenuity tempered with a dose of devious scheming, had come to his rescue. Even though it was a plan devise by his friend the harbormaster, Alfred saw no reason not to take credit for it, at least in the eyes of his father-in-law. All that remained now was for Johann to send his instructions to Norway. The rest would be easy enough to do once the boat arrived.

Later that summer *Vega* left Ølve on what would become her final voyage under the newly reinstated Norwegian flag. She was lightly loaded with a cargo of dried fish destined for Bergkvara, Sweden. The voyage was an uneventful one, with fair winds and calm seas. On arrival, her cargo was quickly off loaded. Later that same day, the boat went round to the pier beside Alfred Olsen's boat yard. On the next high tide, *Vega* came out of the water on Olsen's marine railway. Once high and dry, a gang of shipwrights randomly removed several hull planks exposing the frames of the boat for inspection.

Early the next morning the local surveyor and the harbormaster made an official visit to Alfred's boat yard. Places like Bergkvara are only large villages where the entire population know each other, and are usually interrelated. With a nudge and a wink, due to some mysterious internal damage the local ship surveyor solemnly declared *Vega* an un-repairable total loss. The harbormaster duly affixed his seal to the surveyors report as a witness. That done, the three men retired to Alfred's office for a well-earned glass or two of aquavit and a cigar, both of course were cheerfully provided at Alfred's expense.

Later, when the two men left Alfred's office they each carried a cloth bag containing two large bottles of Johann's Scotch whisky, and an envelope filled with bank notes. That night, Johann celebrated with a glass of real Scotch malt whisky, not the cheap stuff he had so generously given to the two paper pushing officials. As he sipped the golden liquid, he puffed contentedly on an imported cigar.

Based on the surveyor's official declaration, duly registered, and witnessed by the local harbormaster, *Vega* was removed from the Norwegian Registry of Shipping. As far as officialdom was concerned, another tired little boat had reached the end of her working life and would soon be broken up for firewood.

To quote Lars Nerhus, "I was always told *Vega* was the best and strongest *jacht* he (Ola Nerhus) ever built and all I could find out was that she went to Sweden in 1905 and never returned. This would be told to me in a sad voice by my grandfather and it would always make me sad as if some important part of our family had been lost".

* * *

On the 10th of May, in the spring of 1906 Alfred Olsson's boat yard was a busy place. Not only was a large gang of construction workers busy paving over the yard with cement, but a newly built boat was ready to be launched for Mr. Johan Carlsson. There were flags flying and colored bunting strung around the yard to give it a festive air. Later Johann's daughter *Vega* would launch the new boat. Well, she would launch a more or less new boat. It was a lovely little boat. Over the winter, Alfred had carefully copied her lines and made more than one interesting note concerning her construction.

As Mr. Carlsson's boat slipped into the water, the town band tootled and squeaked while the official party busied themselves drinking and celebrating. No one noticed, or at least no one commented that with the exception of fashion pieces added to her bow and stern this new boat was identical to the one condemned in Alfred's yard only months before. Johann was so pleased with himself he reached into the wrong pocket, only later discovering he had given both the surveyor and harbormaster one of his expensive imported cigars rather than the cheap ones he always carried for such occasions.

From that unusual resurrection, *Vega* continued life under the Swedish flag, eventually becoming the famous *Vega of Bergkvara*. She faithfully transported cement, building stone, bricks, and other heavy loads until 1938 when Olands Cement AB of Stockholm purchased her from Johann's son. Olands operated her until 1949.

In 1928, *Vega* was equipped with a one cylinder, twelve horsepower diesel engine later upgraded to a mighty fifteen horsepower single cylinder engine in 1939. Today we laugh at such a small horsepower ratings, yet those engines pushed the fully loaded boat every bit as fast as the current six cylinder, 215 horsepower Perkins engine, and at about one-fifth of the hourly fuel consumption. It would seem that horses have become smaller these days, while consuming a lot more than they did back then.

As the demand for small wooden cargo *jachts* declined, *Vega* soon found herself employed as a "stone fisher". Stone fishers haul a steel dredge bucket across the bottom of the shallow North Sea collecting the round glacial stones that litter the sea floor. Once the hold is full, those stones are traded against hides and dried fish. It is a hard and dangerous profession well known as a "ship killer".

The work is brutal, the profits small, while the wear and tear on the boats is enormous. Most stone fishers end their lives on the bottom of the North Sea having been broken by the concentrated weight of their own cargo – a cargo they were never designed to carry.

Designed and built for precisely that type of cargo, *Vega* was fortunate. She survived. In 1989 still carrying a modest sailing rig, *Vega* became the last wooden sailing boat to work as a stone fisher. In early 1990, still strong but showing the scars of her long hard life, *Vega* was sold to a new owner who soon began a complete restoration of her hull and rigging. The restoration of her hull was a success; however that of her rigging (she was re-rigged from a cut down Galleass to a cutter), left much to be desired.

In 1996, her owner set out from Sweden intending to sail *Vega* around the world alone. For many reasons that dream was to prove impossible. Having motored most of the way to the Canary Islands his impractical fantasy was abandoned. *Vega* was unceremoniously hauled out on the hard where she sat forgotten, ignored, and neglected under the scorching Spanish sun for the next five years.

Chapter 1

Sun, Stars, and Hope

A wave slammed against the hull. The resounding thwack snapped me out of my exhausted trance with a start. It was my turn on the emergency steering tiller, and I was worn-out. Falling over with hunger and fatigue, I desperately needed sleep. My ribs hurt from a fierce crack against the wheel. Dried blood matted my hair. The small hand compass I was steering by had become little more than a blur a meter or so away. Constantly blinking my eyes and wiggling around on the where I sat, it was all I could do to keep my eyes open.

Somewhere south of the Seychelles a full-blown Indian Ocean cyclone by the name of Gafilo had mercilessly battered our small wooden boat for three endless days and nights, a seemingly eternal episode in my life, punctuated by one life-threatening emergency after another. Living from second to second, we had existed in constant fear for our lives. Now the wind had fallen noticeably, and the seas were calming. Somehow, we had survived those stress-filled days, but the danger was not yet over.

Considering there are so many experiences in life you can happily do without, a big storm at sea must surely rank among the top two; right along with getting your privates caught in the zipper.

Cyclone Gafilo provided us with the kind of days that build character, or so they say. If you ask me, those days were the type of brutally raw experience that make you wish you had bought a date farm in the middle of the Gobi desert, rather than a deep-sea sailing boat. While you are at it, make that a farm on top of some very high mountain.

Just after dawn, I changed our course. Our new heading was more toward the north, a direction that agreed well with the wind and reduced the loads on our crippled steering gear. What we desperately needed was a safe port, one where we could repair our shattered hydraulic steering ram and rudder. We also needed a place to recover from the storm's vicious battering.

The closest safe haven was Victoria harbor on the island of Mahe in the Seychelles. With the fragile state of our steering, winning those few hundred miles would be a difficult – perhaps even impossible – task.

Covered in bruises, cuts, and scratches we were all struggling along on the last of our energy reserves, and those supplies were fast running out. If you put the four of us together, we might have been able to muster one competent crewmember and the cat, just.

In normal circumstances, we only need one person on watch, with a second down below in the salon on standby, usually sound asleep on the sofa. Now with the steering broken we needed two people for each watch. One crewmember was needed up on deck trimming sails, watching out for ships, and any other dangers, while a second crewmember was required down below to manage the emergency steering tiller.

The emergency steering demanded so much physical force, even with the relieving tackles rigged, that steering for more than one hour at a time was simply impossible. Even by rotating between two one-hour stints at the steering and two one-hour stints on deck each four-hour long watch was a purgatory for us all.

Four hours on and four hours off gave us precious little time for any meaningful sleep between watches. Deep-seated fatigue had us moving around like zombies on Valium.

All four of us were severely bruised and battered from the storm. Suffering from painfully sore muscles brought on by the intense effort needed to steer, eating paracetamol tablets as if they were candy, and in general dead on our feet. If a troop of pink elephants had ridden by on unicycles they would have fit right in.

I doubt we would have made it safely into the harbor, had it not been for two amazing young men occupying a small apartment in London. They were the sum total of the Call Center and information service for our Iridium Satellite telephone system. As the Irish say, 'May the good Lord set a flower on their heads'.

At the height of the storm, we discovered there were only three minutes of credit remaining on our satellite phone. That phone was our only viable means of communicating with the outside world. It would be our only dependable means of calling for help should the boat begin to sink. Of course, in an emergency, we would also try the VHF radio, but its limited range was not encouraging.

In desperation, I dialed up the Iridium call center and explained our situation. I chose the Call Center because those calls are free. I will never know if it was pure boredom, an honest desire to help others in trouble, or perhaps a combination of both, but those people really came to our rescue.

For the next two days, they checked in with us every hour on the hour, never missing a call. Each time we would update them on our situation and the local weather. It may not seem like much, but just knowing someone was actively following our progress gave our moral a big boost.

Thanks to the constantly updated weather reports and advice they provided, we altered course to avoid the worst of the storms violence. Those reports also gave us hope. Knowing the best course to steer and when we could expect the storm to pass, made suffering through the present an easier burden to bare.

At the time we were unaware those lads had pulled out all the stops, tracking us hour by hour on a big map they found somewhere, downloading all the latest satellite images of the area, and even enlisting the advice of an expert on tropical cyclones from the World Meteorological Organization.

There was also information they did not share with us, the gigantic bulk carrier that broke up and sank not far from where, the offshore ferry that was lost, or the many other vessels that were screaming Mayday at the time. What they knew, and we thankfully did not, was that Cyclone Gafilo was the most violent cyclone to hit the Indian Ocean in recorded history. A real category 5+ monster that was as busy breaking records as it was tormenting us.

As the storm began to abate we needed to make port as soon as possible for repairs. Once again, our friends in London came to our aid. Deciding that Victoria in the Seychelles was our best option, they contacted the port authorities and Coast Guard in the Seychelles advising them of our location, current course and speed, and intention to enter their port. They also advised that we had serious steering problems, which might make maneuvering in tight places difficult if not impossible. It was a good thing for us they did.

Three days later, we arrived off the entrance to Victoria Harbor. By then we had established constant contact with the port authorities and Coast Guard using our VHF radio. Both services proved to be very professional and extremely helpful. The Coast Guard sent out a boat to meet and guide us through the reefs at the harbor entrance. When they saw how bad our steering was, they decided it would be safer to tow us in. That decision made sense to me, but still did not solve our steering problems.

Entering the harbor was a stressful time for everyone on *Vega*. With the head of the rudder loose, steering was at best a hit and miss option. Try to imagine pushing the tiller a few degrees to one side or the other was no guarantee that the actual rudder would move. Most of the time the rudder head would cant to one side, but the actual rudder would not pivot. So, when nothing happened after a correction, we would add even more correction. This would go on until all of a sudden the rudder would actually pivot, usually much more than desired. The result was *Vega* making her way through the reefs, zig-zaging like a drunken snake. It was a miracle we made it through that channel without running aground.

Once inside the harbor our troubles were just beginning. First, we had to dodge around an enormous yellow oil tanker mooring. After a rather exciting few minutes we managed to miss it by about fiver meters. I swear at one point the fellow on the back of the Coast Guard boat was ducking down with his hands on his head, the universal sign of impending disaster.

Then we turned toward the small boat anchorage. Fortunately there was only one other boat there, a small fiberglass sailing sloop. As we approached, a man came out on deck to urinate over the side. At first, he did not see us approaching, but when he finally did, he gave such a start he must have jumped half a meter into the air, while giving himself and the deck a good hosing down.

You can imagine his consternation at seeing this rather large, heavy boat headed directly at his floating home with apparently no intention of turning away. Mind you, at the time I was having apoplexy yelling down to Meggi, who was on the tiller, to turn. It was only at the very last second that our rudder flopped over and *Vega* sheared off to pass behind the small yacht. I feel certain the fellow on board that yacht found it easy enough to urinate while all this was happening. I just hope that later the laundry did not refuse his linen.

The rest was rather anti-climatic. We found a nice spot, dropped the anchor, and all together heaved an enormous sigh of relief. Once we had thanked the Coast Guard lads for all their help, and established anchor watches the rest of us promptly fell out, dead to the world. Anchor watch aside, I think I slept solidly for the next 36 hours. When I finally made it back to the world of the living, one look around convinced me the Seychelles are beautiful.

How easily sailors forget. I think having a short memory must be some sort of prerequisite for the job. One day – with seas rough enough to make a whale puke – there you are, swearing to all and sundry that once you get to land you will never set foot on a boat again, not even if it is a rowboat at the county fair. Then the wind drops and the sea calms down again.

Minutes later, all is forgotten, and it is back to business as usual. As crazy as it may seem, that is exactly what happened on board *Vega*. After such a harrowing experience, we were all so pleased to be alive; the last week of hardships simply did not seem real.

We spent almost one month in the Seychelles, making repairs and in general recovering from our nautical tribulations. Mind you, there are few places on earth better suited for the rest and recuperation of storm-battered sailors than the Seychelles. The sunny climate and friendly, easygoing people were precisely what we needed. If you add to that the fact their women are generally some of the most attractive you will find anywhere, little wonder the place is famous. I saw more than one of those lovely island beauties that could curl the toes on a plaster saint, with only a smile.

As to friendly, several days after we arrived I stumbled onto the local newspaper office. I forget what I was looking for at the time; it could have been anything from the local version of a supermarket to a public toilet. In any case, once there I had the bright idea to ask if there was some way we could publicly thank the port authorities and Coast Guard for all the help they gave us.

The way that editor jumped on my idea…it must have been the slowest news week on record. Next thing I knew, it was me giving them a full-blown interview and a photographer roaming the boat, snapping pictures of everything including the cat box. A few days later, there was a picture of *Vega* right at the top of the front page, followed by half a page of my ramblings. That same afternoon we had the local television station out for another interview where we once again praised the local port control and Coast Guard then thanked the island population in general for being such nice people.

The result of those two articles was amazing. Everywhere we went people would approach to commiserate over the storm or make suggestion on how to fix our damaged rudder. Most of them acting like they had known the four of us for years, and calling each of us by name. Just walking through the town people would smile and bid me "Good morning Captain Shane!"

Between sudden fame and hard work, we somehow managed to get the rudder repaired, along with a few things that had bothered me during the last voyage.

By early April 2003, we were once again ready to set sail for Malaysia. What with loading fuel and water, it took us two more days to prepare our departure. The day before our departure, we received a pleasant surprise. Employees from the Seychelles Commodity Board had all chipped in to make up a care package of food and other necessities for our trip. It seems that in one of those interviews I had mentioned our pockets being for rent and how it would be beans and rice from the Seychelles to Malaysia. They delivered that bounty in a panel van, chock a block with boxes and bags. It was a happy crew that loaded those supplies on board *Vega*. The number of times we blessed them during the next month were uncountable.

That same evening we cast off our lines, setting out on a month long odyssey mostly on calm seas under clear blue skies, a journey where little or no wind was the norm. We spent most of that time aimlessly drifting around the Indian Ocean, with only heavy North Sea canvas for sails. Not one of the nine sails we had on board at the time worked well in light winds.

Unfortunately, there is no such thing as a sail that works well in all weather conditions and that trip was the perfect example. Sails are designed for different wind conditions. They range from big ghosters built from very light cloth for the lightest of airs to tiny storm sails constructed from canvas as heavy as cardboard, over engineered to take anything Cape Horn might throw at them.

The reason for this has more to do with how sails work than anything else. You see, a sail is not much more than a vertical wing made from cloth. An aerodynamic shape, and how you present that shape to the prevailing wind, generates most of a sail's driving power.

In the majority of cases, it is not the wind pushing on the back of the sail, but the "lift" created by wind flowing over the front of the sail that causes a boat to advance through the water. In light air if a sail is too heavy it just hangs there looking like someone's damp laundry and is, as far as moving the boat is concerned, just about as useful.

A lighter cloth assumes the proper shape in lighter wind and begins to provide drive long before the heavier sail has even started to take on a shape. Size also plays a big part in sail design. But, that rant can wait for another time.

What really mattered for us on that long drift across the Indian Ocean was that our sails had originally been made for the North Sea. They were not at all suited for the light winds normally found around the tropics.

One night I overheard a crewmember singing to pass the time on watch. His little ditty summed up that trip quite nicely, "Drifting, drifting, over the flaccid main, the skipper says to get it up, but all it does is hang…" He made up a few additional verses, most inventive they were. Some of the vivid descriptions he came up with for various anatomically impossible sexual acts were quite ingenious. But, those will have to wait for the X-rated version of this book soon to be available in a plain brown paper wrapper.

Chapter 8
The Fine Art of Naviguessing

People are always asking me if I ever become lost. It's an understandable question considering often being out of sight of land for such long periods. The truth is: *never*. I always know exactly and precisely where I am. Mind you, from time to time the rest of the world becomes misplaced in a most disconcerting manner. But, I can always tell you within centimeters exactly where I am.

The problems occur when I have to relate the position I am currently occupying to one on a chart. Once I have charted that position, the theory says it will tell me exactly where the land has gotten off to while I was out at sea, and not keeping a close watch on it. You would be amazed at how fast a well-known piece of land can drift around if you are not paying careful attention. I just find it strange how it took all those brilliant scientists so long to discover continental drift when any uneducated illiterate seaman could have told them about it ages ago.

Navigation is not only the fine art of knowing exactly where you are, but also where you are not. Knowing where you are not is a position vastly more important than most people give it credit for. There are also the meta-positions of where you have been, want to be, or wish you were that need to be carefully considered in any navigational equation. Hence, the age-old accolade of "Naviguesser", an honorific – more or less – traditionally applied to whoever is in charge of knowing where the land is in relation to the ship.

Over the centuries, various academic types have attempted to make a science from the ancient art of navigation. Since the vast majority were the kind that get seasick in a rocking chair, I can only surmise their attempts were designed either to create another chair at the university they infested or to get themselves on the cover of the local sensationalist magazines in order to impress the girls.

Truth be known; navigation is still an art. It still relies heavily on the old MK-1 eyeball and a large dose of practical common sense. Maybe the latter is why many modern yachties have so much trouble understanding it. Common sense being one of those things that does not come with a manual of instructions complete with 32 pages of legal disclaimers and safety warnings like *Warning: running hard aground at full speed can be hazardous to your wealth.*

Sure, there are scientific underpinnings for navigation that every sailor should be fluent in, and they help a lot. But, those are simply the rules and techniques a navigator needs to understand. Rules that are more in the nature of guidelines, designed to be employed with great caution and more than a few judiciously applied grains of salt. Remember you do need to have the technical bits down pat, but almost as importantly you need to know how and when to employ the various aspects of those techniques. It also helps to be a bit paranoid. Is it still paranoia if you know the sea really is out to get you?

And, people wonder why I have so many grey hairs. It is a miracle I have any hair left at all. Amazingly, I have not chewed my fingernails all the way down to my elbows by now what with some of the places we go and the state of the navigation equipment I have to work with.

Chapter 9
Calm Before the Tsunami

Sitting on the terrace of the Royal Langkawi Yacht Club, with a cold Bombay Sapphire G&T in one hand and a triple-decker club sandwich in the other, I was surrounded by the sweet-smelling aroma of tropical flowers, mixed with the salty tang of the sea, and feeling content.

A golden fish eagle effortlessly gliding above the marina suddenly stooped. Its feet barely touching the water only meters from where I sat before several beats from those mighty wings effortlessly bore it aloft again, talons like daggers tightly gripping a small fish.

All things considered, at that moment life was looking good. From where I sat in a comfortable wooden chair with a nicely padded cushion, events of the past month seemed like a dream. Had we really just arrived safely from a rather boring month-long journey across the Indian Ocean?

When, like all sailing voyages, our odyssey from South Africa to Malaysia finally ended we were well over due for a few of lands luxuries. I for one was dreaming of something long and tall with ice in it and a massive plate overflowing with fried potatoes, as we limped into the Yacht Club, on Langkawi.

Once the boat was safely moored to a pier, it did not take us long to find the yacht club bar and restaurant. What the other patrons of that august yachting establishment thought of the bedraggled, somewhat scruffy, and slightly whiffy new arrivals they politely kept to themselves. Although one or two did, rather artfully, shift themselves up wind.

After ordering a drink, and acquiring a few important directions from the friendly barman, cold drink in one hand, towel and soap in the other, it was this little boy off at a trot looking for the nearest shower sporting hot water.

Still clutching my cold drink while successfully imitating a recently rescued castaway, I found a comfortable looking shower stall. Then with no further ceremony, I stripped, turned the water to its hottest setting, and lay down on the floor with my feet propped up against the opposite wall. I shall never forget the glorious feeling of luxuriating in my first hot water shower in almost a month. I was in paradise, that is, until the hot water ran out.

Meggi and I spent almost a year in Langkawi, sorting out various urgent problems such as the fresh water and toilet systems, while making a few badly needed temporary improvements to *Vega's* very rustic accommodations. When we first acquired *Vega*, her living spaces were a cross between an Afghan goat shed and an African chicken coup. I think the chickens were winning, by the way.

During that time Meggi industriously spent long days in front of her computer, diligently creating drawings and manipulating ideas for *Vega's* accommodations. She was determined to make the maximum use of every available centimeter of space. Often it seemed that when she had a good idea for one end of the boat, the various allotments of space obliged her to change the whole layout, all the way to the other end. More than once, she complained that a boat interior is nothing more than a one big complicated piece of furniture.

If our only problem had been *Vega's* accommodation spaces, then we would have been a content crew. As it was, while Meggi was busy arguing with angle and curve, I was occupied with rigging and a myriad other things that all urgently needed attention. The electrical system alone was enough to send an Italian spaghetti chef into fits of rapture.

In reality, the task we faced was no less daunting than a complete refit of the interior and an almost complete re-rigging, including a new mizzenmast with its accompanying spars, sails, rigging, and irons. I will not even go into all the various systems and electronics that needed a complete overhaul or replacement.

By then, our few surviving sails were a collection of crudely patched rags. Replacing them on our severely limited budgets was an impossible dream. Fortunately, we did manage to acquire several used headsails of lighter material. They were not pretty, but they helped immensely when it came to moving *Vega* in light wind.

Right in the middle of that seemingly endless struggle, a natural disaster occurred of such colossal proportions its aftermath resonated around the world. That event completely changed the direction of our lives, and the future of the *Vega*.

Chapter 10
The Great Tsunami

The afternoon of 26 December 2004 brought an inundation of sudden death and massive destruction that quickly resounded around the world. In Langkawi, it started out as another lovely tropical day. One of those days set against a deep blue sky with only a few scattered clouds and a light breeze. It was impossible to foresee that within seconds the normally placid marina waters would become a maelstrom of vicious swirling currents.

Hundreds of miles from where we were peacefully enjoying the sunshine and a gentle breeze, colossal waves were mercilessly battering the island of Sumatra with devastating force. Unstoppable killer waves, often over 10 meters high, thundered ashore without pity, wiping out the lives of over a hundred thousand people in a matter of minutes. Entire cities were utterly demolished. As far away as East Africa, Sri Lanka, and Thailand people felt the effect from those murderous waves.

As luck would have it, we were in the Langkawi Yacht Club when the first surges struck. Meggi and I were preparing for a well-earned siesta when without warning, *Vega* slammed brutally against the pier. Her mooring lines screamed against the bitts as the first of several massive, undersea earthquake-generated tsunami waves struck.

And so started one of the most unusual afternoons of my life. As Meggi and I raced around doubling mooring lines, in the end we had a cat's cradle of lines a drunken spider would have been proud of, and doing our best to keep fenders in place we had no idea what was happening. The rapidly repeating tides were vacillating from extreme high to extreme low in only minutes. The marina was filled with raging currents and whirlpools. The air was alive with a cacophony of sounds, a bedlam of banging halyards and screaming mooring lines over laid with the urgent calls of sailors fighting to save boats that had been poorly moored.

For all of us who struggled from moment to moment that afternoon there was one all-encompassing question: *What the hell is happening?*

Meanwhile with half the coastal population of Southeast Asia running for their lives in panic, we were more worried about damaging the Yacht Club pier. I am still convinced, they would have found a way to make us pay for it. At one time, I had *Vega*'s engine warmed up, ready to slip our lines as the floating pier came within half a meter of lifting free from its steel piling.

While we were lucky to escape with only a few scratches in *Vega*'s paint and one or two broken mooring lines, many were not so fortunate. Both of the other marinas on Langkawi were completely devastated.

To understand how that happened, you need to understand how a modern marina is constructed. Floating piers ride up and down with the tides on massive pilings driven deep into the seabed. The height of those pilings above water depends on the highest predictable tides. Based on the highest predictable tides, the designer adds a safety margin to the height of the pilings so that the floating piers with boats tied onto them cannot escape.

Should the water level exceed the height of the piling, then the pier – boats and all – can float off the pilings and drift away. The tidal surges created by that tsunami were *twice* the height of a normal high tide. When the floating piers came adrift from their pilings, over a hundred boats were washed out to sea, many still attached to piers. Some of those boats survived. Driven by those giant tidal surges other boats were washed ashore, hopelessly grounded well above the normal high water level.

Through it all chaos and confusion reigned. You see, although we could see *what* was happening at any given moment, we did not know *why* it was happening. A subtle, but important difference that is. When it finally occurred to me to switch on our marine VHF radio it was alive with frantic calls for assistance and the latest disaster reports. That was a day of pure bedlam as bystanders, yachties, and other boat owners did their best to assist each other and boats belonging to owners who were not on board at the time. It was a heroic effort, one that resulted in many boats being saved, even though many would also eventually be lost.

Over the next few days as the magnitude of this monumental natural disaster and its toll in human suffering began to filter in, many people volunteered to help alleviate that suffering. In their generosity, they stood poised to help the victims in Sumatra by sending them donated food and medical supplies.

Having seen firsthand the damage inflected on their own island, the people of Langkawi were prepared to help others who had lost everything – homes, families, everything – in those few brief moments of devastating horror.

Suddenly, race or nationality no longer mattered. No one cared if you were Christian or Muslim, Chinese or European or even purple with bright green stripes, we were all human beings, and some of us urgently needed help. The more fortunate readily rendered assistance as best they could. The problem was how to quickly transport and distribute that support to those who needed it most.

Since *Vega* was one of the few boats capable of carrying enough to make the thousand-mile return trip worthwhile, and willing to volunteer, we quickly found ourselves the focus of an ad hoc relief operation.

Between the Chinese business community in Langkawi, the Sikh community on the mainland, and a multitude of willing Malaysian shop owners we soon had almost 22 tons of food and medical supplies committed for what became our first Mission of Mercy. Over the next few days, a constant stream of donated supplies poured into Langkawi on the fast ferries from mainland Malaysia. In a show of solidarity, ferry companies transported and stored those supplies for us free of charge.

The plan was a simple one. We would deliver our relief supplies to the island of Pulau Weh, located just north of Banda Aceh. Although severely damaged by the tsunami, Pulau Weh still had a functioning port where we could transship those supplies onto local cargo boats. Those local boats would then distribute the food and medical supplies along the devastated west coast of Sumatra.

The plan seemed a good one. To those of us sitting around a table in the air-conditioned office on Langkawi we had dubbed "The Chaos Control Centre", it made a lot of sense. What it failed to consider were the vicious seas around Sumatra's northern coast – some of the nastiest waters you will find anywhere outside the seventh circle of hell. That Greek lad in *The Odyssey*, the one who was always getting into trouble, would have loved the place.

Our brilliant plan also failed to consider how lightly built most Indonesian cargo *phinisi* are. They may look big, and have impressively thick planking, but, all things considered, those boats are not designed for the same consistently rough seas as a boat like *Vega*. Then again, at sea you can never forget the element of luck.

Chapter II
Loading the Beast

By now, you are most likely imagining *Vega* parked placidly alongside some tropical pier with a constant stream of food and medical supplies streaming into her cargo hold. If you have a vivid imagination, you may have peopled that image with Meggi holding a clipboard, where she busily notes each item as it is loaded onboard by a merry band of well-muscled Malaysian sailors. Of course, you would also add the vessel's jolly captain strolling around puffing on his salty pipe while in general managing to get in the way of those with real jobs to do. At least you have the latter part more or less correct, although contrary to what some seem to believe – I do not smoke a pipe.

Looking back, the truth was a far less romantic mixture of panic, chaos, and bedlam all rolled up with tons of rice, sugar, and other assorted eatables. If anyone knew what was happening from one minute to the next, we never met. I think the only thing missing was a rabbit in a hat inviting us to his tea party. The medical supplies were perhaps the easiest to log and store. At least they came neatly boxed and well labeled.

You see, it was not as if we could ring up the local supermarket and order several truckloads of food, even if we had somehow miraculously found the money to pay for it all. On the contrary, the supplies we would be delivering arrived in so many various ways, shapes, forms, and quantities it was almost frightening. Everything from pallets of rice, arriving on the fast ferries from Penang, to individuals bringing in small bundles or bags containing a few assorted items was arriving daily. Everyone wanted to help, and did help, to the best of their ability.

What I remember most are the normal everyday people, bless their hearts, who reached into their pockets and made a sacrifice to help others. Small shopkeepers, gardeners, lorry drivers, maids, and ditch diggers who unselfishly gave what they could. Although we preferred things in case lots or full bags of rice and sugar, every time someone would pitch up with a small bag of mixed provisions, or a cloth folded and knotted around a few hands full of rice and a small tin of tomato paste, I could easily understand their desire to help. I also understood that the bag they delivered represented the best they could manage within their means.

This of course meant we had to spend hours repackaging small bundles of bulk items like rice or sugar and then sorting other items like canned goods into boxes or bags we could easily manage.

Two days before we departed *Vega* was so full it was almost impossible to move around down below. All of the cabins and even the toilet were chock a block with bags of rice and sugar, boxes of canned goods, cases of baby formula, and of course medical supplies. Meggi had the salon, which in any case was more or less a vast open space, packed to the beams. The only clear space remaining consisted of a path leading to the galley and engine room.

Of course, just about the time we sat back and started patting ourselves on the back to celebrate getting it all in, our friends from the un-official Chinese business community in Langkawi brought along their contribution. I thought Meggi was going to have apoplexy when they proudly showed us two tightly packed panel trucks full of food.

People often joke about how tight fisted the Chinese can be, and it's true, they *are* sharp business people who can drive a hard bargain or squeeze a coin so tightly the kings nose starts to bleed. On the other hand, I have found them to be quite generous and open hearted when it comes to helping others less fortunate than they are, and damn smart when it comes to organization.

While we had been busy stuffing the boat and getting ready for the voyage, every Chinese counter jumper, and Malaysian shopkeeper on the island had been participating in a whip-around, the splendid results of which was now giving Meggi migraines just to look at.

As we were busily unloading boxes into the yacht club trollies one of our friends made a comment I have never forgotten, "We Chinese do not like donating to big charities. They might use our money for anything. With you we know our help will go straight to those who need it most". I did not realize it then, but his summation was the heart of a concept Meggi and I had been trying to put into action for years.

We soon had all five of the yacht club trollies industriously trundling back and forth delivering boxes of food to *Vega*. Meanwhile, as the pile of cargo grew beside *Vega*, Meggi was muttering and mumbling about us needing a basement if we were ever going to stow it all onboard. Those two and a half ton panel trucks may not look very big, but you would be amazed at how much they will hold when tightly packed. Then again, *Vega* does not look very large either, yet somehow Meggi managed to pack away every bit of that load. If I did not know better, I might easily assume she flew a broom at night and danced around naked during the full moon. Twenty years we have been together, and the woman still never ceases to amaze me.

Of course stuffing the boat was only one facet of the problem. Our navigation equipment was a disaster waiting to happen, and, well you try finding charts for Sumatra, which by the way is in Indonesia, when you are on a small island in Malaysia and see how easy it is. Then there was another important question: were those charts still accurate. What we had seen as a torturous series of gigantic waves was really the result of a massive undersea earthquake occurring not far from the northern tip of Sumatra. Nature had only thrown in the waves as an afterthought.

Experts were already speculating over what effect that massive shifting of tectonic plates might have on the surrounding islands. According to them, the land was either raising, or sinking, or perhaps strolling out for a cup of tea. It all seemed to depend on which talking head you happened to catch and or his luck in the singles bars the night before. Trying to make heads or tails out of all that pseudoscientific babble was enough to have a bronze statue searching for the paracetamol bottle.

We would be going into a small port on the island Pulau Weh whose entrance was already complicated enough, what with the sunken fishing boats and collapsed piers, without having to speculate over changes in the seafloor. A problem that would translate into water depths being different from those shown on the charts. With our depth sounder working only when the cursed thing felt like it, you can imagine the importance of such minor details.

More than once, I gave thanks to my lucky stars that we would not be going down the West coast of Sumatra where the geological changes would be more pronounced. I could easily imagine some of those small bays that provided the only safe anchorages, fouled by earthquake-generated landslides or the detritus of whole villages.

While we were getting the boat ready, our friends from Sikh Aid had dispatched an envoy to Pulau Weh. His job was to prepare for our arrival, navigate through the inevitable Indonesian maze of rubber Stamp-o-paths, charter a local cargo boat to distribute the supplies we would deliver, and in general make himself useful. Overall, Richie did a great job of keeping us informed and clearing away the various official impediments that arose.

Ten days after the tsunami struck, we had the boat fully loaded and ready for departure. I wish I could say the town band turned out to see us off, although having heard the town band I would have been satisfied with a few dancing girls, a bit of flag waving, and a short speech by the mayor. The fact is, no one turned out to see us off. We just decided it was time to leave, cast off our lines, and set a course for Sumatra.

Chapter 12
A Mission of Mercy

With *Vega* so heavily loaded, the trip from Langkawi to Sumatra was a slow one. Through a miscalculation on my part, we had loaded her about a half strake down by the bow; rather than the usual one strake down by the stern she just loves. This made her sluggish, and a little hard to steer. As we puttered along at between 4 and 5 knots the crew we had hastily scraped together for the trip proved themselves champions.

Andy Parsons, an inveterate British adventurer, had years of experience at sea. Of medium height with gentle brown eyes, Andy is one of those people who are always in motion, radiating an abundance of energy, and an intense curiosity for every experience life has to offer. No sooner had Andy stowed his gear than he had taken charge of our binoculars. He always wore them whenever on watch like some esoteric badge of office. A trait that quickly earned him the nickname of Mr. Binocs.

Singaporean John Heng was just launching his career as a photographer. With black hair and an expressive face, John always seemed to find a smile. He had joined us at the last minute, eager for a chance to photograph the aftermath of the great tsunami close up.

Everything that could float, and many things that were not meant to, were drifting on the ocean in those days. Whole trees, overturned fishing boats, even the complete roof of a Thai house drifting along with a few forlorn chickens and a duck sitting on top of it soon ceased to have any interest, other than as objects to be avoided.

For me those long nights, darker than the halls of doom, were the most nerve-racking part of our journey. With no moon, and half the detritus of Southeast Asia drifting around the risk of a serious collision was very real. All of us knew it, and accepted at any minute there might be an almighty crunch that would soon see us standing off in the dingy watching the good ship *Vega* in her final moments. We made jokes about it, as people will in those circumstances, but the reality of that constant danger was never far from our thoughts.

Our voyage from Langkawi to Pulau Weh was rather anticlimactic. The seas were calm and the wind lighter than I could have wished. The only real excitement happened when I mistook one of the crew with a rather spectacular attack of flatulence for an approaching thunderstorm. Just be warned: it is never a good idea to serve sausages, beans, sauerkraut, and brown bread on a boat. It may be a German specialty, and great eating, but it sure gives a whole new meaning to the term "Musical Meals".

We did have one other bit of excitement when an American aircraft carrier sent a helicopter to have a squint at us. It was one of those bizarre looking things festooned with rockets, guns, and a strange assortment of pods that might have contained anything from chewing gum to nuclear weapons for all we knew. I could just make out the pilot and gunner all kitted out like Arian Gods of War, as that strange beast came to a hover in front of us.

A load hailer ordered us to contact them on VHF channel 16. Which, taking my own sweet time, I did. As the radio came on there was an arrogant voice informing me that we were entering restricted waters and had to turn north at once, If you ask me he sounded exactly like he had swallowed the poker, along with all that "policeman of the world" propaganda he grew up on.

I could just picture those two lads sitting up there proud as Lucifer in their Star Wars machine. You know the type, for sure. The ones that always make top marks in civics, play football (yank style), and have a hankie embroidered by their dear old granny saying "My country right or wrong" hanging in a frame over the bed; in other words, what the rest of us usually call, right prats.

You see, I tend to be one of the billions of people on our planet who do not appreciate that type of blatant arrogance, even if it is legal. In this case, it clearly was not.

Since we were heading west, having a hard enough time of it without going out of our way, his suggestion was not an idea I could grow to love.

I politely informed them we were carrying food and medical supplies on an emergency relief mission, and that I was navigating along a clearly defined international shipping lane, that happens to be one of the busiest in the world. In addition, even if the above were not applicable, I was in Indonesian national waters.

Since they, for a certainty, were not the Indonesian Navy, or the Coast Guard, or even the 'Indonesian Society For the Prevention of Cruelty to Animals', I fully intended to maintain my current course and speed along my lawful route.

In essence, I gave him the verbal version of that ancient, time honored, single finger salute, minus the usual accompaniment of four letter words, and pointed comments on genealogy. There is such a thing as good form, after all, even when dealing with Yanks.

Clearly, they were intent on playing a game of silly buggers - even if they did not have all of the pieces – or even understand the rules. As far as I was concerned, it was going to be a one sided game. So there and then, in the best spirit of international relations, I tried a different tack.

Oh dear, says I in an innocent voice, if they were so afraid of a 100-year-old wooden sailing boat that could barely make 4 knots, a sailing boat that was currently dead downwind of their infestation, perhaps they should rethink their entire range of defensive measures.

I also informed them, in what I hoped sounded an offhand manner, that the whole conversation was being filmed by the BBC, at which point John, taking his cue like a good'un, went up on deck and pointed his rather large video camera at them. Amazing how fast a little video camera can put the wind up such a big expensive war machine.

In short, we sent them a polite, yet well-deserved, rude raspberry delight, with a well-thumbed nose topping, and never deviated a single degree from our course.

Somewhere, someone on that aircraft carrier must have had an attack of common sense. Perhaps one of the cooks, or a plumber, was wondering through their radio room at the time. I know for a fact, common sense in the military is such a rare occurrence that the culprit most likely had to spend days filling out reams of forms and apologizing profusely to all and sundry, before being reassigned to an obscure weather station at the North Pole.

In any case, without another word that great fuel wasting monster did a rapid turnabout before lumbering away never to be seen again. We did wave them good-bye, Andy and I both showing only one finger on each hand as we did so.

We never did see their famous aircraft carrier. Which I figure was most likely off busily bombing someone in a mud hut who had the nerve to disagree with their philosophy of The World for US, and the rest of you can have back the scraps. As long as you do what you are told, and grovel properly when we condescend to throw you a few. Arrogant lot those yanks, almost as bad as lawyers or Eskimos.

Chapter 13
Into the Jaws of Hell

It was early morning when we arrived at the lovely old colonial town of Pulau Weh. Picking our way around sunken boats and other debris, we tied up to one of the few piers that were still serviceable. No sooner had we arrived than Richie; our Sikh Aid liaison came to meet us. Richie is a big jovial man sporting the obligatory Sikh turban and beard. Although clearly a man who spends a lot of time smiling, that particular morning he was not in a very cheerful mood.

His news was not encouraging. Both of the local cargo boats hired to carry supplies down the west coast had been damaged so badly by the rough seas, they were forced to turn back. We could offload our supplies into a local warehouse, but he was not at all sure how those supplies could be delivered. He then went on to brief me on the local situation. It was by then certain that the hardest hit communities were along the West coast of Sumatra.

Television had the entire world focused on Banda Ache as the center of devastation. The truth is all the journalists were huddled together in Banda Ache's two remaining hotels, where they could enjoy air conditioning, hot meals, and a bar with iced drinks. Few, if any, ever ventured further than the town limits. None went to the West Coast.

In fact, if you know Banda Ache you soon enough realize the most famous news footage was shot from the roof of the town's best hotel. Don't look at me; I never said those high paid disaster journalists were dumb - just over paid.

While Richie was busy explaining the situation, I noticed a dugout canoe slowly progressing across the bay. An old man called out something from the canoe. Out of the corner of my eye, I saw Andy who speaks a little Bahasa go to the side. Then John disappeared down below on the run, quickly returning with a bottle of water. The water promptly vanished over the side. Being curious, I excused myself, crossing the deck to see what was happening.

There tied to *Vega*'s side was an ancient dugout canoe. It contained an old man and a young boy dressed in rags, more a collection of holes held together by random threads than clothes. They both looked dead tired as they passed the water bottle back and forth between them, having the good sense to sip rather than guzzle from it.

After the usual half-hour of hi, hello, and how are you the local culture requires, Andy figured out their village had been destroyed by the Tsunami, while they were out fishing. Being the only boat to survive those monstrous waves of doom they had set out looking for help. Since then, they had been paddling their small canoe through some of the world's most difficult currents and waves, passing one devastated village after another, in their search for help. While we were talking, the boy passed out from exhaustion in the bottom of the canoe.

These were not beggars. They were proud honorable people, who had been peacefully going about their lives until fate thrust them into a natural disaster far beyond their wildest nightmares. Dehydrated, scared, hungry, and bone tired, yet still pushing on, they had made it this far. Could we possibly refuse to, at least, try to make it down the west coast with the sorely needed food and medical supplies we had onboard? That was, after all, more or less exactly what we had come to do; providing you ignored the bit about rough seas, rip tides, 5 meter tidal bores, whorl pools, and standing waves.

I knew *Vega* was built to withstand the North Sea, and violent Arctic storms, while fully loaded with heavy cargo. We had already seen her doggedly fight her way through a cyclone in the Indian Ocean. If any boat could make it, she could. The real question was could we? I readily admit being apprehensive at the prospect of undertaking such a voyage.

You see, I never claimed to be one of those heroes always ready to stand tall and full of courage in the face of dastardly hardships. If my country was at war and called me, they would get the answering machine saying I had moved to Port Stanley in the Falkland Islands (beep, beep). Meanwhile I would be busily making my way toward some remote tropical island in the Pacific, on a tramp steamer with a broken radio.

The thought of sailing through one of the nastiest little stretches of water on the planet, in a boat loaded almost to her limit, fairly gave me the screaming jeebies.

On the other hand, there are times when you have almost sauntered your way around the corner to a place where you can start legging it at full speed towards safety, when real life taps you on the shoulder with a task only you can do. Should you not do it, well that just does not bare thinking about. Not, that is, if you want to continue looking other people straight in the eyes. The most important eyes, being the ones you see in the mirror every morning.

There are people who could easily have turned a cold shoulder on those hungry souls. Me? I am proud not to be one of them. I may not be the bravest person around, but I congratulate myself on still having a few strains of humanity left. Maybe it is some lingering sense of responsibility as a human being, or in this case a serious attack of temporary insanity.

As much as I felt this might be the dumbest thing I would ever do, I also knew I would put on a brave face and get on with it, all the while hoping and praying for the best.

We brought the old man, and what turned out to be his grandson, on board *Vega*. While they were being fed, I called a crew meeting. I usually do not subscribe to democracy at sea unless it is one man, one vote, and I am the man with the vote. On a well-run boat, there is only one captain, who makes all the decisions. Right or wrong, I am responsible for the outcome. I will listen to suggestions, if there is time, but when the chips are down it is my call, and my responsibility.

In this case, the decision was so momentous and the potential hazards so genuine, I felt we should all agree if *Vega* were to continue down the west coast to deliver our supplies. With the crew sitting around on the cabin roof, I did my best to explain the conditions, the dangers as I saw them, and what I thought our chances were.

Just so you know I was not the only one ready for the hatters ball, we all agreed we should go. So, early the next morning, with the skipper's knees merrily knocking out a symphony of apprehension, we set off on what was to be one of the hardest voyages I have ever sailed. Rip tides, standing waves, currents, cross-seas, whirlpools, and tidal bores all awaited us as we set out. The old man and his grandson wisely elected to stay with family on Pulau Weh, at least until they could recover from their ordeal.

I am not going to preach about the rampant devastation and suffering. If you were there, and saw it, then you know, and are scarred for life by what you saw. If not, then just be glade you missed it. Suffice to say, we made it down the west coast, , where we delivered our supplies. I hope that voyage saved a few lives, and helped a few people get back on their feet.

I know I shall never forget all those stunned blank faces. People so completely overwhelmed by events, they were unable to fathom what had or was happening to them, much less put a why to it. Talk about a landscape from the gardens of hell, families had been ripped apart, whole communities destroyed, futures obliterated, leaving the survivors so badly traumatized I doubt they will ever fully recover.

They say war does that to people, but so does nature. The only difference I can see is that nature is not looking to make a monetary profit from all the suffering and waste. Nature just does it because; well that is nature for you. No wonder they call her a mother. Even so, when you see firsthand, the results of nature on the rampage, it is just as horrifying as any war.

Chapter 14

Of Standing Waves and Whirl Pools

If our journey down the west coast of Sumatra was rough, the return trip was a voyage from hell. In all my years at sea, never have I encountered such an intense concentration of nautical horrors, all busily infesting one small stretch of water. We spent almost four days trapped in a series of nautical nastiness' that would have given an optimist on valium nightmares. Even now, sitting in the safety of a calm secure harbor, I still get the screaming jeebies just thinking about the northern tip of Sumatra.

Mind you, the seas must have been just as bad on the way down, although with the wind and waves coming from astern their effect was not so pronounced. Now that we were heading north, the whole miserable boiling was conspiring against us. Between slamming into head seas, trying to climb over the odd standing wave, whirlpools diligently spinning us in every direction, and the ever-constant wind holding us back, there were times we cheered when the speed over ground exceeded one knot. We had one stretch where with the engine roaring away and guzzling fuel like a thirsty camel; it would take several minutes for the boat to fight her way over a single standing wave.

If you never had the pleasure of sharing the same stretch of water with standing waves let me explain why you have not missed much, that is, unless you happen to be a sea going masochist. Standing waves form where two strong currents meet head on forcing up a steep hill of water that usually stays in one place. The fact they are not moving is what makes them so hard for a boat to manage.

Normally at sea, the waves are in constant motion traveling along at a speed in proportion to their height. A moving boat that encounters one of those waves head on simply goes up and over it. Or, as frequently happens, if a boat simply waits around long enough the wave will get bored and go away of its own volition.

When you encounter a standing wave, it is almost like hitting a watery wall. Since the wave is not moving, the boat must drag its entire weight up and over the top unaided. Of course, when the boat reaches the wave crest it becomes like a plank on a seesaw balancing there with the propeller well and truly out of the water. If your floating palace, complete with screaming engine, does not have enough inertia to make it over the top, it drops back and the whole nerve racking process starts over again. Oh, and did I mention that once the little dear finally does tip over the top she drops down the other side like some demented ten year old with a big hill and a new skateboard.

The potentially destructive stresses and strains this puts on a boat's structure are enormous. The screams and groans of tortured wood are deafening. Broaching is a very real danger. Each individual standing wave demands the utmost care and personal attention. Each is a life-threatening situation. Little wonder those two big phinisis were so badly damaged. Fortunately, big standing waves are rare, even along the west coast of Sumatra. Then again even one as small as two meters and become a right house of horrors. And, just to make it even more interesting, standing waves form where two strong currents meet, one of which is always against you.

Of course, where you get two strong currents meeting you also get whirlpools. Nasty little devils that can spin a boat in a full circle faster than you can say Hollywood, that is when the riptides are not doing an admirable job of shaking the fillings out of your teeth. Given a choice, I would gladly chose a seaside resort with pretty girls in skimpy costumes serving me cold drinks, and maybe even a relaxing massage. As I said, just thinking about that trip still gives me the willies, and the sudden desire for a large tot of brandy.

I will not bore you with the details of that voyage. Truth be told, those days and nights are only a blur of disparate panics and general misery in my memory. Mind you, it is a blur carefully sealed in one of those mental compartments with ten padlocks and a sign swinging on the door saying, "Warning to self, DO NOT repeat this experience, never, not even on a bet, honest, I'm not kidding me".

When we finally limped into the harbor of Pulau Weh our little ship and her crew both looked like recently rescued castaways. We were all covered in black and blue bruises, our variable pitch propeller unit had jammed, the elbow in our engine exhaust was cracked, and more than one part of the rigging needed urgent attention, yet all things considered, *Vega* was still afloat and we were still alive, a feat that must count for something.

Pulau Weh, especially right after the tsunami, was not exactly an industrial center overflowing with spare parts, or available engineers. Over the next few days, Meggi, Andy, and I did our best to get *Vega* back into some sort of seaworthy condition. We soon had the rig repaired, and the engine elbow wielded. Try as we might the variable pitch propeller successfully defeated Andy and me both. It simply needed parts we could not even hope to find where we were.

John, being Singaporean, was about as much help as a priest in a brothel. Great person, mind you, and he was always ready and willing, but the Singaporean idea of fixing something usually consists of finding the hand phone number for a nearby technician.

It took us four days to make the trip from Langkawi to Pulau Weh fully loaded. The return voyage took us almost a week, and what a memorable journey that turned out to be. Shortly after leaving Pulau Weh, the exhaust elbow broke again. That coupled with the frozen variable pitch propeller, which had of course jammed in course pitch, meant that the engine being overloaded by the propeller was constantly belching out black smoke. Most of which, I might add, was hard at work happily depositing a black oily film on every available surface in the boat.

The propeller pitch was so course it prevented me from using more than about one thousand RPM. That is only slightly above idle speed. Oh, I could push the throttle further along, but all we gained was more and blacker exhaust fumes. Just about that time the North East Monsoon decided to set in hard against us bringing with it a nasty short steep sea.

All in all, we were once again reduced to urging the boat along by shear will power and cheering when the speed surpassed anything over two knots. It was impossible to sleep down below and cooking became a drudgery. Our food tasted of exhaust, our clothes smelled of exhaust, and we all took on the appearance of coal miners just coming off the night shift. As I said, lovely little voyage that one was.

On the plus side, Meggi and I discovered that a little boat like *Vega* could make a big difference for people living on remote islands. Bye the time we suffered our way back to Langkawi, a plan had evolved. Granted it was rough, and would take us years to refine. Yet ten years later, that basic plan is more or less precisely what we do every year.

Chapter 15

The Art of Making a Difference

The 2004 tsunami had been a turning point for Meggi and I. It demonstrated firsthand how a little boat like *Vega* could make a big difference by carrying donated educational and medical supplies to remote communities.

From our years living in Africa, Meggi and I knew what actually helps people, and what type of projects are designed to help aid workers and their agencies worm more money out of innocent donors. You would be amazed how much hard work that lot put into insuring job security, paying themselves exorbitant salaries with incredible benefit packages, and wasting money in general– all tax free - bye the way. It is a shame they keep forgetting about the people they should be helping.

Over the ensuing months, we developed a simple concept of how *Vega* could make a meaningful difference in the lives of communities on remote islands. That basic idea, with a few refinements, is what we do today. You see, no one understands the needs and priorities of a remote community better than the people living in that community do. If you really want to help, you can always make a good start by asking *how* you can help.

Based on that simple premise, we visited several remote islands in Eastern Indonesia talking with village leaders, teachers, and health workers. We ask one simple question; what do you need to do your job, and improve your community?

We started with two islands, where we gathered lists before returning north to Singapore, Malaysia, and Thailand. There we approached friends who had been helpful during the tsunami to see who was willing to provide the supplies needed to fill those lists. The response was modest at first, but encouraging. When we returned to our two islands the next year, loaded on board were many of the items they had requested.

Delivering those items, we collected new lists. That year we also visited two new islands, where we collected additional lists for delivery the following year. Since then the process has been repeated every year, and every year, as our capacity grows, we add new destinations to our route.

Our first year we delivered two bags of expired medical supplies and 12 boxes of basic school supplies; in 2014 we delivered over 120 complete comprehensive midwife and health worker sets. All the pharmaceuticals were new and in date. Each of those kits weighed an average of 20 kilograms. Moreover, that was only part of the roughly 24 tons of medical and educational supplies donated to us by our supporters, and delivered directly to those in need.

We never waste space, or transport useless cargo. Someone is waiting for, and needs, every item we deliver. On a boat the size of *Vega*, we cannot afford to waste valuable volume on unimportant items. Hence, we never carry old clothes or other high volume low intrinsically useful items. We far prefer to carry antibiotics, or other important necessities in that space.

These days we usually have a volunteer Indonesian doctor along on our deliveries. The doctor holds clinic for the remote communities on our route, and provides training for the traditional midwives and health workers. Not at all bad, for a little boat struggling along with a volunteer crew on budgets you need an electron microscope to find, that is if there is anything available to be found.

Chapter 16
Life on the Bounding Main

Sailing a boat like *Vega* is not all-hard work, although for sure we get a healthy dose of it. There are also moments of hilarity on board, such as the time one stalwart volunteer crewmember decided to adjust the main sail peak angle all by herself. She could have done it, mind you, with the help of a belaying pin to control the halyard.

All she really wanted to do was slack off the peak halyard a smidgen so the sail would set better. It seemed such a simple job; she did not want to disturb the rest of us to help her with it. Everything went perfectly; right up until the moment she cast off the halyard.

One minute she was standing firmly on the deck; the next she was about three meters up in the air with her legs tightly wrapped around the mainmast, hanging on to the peak halyard for dear life and yelling for help. You might find it interesting to note that we regularly lubricate the masts with Vaseline to help the mast hoops slide up and down, so she was slowly slipping upwards as the descending gaff peak set the mainsail flapping and banging.

Of course, what with the banging of the sail and her ardent scream the rest of us all spilled out on deck in a rush. Seeing no immediate danger to boat, life, or limb, we proceeded to mill about rendering helpful advice, and making various sailorly suggestions.

Things like, "Shall we send up your lunch now or later". "Can you see land from there at all?" "Do you want me to make a picture? You have to smile if you do." All punctuated by the victim's shrill complaints and muttered curses, often accompanied by some rather dubious comments on our genealogies.

I mean really, can you imagine cross breeding a bald headed buzzard with a pink hamster? Well, she could and told one of the crew about that particular family relationship of his in exquisite detail. All of which she mixed with plaintive entireties to be hauled down. I think sometime before sunset was clearly her preferred choice.

Although old sailing boats were carefully designed to keep the sailors in and the water out the forces on *Vega*'s sails can be enormous. Those forces easily surpass what the average person can control with brute strength alone. Forgetting that fact is something, you do at your own peril.

Beyond a doubt, life on an old sailing ship can be dangerous. However, properly managed *Vega*'s lines are safe, and not at all difficult to handle. That is, unless you forget the basics in a moment of stress. That happened to another of our female crew one night, an event that provided the rest of us with a handy source of jibes and jokes for days afterward.

When a sudden squall comes up, or any other urgent "all hands on deck" situation, every one tumbles out in whatever they happen to have on. A nasty 3 AM thunderstorm might find more than one of us out on deck struggling with the sails while dressed in noticeably less than our mothers, or the local preacher, would consider appropriate attire.

The thing is, and this is all part of the sailor's ethos. In those moments, you do the job in front of you with no lechery allowed. Not even a little peek, Scouts Honor, and all that stuff. It is simply another one of those adaptations to the realities of being at sea on a traditional sailing ship. An adaptation that evolved to get the job done quickly, without first having to wait for the wardrobe department to tart everyone up.

Besides, it really is rather difficult to rubberneck someone in the dark when the wind is howling a wholie, even if they are standing right beside you sticking one in your ear. Soaking wet, hauling your heart out on a line is just not one of those magic moments, although any unauthorized perving of nature's bounty might quickly earn you a short sharp kick on the shin.

Well kiddies, it was just such a 3 AM squall, black as the inside of a tar barrel, with the wind wailing fit to blow your hair off, and water flying about by the bucket full, that found us all out on deck reefing like loony's, while tacking at the same time. Suddenly through that bedlam of natural noise, we all distinctly heard a definite squeal, followed by a rather loud squeak, in a manifestly female voice. It was coming from the windward sheet handler.

She was a young woman of great energy and dedication. She was also, what you might politely call, "rather well endowed". In her haste to help the windward jib across, she had forgotten her own position in the whole maneuver. When the sail filled, suddenly jerking sheet and all hard over to the downwind side, she was standing in the wrong place - topless.

Out of control, the sheet paid out rapidly. Whipping as it did so right across both of her rather prominent endowments. The result was a loud squeal and a spectacular rope burn. To her credit, and mind you she was not a very happy camper at that moment, she finished her job.

Once we found she was safe, and more or less sound, the off watch went back to bed. Nothing more was said, until the next morning that is, when the good-natured teasing and crew jibes began. "Wow! That was nasty did it hurt. Can I have a look"? "Are they Ok? Maybe I should have a look to check for you". "Want some help rubbing in that ointment?" Or, the more basic version of, "Hay, show us your rope burns". It was amazing how many volunteer doctors we suddenly had on such a small boat.

Fortunately, she had a good sense of humor, and the rope burns were not serious. Within a few days, they had healed nicely, with no sign of any enduring insults. That did not stop the good-natured teasing or the jokes, mind you. But, it was important to her, for sure.

You may have noticed from the above that sailors in general are a gentle, caring, lot who would never stoop to blatant inyourendos. Just as they would never take advantage of another's awkward position to tease. At least not much, in any case!

Nor, do these things always happen to the girls. More than one young lad has answered the all hands call in boxer shorts and received a nasty surprise when he realized the split in front maybe handy, but it does not always keep things in, or protect you from flailing lines and flying blocks.

More than once the old sea ditty, 'heave ho the jib halyard, heave ho the jib halyard, my finger is caught in the block' has been modified and sung on board, usually by the female crew, much to the indignation of some poor red-faced fellow bravely hobbling along, all stooped over with his knees tightly pressed together.

Mind you, those are the times when the girls get back their own, and with a vengeance. Comments like, "I didn't think it would reach that far." or "Don't worry, no great loss."

Me? I wear the nice snug jockey type knickers and glad for them. You see once years ago I tried the hippy thing of sailing nude, for a while at least. Until...Well, that's a painful story best saved for another day, or the uncensored XXX-rated version of this book soon to be released in a plain brown cover.

Chapter 11

Jakarta

Jakarta gives a completely new meaning to the expression "love-hate". Who ever said, "I used to muck about in boats, now I boat about in muck" must have been a yacht owner from Jakarta. The traffic alone is enough to give you nightmares worse than lobster and cheese. A cloud of brownish grey smog constantly enshrouds the whole place. Of course, since the land is sinking and the sea level raising at an alarming rate, air pollution may soon be the least of their worries.

As much as we enjoy the lovely place where we moor the boat, and our many friends, it is always a pleasure to escape from that great seething mass of humanity, all jammed together by the millions.

The seawater is so dirty no one ever volunteers to clean the prop. We usually draw straws for that job. As Meggi once commented, the almost total lack of visibility under that water may be a good thing. At least, you cannot see what you are sharing the water with.

Whoever finally gets stuck with that exasperating job runs for the shower once they finish like all the demons of hell are after them. If by demented demons you mean a vast assortment of viruses and germs, then maybe they really are.

One thing for sure, no one opens his or her mouth in that water. One small sip would most likely lead to weeks in the intensive care ward. Complete with doctors looking serious while shaking their heads, and a whole troop of attentive young medical students coming in to see the strange new developments. Or more likely, to check if you are cyan, fuchsia, or perhaps sporting pink polka dots with green strips that day. For sure, they would compose a few curious new write-ups for the medical books.

Jakarta is a place without a single marina, or at least a marina that is not falling apart or half flooded every time the tide goes a little above normal. Fortunately, our friend Pak Jusli invites us to use his private pier on the exclusive island of Pantai Mutiara.

That pier forms part of his charming Jet Ski Café. Jet Ski Café is the "In place" on an island with what looks like the highest concentration of wealth per square meter to be found anywhere in Indonesia. It is also home to the Pantai Mutiara Harley Davidson motorcycle club.

This is a place where almost every night we see Ferraris, Maserati's, and every custom made form of personal transportation you can imagine. Although I must admit, the Sunday morning Harley Davidson Motorcycle Club meetings are my favorite.

So many lovely motorbikes, all polished to the nines, line up as their happy riders take a break from running Indonesia to go riding, in real style. Imagine everything from sleek cut down choppers to what can only be Harley's answer to the space shuttle, all lined up on display. I am sure you can also easily imagine me wondering about drinking the free coffee and drooling on the chrome work. Ah! If only I was 24 again, and had the keys to one of those magnificent monsters.

The thing is, although dressed in their scruffy leathers many of those rowdy looking bikers, who happily give the bikers handshake, are some of Indonesia's toughest executives. During the week, when they occupy all those top floor offices with acres of expensive carpet and desks you could host a football match on, with a small army of beautiful secretaries to run around making coffee and doing all the work, these guys have noses so hard you could sharpen knives on them. Away from the office, dressed in their leather "colors" for the bi-weekly Harley Club meeting, they are some of the friendliest people you will ever meet. Over the years more than one of those men has become an ardent supporter of our work.

For us Jakarta is a very important stop over. That is where we purchase all of our pharmaceutical supplies, seeds, tools, and most of the educational materials that need to be in Bahasa Indonesia. We purchase our pharmaceuticals in Jakarta to insure the Indonesian Ministry of Health approves, and the instructions are in Bahasa. It also helps that one of our Harley riding friends owns the largest wholesale supplier of pharmaceuticals in Indonesia. He gives us supplies at his cost, when he is not outright donating a few of them, just to help the cause.

Jakarta is our final chance to do last minute stocking up on provisions for the long months ahead when we will be thousands of miles away from the next super market. Jakarta is also a place where I usually wind up giving talks on practical ship design at the University of Indonesia, addressing women's clubs, schools, and in general singing the song and dancing the dance or as one friend puts it, blatantly mooching and begging.

My main rant at the university is usually along the lines of, "ships are tools meant to do a job. So how can you possibly hope to design a proper tool if you have never used one?" Of course all those intent young engineering students look at me as if I am ready for a padded room complete with sleeveless dinner jacket, but then again who knows. Maybe one those bright young people will get the idea and some poor sailor will have an easier life for it.

When we leave Jakarta the boat is loaded to the deck beams. Every cabin, even the toilets, are packed solid with supplies destined for the islands we assist. A claustrophobic path between all the boxes and bags provides access to the galley, chart table, and engine room. With the boat so well stuffed this is a time when we all freverently pray for dry weather and calm seas. Prayers that are seldom answered.

Chapter 18
Rough, Wet, and Wild

Our yearly slog from Jakarta to Pulau Medang takes place against a backdrop of rugged mountains and stunningly beautiful scenery, a panorama where active volcano's and lava flows are daily companions. A rare insight into the world as it must have been when still new and raw. Indonesia is one of the most geologically active places on earth. Here is a land still being born where earthquakes, mudslides, belching volcanoes, flaming lava flows, and tsunamis are commonplace occurrences.

If the sobriquet Ring of Fire conjures images of volcanoes curving away into the distance for thousands of miles, the reality is even more impressive. Several geological collision lines, which stem from three tectonic plates pushing and shoving against one another like a pair of dowager duchesses locked together in a small closet, are still struggling to form the Indonesian archipelago.

A look at the underwater geography of Eastern Indonesia shows a mass of swirling arcs where vast underwater rifts plunge to depths of over 5,000 meters and gigantic volcanic mountains, well over 6,000 meters high, are thrust up from the floor of the sea. Damned impressive place, if you want my opinion. Just try not to be around when one of those volcanic brutes goes boom, as Krakatoa did some years ago, or that big bruiser on the island of Bali that lost over 700 meters from its top in one impressive detonation.

That one was a bit like a champagne cork going "POP". One day there was this normal pointy toped mountain minding its own business and the next day it was missing a few hundred meters off the top. Mind you, there was an impressive "BANG" somewhere in between. As these vast panoramas of natural beauty unfold, and then slowly slip into the past along our starboard side they break the monotony of a long tedious voyage, a journey where creature comforts are rare.

This is a time when we are either sleeping out on deck, or huddling down below on top of our cargo wishing we could sleep out on deck, where it would be cooler. Heavy seas breaking across *Vega's* bow, sending sheets of spray flying back along the decks may have something to do with it, but I always find that stretch of water the harshest part of the year. The seas are not the roughest, nor the biggest, but those miles are frequently the most uncomfortable.

We really have no other choice than to continue banging away for days at a time, fighting against the wind, currents, and head seas; enduring speeds that often fall below two knots with the engine howling away in our ears as it guzzles fuel like a thirsty drunk in a brewery. All we can do is endure, until finally the long thin island of Java slips astern and we turn into the Bali Sea. You may laugh, but there have actually been cheers when we managed to increase our speed over the ground from 2.0 to 2.5 knots.

Forget all the romantic images of sailing along this stretch. With the South East monsoon wind dead against us the miles we win are all thanks to "Mr. Perkins"; the name we lovingly christened that fuel-guzzling metal monstrosity infesting our engine room with. I can imagine what it must have been like in the old days of pure sail when square-rigged ships had to force their way along this stretch of contrary winds, currents, and seas. Of course, they would never have been mad enough to try it after the turn of the monsoon, as we are usually obliged to do.

The first indication of glorious salvation comes within an hour of passing through the Raas Straights, a narrow passage between the islands of Pulau Sapudi and Pulau Raas, two attractive little islands formed by the same mountain range as Java, a chain of islands separating the Java Sea from the Bali Sea.

There are times when two seas have different names simply due to their location, or some ancient geographer's fantasy. In this case, the Java Sea and the Bali Sea are so different in consistency and nature they deserve their individual monikers.

Passing from the Java Sea into the Bali Sea the water magically transforms from a murky dark green into a clear deep blue, with a much friendlier swell. Rarely do we transit the Raas straights without being welcomed into the Bali Sea by flying fish and dolphins.

On average, it takes us about a day and a half to cross the Bali Sea. By the time we reach our first delivery stop on Medang Island, the sea has changed dramatically. And a welcome change it is, after the hardships of beating around Java. From that point onward, there might be days when the weather is disagreeable or the seas a little uncomfortable, but at least we have the consolation of knowing the worst is now behind us.

The stretch from Jakarta to the Bali Sea does have one advantage, it provides a chance to judge who among our volunteer crewmembers is helpful and whom we need to replace as soon as possible. You would be amazed how many people are simply incapable of fitting into a small tightly knit team where their every action has an effect on the others around them. In any case, the trudge around Java is a real life test of who will make it and who will fall by the wayside.

Once in the Bali Sea we are usually blessed with wind we can use for sailing. Nothing to get excited about, mind you, but it does give everyone on board some good honest exercise, along with a chance to start learning how that mystical spider's nightmare of lines really works.

Chapter 19
Her First Day on the Job

A small fishing boat, redolent with the smell of ancient fish and rotting seaweed slowly approached the dilapidated wooden pier. Around his head, the owner wore a brightly colored headscarf. Tightly wrapped in the traditional Bugis fashion, his sarong provided a vibrant contrast of colors. With the skill born of a lifetime on the water, he nudged his small boat closer to the rickety wooden structure. At 34 years old, Ahmad Fajir spent most of his days fishing, but he was not at all abject to using his boat to play ferry should a fare be on offer.

Busily offloading a consignment of mixed goods was the piers only other occupant, a modest wooden cargo boat, badly in need of a little paint. From deep in its cargo hold colorful bundles and bales were flowing ashore along a chain formed by well-muscled sailors clad only in their wrap around sarongs and a head clothe. Their golden brown bodies glistened with sweat under the tropical sun. The cargo handlers teased and joked with each other as they worked. A group of happy children raced along the beach, deeply intent on whatever it was they were doing. An old man sat in the shade of a tree repairing his fishing net, a hat woven from palm fronds on the ground beside him.

Wiping sweat from his eyes with the tail of his headscarf, Ahmad looked to the bow of the boat where a rather attractive young woman was standing. She was dressed in a modest white blouse and long comfortably loose black pants. As he watched, she tied back her hair with a bright green hairband then donned the traditional Muslim headscarf most of the local women preferred for traveling.

Her husband and two children were still huddled in the middle of the boat under a blue plastic awning. Ahmad had borrowed that ragged plastic sheet from his friend Habib. He knew from long experience that during the often-boisterous crossing from Sumbawa to Medang, without protection his customers and their meager possessions, would soon have been drenched by splashing waves and flying spray. Today the seas had been unusually calm, the passage a comfortable one. Even so, he suspected the youngest girl among his passengers had been mildly seasick.

Standing in the bow, a small frown creased the young woman's brow. Here she was, a fully-fledged midwife and nurse arriving at her first official posting. She should be proud of her accomplishment, yet she could not help feeling a twinge of anxiety. At the foot of the pier, slightly off to one side, a group of women sat companionably on a large plastic sheet. They were ostensibly sorting seaweed and preparing plastic water bottles to be used as floaters for their seaweed farms, she knew they would be busily gossiping.

Mitha smiled to herself. She had been born on an island like this and was well aware of how community politics worked. Sitting in companionable comfort under a shady tamarind tree these were not just any women, these would be the island matrons, come to inspect and pass judgment on the new midwife. Although this was her unofficial reception committee, she knew that unless she spoke first those women would studiously ignore her, while doing their best to sneak surreptitious peeks.

But, first things first. As daunting as her initial meeting with those powerful old women might be, negotiating the rickety wooden pier had to come first. To Mitha that prospect was even more frightening. There did not seem to be a single nail in the entire construction. Mitha could see the pier sway and shake every time one of the sailors carried a load across it. She wished there was another way ashore, one that looked less likely to dump her unceremoniously into the water. She chuckled to herself. What a memorable entrance that would be.

Mitha smiled, she could hear her little family emerging from under the plastic cover. The children commenting excitedly on their new surroundings. Her husband, she knew, would be quietly taking it all in without comment. She turned to search him out, their eyes met, he nodded slightly. Supportive as always, he began to hoist out their meager belongings, passing them up to willing hands on the swaying pier.

Taking a deep breath Mitha did her best to scramble up onto the pier and into her new life in a dignified manner. With a toss of her head, she adjusted her headscarf, and then with another deep breath and a silent prayer, she headed for the women sitting in the shade. With a slightly forced smile illuminating her face, Mitha called out to them, 'Salamat Pagi'. The women cheerfully answered her greeting.

Shifting ever so slightly, they opened a place for her in their circle. Taking her place Mitha unconsciously began sorting seaweed, a chore she had grown up with. Out of the corner of her eye, she saw one of the women give a slight nod of approval. Within minutes, Mitha found herself the focal point in a lively conversation. Although the questions seemed innocent enough, Mitha knew she was being tested.

What the matrons of Medang saw was a polite vibrant young woman with raven colored hair and sparkling brown eyes who radiated a friendly no-nonsense confidence in herself and her abilities. They already knew much about her from the last midwife. A certified nurse and midwife, this new girl had graduated from her official Ministry of Health training shortly before being assigned to their Island.

For Mitha the next few hours were a blur. Taken on the official rounds she diligently met all of the island elders and drank the appropriate cups of tea. She was surprised, yet inwardly pleased to discover she liked the people she was meeting; they made her feel important. Young as she was these respected community officials were accepting her as an equal, an important addition to their little community.

While Mitha was busy shaking hands and drinking tea, her family and their baggage were conveyed to the official clinic and residence for the midwife. Taking one look around the place, her husband stoically shook his head then set out to borrow a shovel and some tools from their nearest neighbor.

The children he set to sweeping the front yard with an old broom. Within minutes, other children joined them. Soon there was a brigade of happy children all diligently chattering and sweeping. Judging by the amount of dust they raised, each one of the children had brought their own broom. If the noise was any indication, they were sweeping the entire village.

Exhausted from her official rounds Mitha arrived at her new home only to encounter a sad reality of life on a remote island. The further you are from the main population centers, the easier it is for the Ministry to forget about you. Her small rural clinic, consisted of an empty three room building, the whole interior now covered in dust. The front yard was neatly swept, but her husband had forgotten to close the front windows while the children were sweeping. She smiled and shook her head.

At a stretch, that building might accommodate her family. A broken storage cabinet in what had once been the examination room was completely eaten away by termites and starkly barren of supplies. Its door hung at a forlorn angle from a single hinge. When she went to open the back door, it fell off in her hands.

Although she was dedicated and well trained, Mitha had been sent to a place where there was absolutely nothing to work with.

Standing where a back door should have been, she hung her head. This was not how she had imagined her first posting. An arm reached around her waist. Her husband hugged her. She turned and leaned her head against his chest. That was when she felt the tears begin to form, tears she valiantly fought to hide.

On her own, with an entire community now dependent on her for medical care, she felt powerless. Looking up into the kindly eyes of her husband, she allowed herself a tiny smile. Frequently during her life Mitha had been called stubborn, willful, and even proud. Fortunately for the people of Medang, all those accusations were somewhat true. And so it was that faced with an impossible task a young woman squared her shoulders, took a deep breath, and never looked back.

While her husband repaired the back door, she would need a bucket and lots of soap. She would also need bleach, the ceramic wash basin was almost beyond salvation and the floors were thick with grime. That first night they slept on a clean bare floor.

Squeezing her small family into one of three rooms in the official health post, Mitha dedicated the front two rooms to her "clinic". What should have been the family's parlor became the waiting room. The front bedroom became her examination and delivery room. Although her family had only mattresses on the floor, with the help of those stately village matrons, she managed to furnish the examination room with a wooden bed, a stool, a small table, and a cabinet to store the meager supplies she brought with her. Supplies she had purchased with her own money.

A year rolled bye and still Mitha struggled to do her job. There were times when she was so deeply frustrated she swore she would quit, but her inner strength, and a strong stubborn streak, refused to let her. Here she was respected and needed, and here she would stay doing her best. Then, on the day two foreigners from an old sailing ship appeared at her modest clinic, a miracle happened.

Chapter 20
Befriending Paradise

Arriving from the sea one quickly notes how every island has its own special aroma. Volcanoes have their strong smell of sulfur and steam often in stark contrast to the verdant scent of land and forest. On more settled islands the rich fragrance of tropical flowers mingles with the aroma of cooking fires and exotic spices.

Once on land it is no longer the fragrance we notice, but the sounds of an island - a polyphonic orchestra ranging from a deep geological rumbling to high-pitched birdcalls. The wind in the palm trees, the surf on the beach, all blend to form each island's distinctive song. An all-pervading undertone to the village life each island supports.

After the long hard slog around Java, the island of Medang is a welcome sight. Located North West of Sumbawa between the Bali and the Flores Sea; the island of Medang is so small you will have trouble locating it on most maps. Here the seabed gently slopes upward, forming a crescent shaped bay surrounded by white sandy beaches lined with coconut palms. At last, we can relax a bit, cheerfully returning to the pleasures of life on the water in one of the world's most beautiful maritime regions.

After a week at sea, plodding along through water that could do with a good flushing, followed by a healthy dose of toilet bowl cleaner, the crystal clear water of the Bali Sea can come as a shock. When you know the depth where the boat is anchored to be almost ten meters, looking over the side and seeing giant coral heads that appear to be only a meter under the surface, can be more than a little disconcerting.

*　*　*

There are two villages on Medang Island, although Bugis and Bajo are really just one long village with two distinct ends merging somewhere in the middle. The islanders claim that both are very different, that each community has its own distinct culture and traditions. Strolling down the road it can be a bit surprising when the architectural style abruptly changes from one house to the next as one village suddenly becomes the other.

The Bugis are Indonesia's traditional boat builders and seafarers. They tend to be fishermen and sailors. For thousands of years these hardy people have built and manned the trading craft and larger fishing boats of Indonesia. Someone once said the Bugis people sprang from a cross between cats and fish. Seeing how at home on the water they are, I can almost imagine some truth to the story.

Historically those inveterate sailors were also the most adept of pirates. Bugis pirates were the origin of the term "Boogieman". Although they were never much for hiding in closets and jumping out on naughty children, they did invent the traditional black sails Hollywood now installs as standard equipment on every well kitted out pirate vessel.

From time immortal every Bugis boat had two occupations, each based on age-old cultural tradition, as well as the size of one's boat and its crew. If the other boat was smaller, those on the larger boat instantly became pirates. If the other boat was bigger, or had a larger crew, the smaller boat suddenly became innocent traders going about their lawful business.

Of course, as innocent merchant sailors they would run for dear life as fast as those big black sails would carry them, because by then the bigger boat would be busily chasing the smaller boat according to traditional job description number one. In many ways, they were almost like the British in that sense.

Lovely lot those old time Bugis sailors were; Just the thing to scare reticent kiddies into bed at night, or make them eat their greens. Mind you, they still have that rugged well-muscled look, with the long black hair, flashing black eyes, and stringy beards.

It does not require a great leap of imagination to envision any one of today's local fishermen dressed in a tightly wrapped head cloth and colorful sarong. They do that every day, in any case. If you add screaming bloody murder while leaping aboard some innocent - that means smaller – boat while flourishing one of those horrible wavy Kris knives, the only thing missing would be a jolly afternoon of pillaging, plundering, and ravaging.

The Bugis we meet today are directly descended from the intrepid slave hunters whose very name would have the dreaded, jungle dwelling, headhunters of Borneo taking to their heels, with their whole brood in tow. It is not hard to visualize those merciless headhunting savages legging it at speed for the deep jungle, or the safety of some active volcano. Which by the way, the male headhunters considered less of a menace than the Bugis slave trading pirates. What the women thought about it all, no one ever took the time to document.

The people of Bajo Medang inhabit the southern end of Medang and are the stay at home land lover type. Mostly the people of Bajo are from Sumbawa. They operate the island shops, cultivate the gardens, herd the cows, make the palm wine, and in general keep the island from drifting away while the Bugis are off somewhere fishing or trading.

* * *

We go ashore on a lovely beach, located between two clumps of mangrove trees and backed by a stand of coconut palms where the protection of mangrove roots, and the slight tidal current, has created a small lagoon, a place where we can safely tie off the dingy to overhanging mangrove branches.

Just up the beach is a small, rather dilapidated, building on pilings that was once painted bright red. A building I find reminiscent of an African chicken coop. Leading away from this picturesque little building, with its disintegrating thatch roof, is a footpath that meanders through a palm tree plantation, then into the village of Bajo.

The local architecture consists mostly of traditional wooden houses built on stilts, painted in dazzling colors that would have caused Gauguin to give up on the south Pacific and Van Gogh to forgo the South of France. Moving to Pulau Medang, they could have set up housekeeping together and painted to their hearts content. Mind you, from their point of view the island beauties proudly strolling around in their colorful sarongs would not have put them off either. And, they might also have found the women attractive.

The islanders are friendly people. The younger boys will paddle out to the boat in their dugout canoes, full of curiosity and excited at the prospect of practicing their English. They are happy to exchange a few words with who ever happens to be out on deck, and given half a chance will cheerfully hop on board infesting the place for hours while they practice their modest language skills. Mind you, for them learning English is an important step to a well-paid job in the tourist industry.

Chapter 21

Who Wants an Adventure

"What do you like most about being hundreds of miles from the nearest land?" Now that question is one I have heard in various iterations for years now. Most of the people asking are really hoping I will regale them with tales of death defying feats performed in the face of raging storms.

I don't know why people seem to think I go to sea looking for perilous adventure and excitement, when all I really pray for every time we cast off the lines is a nice dull monotonous voyage; the key operative word in that wish being dull.

Why they insist on confusing my passion for the beauty of old sailing ships with some demented desire for a precarious lifestyle is completely beyond me. You see, to date, I have somehow survived more than enough tempestuous excitement at sea to last me, at least, three lifetimes. The last thing I want is more.

Good grief, if I start looking back over all my adventures, as some people insist on calling them, it's enough to have me searching the yellow pages for remote mountain monasteries. You know the kind of nightmarish recollections that usually come back to you after a late night meal of dubious grease burgers and deep fried potatoes, complete with cheap oil in the sauce, just too nicely muddle your digestion.

All by itself, that Indian Ocean cyclone a few years ago was enough to provide a lifetime supply of palpitations and soiled linen. When you add the likes of hurricane Albertos, and the Great Tsunami of 04, along with the entire wretched congregation of meteorological and oceanographic calamities I somehow have managed to wriggle through with a whole skin, little wonder my hair is so gray. The real wonder is that I still have any hair at all.

What I treasure most at sea are those wonderfully dull moments when the most exciting thing happening is a gentle breeze and perhaps the odd flying fish. Mind you, keep a weather eye on those flying fish. They can be vicious little devils. More than once, while innocently minding my own business, one hurled itself out of the water directly at me. You try having a malevolent half-kilo of piscine kamikaze launch itself at you out of the darkness. Talk about a walloping surprise. Of course, Scourge, our ships cat, thinks they are the feline version of Pizza Express. The freshest meal imaginable, delivered right into her paws.

Ah yes, those cherished moments of dullness enhanced by the shear bliss of letting my mind drift aimlessly through a watch anesthetized into monotony by a study humdrumhumdrum from the turbines of boredom, that's the happy ticket for this lad. In fact, if you ask me, anyone who goes to sea looking for excitement might just as well take up bull baiting or the lascivious molestation of Bengal tigers. Either one would be a lot cheaper, and most likely safer in the long run.

Chapter 22

Welcome to Medang

Knowing *Vega* usually arrives at Pulau Medang in late June, a lookout was posted on the beach to watch for us. Most likely, some student was excused classes in return for sulking around the beach keeping an eye out for our arrival. As a result, no sooner had we dropped anchor off of Medang Island, than an excited young boy was seen racing down the beach, spurts of sand flying from his bare feet. For sure he was off to find Guru Arno. By the time we arrived on shore, a welcoming committee was lined up and waiting for us.

On our first visit to Medang, when we enquired about the island midwife and or health worker, everyone we spoke with steered us to "Guru Arno" at the school. Later we discovered they did this, not because there was no midwife, but because Arno had put out the word, steer all foreigners to him. The reason he ambushed passing visitors was to provide new English speaking voices for the children. In short, having no books or other teaching aids, he needed practice dummies for his students.

That first morning as we strolled down the path that leads to his school, we were guided by two enthusiastic young school girls. They had magically appeared out of nowhere happily yelling "Guru Arno, Merry Christmas, Good Morning" and "God save the King" for all I remember.

Happily dancing along beside us, they were cheerful little creatures. One of them had Meggi by the hand and was diligently dragging her toward the school. Having taken a shine to me the other girl was chattering away in Bahasa with the odd, "My Name Is Good Morning Happy New Year Mister" inserted from time to time.

And so, at the head of a small noisy convoy we arrived for the first time at the school where Guru Arno teaches English. When we first met him, Arno was an English teacher without a single textbook, or any English books, for that matter. He was teaching by repetition. Originally, from Jakarta, Arno is typical of many young teachers in Indonesia. His salary is modest, the benefits few.

Dedicated to their profession, yet finding themselves in a system struggling to provide services for a fast growing population equal in size to Europe and scattered among more than 17,500 islands that are distributed over an area the size of Canada he and his fellow teachers do an admirable job preparing the children for a dynamic future.

From our perspective, the cheerful young teacher we met that day was exactly the type of person we were searching for. Since then we have become good friends, and a lot more island children have learned to speak English.

* * *

As our dinghy approached the shore, I could see Arno and his friends waving a hearty welcome. Waving back, I knew we had a secret. On board *Vega* was a complete computer lab. When the head teacher first asked us for that computer lab, his logic was impeccable. To prepare children properly for the future, they must learn to use computers. Even the lowliest forms of employment require computer skills these days.

Also, carefully wrapped in plastic and tucked away safely on board *Vega* was the LCD projector they had been begging us for. On their previous list, that projector had been underlined twice – in red. Why an LCD projector was such a priority baffled me, but we had found them one, just the same.

It always takes a while for us to arrive properly. Once we have shaken all the hands, drunk enough tea and soda to float a battleship, and enjoyed more than one home cooked delicacy, we are usually well into our second day, happily burping our way from ceremony to ceremony, and trying not to fall asleep during the speeches. Aside from the fact it isn't considered polite, having the guest of honor snoring away during a speech can put even the most diehard local politician off their stroke.

It was not until the third morning after we arrived, that any serious offloading could begin. Boxes and bags of medical and educational supplies were brought up from down below, checked, then loaded into our dinghy. Three trips later, we began offloading the computers.

The whole upper class from Arno's school turned out to help carry things from the beach to the school. With such an abundance of energetic youngsters, we never lacked for willing hands. As soon as the loaded dingy arrived ashore, a whole classroom full of energetic youths descended upon it. Each student would happily take up a package, then set out with it for the school.

The final load contained the packages they were all waiting for. When we began to offload computers and monitors, along with bags containing cables, mice, and keyboards, a little cheer went up along the beach; more than one impromptu dance broke out. That exuberant cheering not only came from the students, a lot of it was from their teachers as well.

As our little parade of computer-laden students proceeded through the village, more than one parent came out to see what all the excitement was about. Most of those curious bye standers soon latched onto one of the teachers who then proudly passed along all the latest gossip. It seems that having a computer lab in the school somehow raised the status of the whole village. It wasn't long until we had everyone including the town drunk coming up to us, saying, "terima kasih", which means "Thank you" in Indonesian. More than one insisted on mauling my fingers, while others tried to shake my arm lose from its socket. Some of those fishermen are stronger then they realize.

By lunchtime, the whole island was aware of the new computer lab. Their children could now learn the mysterious and mystical art of computers. Over the next few days, wherever we went people would come up to thank us for helping the school. I must say we were also rather proud of that accomplishment, although their computer problems were far from over.

Like many small islands, Medang only has electrical power from 5 PM until 10 PM at night. Although that minor technical detail did not seem to worry anyone, I could see where it might prove rather disconcerting for students wanting to learn computer skills during the day. Fortunately, the teachers had foreseen that problem and found a typically Indonesian solution. We soon discovered exactly how important the mysterious LCD projector was.

Chapter 23

A Miracle for Mitha

When we first visited the island of Medang, Mitha Helman timidly welcomed us into her home. With trepidation, she showed us her modest examination room. I was dumbfounded. Out of that small 3-room house, she was providing medical care for well over one thousand people. Meggi and I realized at once that although she had the training and skill, she sorely lacked both the equipment and medication needed to do the job.

Sitting in her waiting room cum parlor, sipping the usual mandatory cup of tea, Arno explained our mission to her. While he was busy explaining, I had a surreptitious look around. I noticed right away that the clock over her examination bed was not working. Hefting a plastic container, designed to hold a thousand paracetamol tablets, I discovered it was empty. Catching Mitha's eye, I could see she was ashamed, not for herself, but for the sad state of her small clinic.

As Arno continued his explanation Mitha was at first leery, then slowly you could see her face begin to register signs of hope. Reflecting that glimmer of optimism, she began to sit up a little straighter, and then her eyes began to sparkle. When she fully realized what Arno was saying, and the objective of our mission, she brought both of her hands together covering her mouth and let out a little gasp.

Mitha looked over to where I was sitting, her dark eyes boring into mine. I could see she was torn between doubt and hope. When I smiled my most encouraging smile and nodded my head in a friendly manner, tears slowly began flowing down her cheeks. Women, half the time if you spank one they love it, but give one something she really wants and she starts crying, no wonder the world is in such a mess.

After a short discussion concerning the problems she faced, and how best to solve them, we ask Mitha for a list of the supplies and equipment she needed to do her job properly. At the top of that list was a neo natal resuscitator, followed by a few other basic, yet important, items. Looking at her list, I knew that dedicated young woman's life was about to change. Most of what she needed, we already had on board the boat. In fact, each of our standard midwife kits contained more than what was on her modest list.

Toward the end of that first meeting, we agreed that Mitha and her husband should visit *Vega* later in the afternoon, which they did. When we dragged out the midwife and health worker kits for her, I thought the poor woman was going to have a heart attack.

One of my fondest memories is of Mitha sitting on *Vega's* cabin roof cradling a neo natal resuscitator as if it were a newborn baby, unrestrained tears of happiness streaming down her face, while she sorted through a complete health worker and midwife kit. Her squeals of delight as she discovered another treasure in one of the bags, more or less made my year.

Earlier in the day, Meggi and I had carefully augmented those kits with additional supplies we felt would be helpful. Every year since that emotional first encounter, we have returned to resupply Mitha's health worker and midwife kits.

Chapter 24

Hot Air, Nails, and Noise

The day after delivering our supplies to the school, one of the teachers paddled out to *Vega* in his canoe He came bearing an invitation specifically requesting that we attend a special community "event" to be hosted that evening at the school. He seemed rather excited about it, asking several times if we would be attending.

Late that afternoon the whole crew, minus the anchor watch, went ashore to see what all the excitement was about. Arriving at the school, we found the quadrangle packed with people. There were flags flying and colorful bunting dangling all over the shop. I would venture to say half the village was there, all milling around the place, and looking pleased as punch with themselves. Well thinks I, who could have imagined a few computers and some other school supplies would get the whole town so excited.

In preparation for the event, they had even built a temporary stage lined with folding chairs and backed by two large poles with a sheet stretched between them.

Every chair in the school was out; all were filled with happy villagers.

The whole thing radiated an air of festivity, with women gossiping, and men standing around smoking and surreptitiously sneaking nips of sopi. Mind you, if you ever want to set up a company selling paint remover, or toilet bowl cleaner, just bottle that stuff to sell, then sit back and watch the cash roll in. At the rate things are going these days, you would soon be the only one around with a product that really works as advertised.

Well what with small children yelling and screaming as they chased each other around the chairs, under the tables, and between our legs, the whole crew were paraded onto the stage, where they duly seated us as the day's special guests of honor. I remember thinking to myself as we solemnly strolled across the stage to our seats, I wonder if they have a toilet, tree, or even a dimly lit wall, somewhere close to hand. As it was I wound up sitting with my legs crossed trying surreptitiously to bounce up and down while speech after speech droned on.

Somewhere in the past, I managed to dominate my fear of speaking in front of large gatherings of people. At least to the extent it involves me having to look sincere while mumbling platitudes and in general boring everyone to tears. The firm decisive expression on my face is normally only me wondering of there will be free food afterwards, or perhaps an acute attack of constipation. The expression I wore that evening was mostly due to my bladder complaining about being charged well beyond its nominal capacity. It was also informing me, in no uncertain terms, that if I did not hurry up and relieve the situation, I had best plan on standing in a puddle.

Now you know why, when it was my turn to speak, up I went with a smile plastered across my face that was only one-step removed from a rictus. I followed the mayor, and a few other long-winded dignitaries, who rambled on like all good public officials seeking re-election. By the time it was my turn I am fairly certain my eyes were turning yellow.

If you want a real tricky one, try speaking to a large audience in a language they do not understand, then waiting until an interpreter translates what you just said, all the while covertly wishing you could cross your legs then bounce up and down. I find the hardest part is remembering what I want to say next, while someone translates what I just said. The real trick is keeping it down to very simple sound bites. That way if you get lost, no one notices.

The other trick is in knowing when you have said enough. Make it too short, and people feel you are not taking the whole thing seriously. Make it too long, and they fall asleep, start picking their noses, or contemplating suicide by boredom. What I do, is watch the audience until I start seeing people raptly staring at their fingernails, or keenly exploring their nasal passages, which is usually as good a sign as any it's time to say thank you and start looking for the food.

No sooner did I finished my bit, have my hand mangled by various dignitaries, and begin looking around in hope of free food, than an energetic troupe of students began clearing the stage of chairs. Taking that as my cue to sneak away, I had just enough time to make a quick dash for the toilet, where my keen sigh of relief must have been heard on the next island.

Returning to the crowd, I saw that our chairs had been removed from the stage, and with great care placed right in the middle of the front row, where, mind you, it would be almost impossible to escape with any dignity. As we waited, I noticed a posse of teachers roaming the crowd shoving woven baskets under everyone's noses.

Here, here, thinks I. This looks just like the plate going round at a "Save Your Soul for $10" tent revival. The reality would prove to be even worse. If I had known what the immediate future held in store for us, it would have been me down on all fours crawling along at high speed under tables and between chairs, gibbering madly while making a frantic dash for the nearest exit, and dignity be damned.

Once the collection brigade was back in front, and after a few quick words from the head teacher, the lights went out. Music, reminiscent of a chain saw hitting a 10-penny nail, began to blare from the schools aging sound system; on the sheet behind the stage an image flickered to life.

. There we sat trapped like rats in a barrel with no possible means of escape, being mercilessly subjected to an ancient DVD copy of a copy of The Sound of Music in Bahasa. Well? You try sitting through 90 minutes of Julie Andrews babbling away in Bahasa and see how long it takes before your brain starts dribbling out of your ears. The things we endure to help these small communities are often unbelievable.

I am proud to say we all sat there, with an assortment of diplomatic grins frozen on our faces, through the entire thing, intermission and all. Of course, this was all part of a plan where the school was using the new computer lab and LCD projector, to raise money for a small generator.

That way the students would be able to use the computer lab during the daytime.

The scheme was simple. They would show movies once a week and take up a collection. The money would go toward buying a generator. Once they had their new generator, the benefits from those movies would be used to purchase the fuel. Their ultimate dream mind you, is a satellite Internet connection so they can watch live football matches. Talk about your community education and cultural development programs.

I found it a rather good idea; and the school did eventually raise enough money to get themselves a generator. Now students can use the computers we brought during school hours, rather than having to come back at night. Personally, I applaud this kind of initiative, but could easily have done without The Sound of Music bit. Then again, at least it was not Mary Poppins. Forget the hot knives and water boards, half way through that one I would have thankfully confessed to anything.

Chapter 25

A Great Day for Sailing

Vega gracefully accelerated as another long six-meter swell rolled under our stern before bowling away in a welter of foam. *Vega* slide into the trough, her bow momentarily pointing skyward before the next wave began to lift her stern. With a difference between wave crests and troughs surpassing 10 meters, this slow stately movement, accompanied by a rather endearing little corkscrew motion, was mesmerizing.

Scourge had herself wrapped around the compass binnacle peacefully snoozing away in one of those positions guaranteed to give any conscientious chiropractor nightmares, or strike envy in the hearts of contortionists the world over. Her front legs were facing in one direction while her aft legs, being contorted 180 degrees, reposed in an entirely different direction. Her paws occasionally twitched, as in her dreams she subdued yet another vicious flying fish, or perhaps she was stalking a giant yellow bag of cat biscuits through some dense pier side jungle. You can never be certain with cats.

With the wind and waves coming from her stern quarter, *Vega* bowled along at an exhilarating pace, propelled by a consistent 20 knot monsoon wind. As each wave reached amidships, a torrent of blue water poured over the rail, bursting into brilliant white foam that sloshed around the deck before draining away through the relieving ports, just in time for the next watery deluge. A sound like muted thunder accompanied the passage of each wave. The rigging whistled a merry tune, accompanied by the creak of wooden blocks and the working of lines. The whole rhythmically changing pitch as the boat rolled with each new swell.

Our little ship was happily racing along with a bone in her teeth and a contented skipper at the helm. She had only her basic working canvas showing. Her tan bark colored sails handsomely drawing against the effort of cracking on at a consistent nine knots. Their reddish tint sharply etched against the deep blue of our surroundings. A random scattering of fleecy white clouds accented the stark cobalt blue dome overhead. What a great day for sailing.

Earlier in my watch dawn had transformed a sea of wrathful malice into a scene of majestic beauty, the stately progression of breathtaking waves mutating with the dawn from a sinister gray into the full grandeur of the open ocean on a gloriously beautiful day. Try to imagine the feeling, a slight trepidation blended with unfettered awe, the whole so magnificent, so vast, that words become impotent, completely failing to capture an emotional essence few will ever experience.

Above me an enormous sky, the deepest blue at its zenith slowly, imperceptibly, fading as it approaches the horizon. You hear about big skies, well take my word for it; the concept has no real meaning until you witness a day like that. And, there I sat at the wheel, trying to find a description for one of the most awe-inspiring sights of my life. The Grand Canyon, the Sahara desert, getting the wraps off that statuesque blonde in Charleston, all palled in comparison.

If only I could take you there, share the sights, the sounds, the motion, a few moments of that grandeur where majestic, grandiose, stately, all those high sounding words become dry empty attempts to package what I was witnessing first hand. One thing for certain, when it comes to the ocean no matter how big a plasma screen television you get, it will never rival the real thing, or even come close.

The only places I ever experienced such awe-inspiring magnificence were deep in the open desert, or at sea. Both of them have in common an uninhibited view to an endless horizon. Places where you realize how small you are, and how immense the rest of the world really is.

But, my God, when you stand there on the fore deck with the heave of the swell and the heel of the deck, the gliding rush of a well-found sailing ship thundering through her element on a welter of foam, it sets your blood to pumping faster. Those are the times when your senses become razor sharp, those fleeting moments that last forever in your memory, the times when you really live.

Well there you have it. I tried. No wonder poets are such a nutty lot; they have trouble describing the smell of green, much less a thumping great real life experience, but with luck, you have the general gist of it. Like I said before, it was another great day for sailing.

Chapter 26
An Arrow Through Time

In utter silence, two hunters made their way along a familiar jungle path. Their handmade hunting bows were tall, powerful enough to drive an arrow through the thick hide of a wild boar. Their razor sharp meter long arrows, were designed to pierce with a spinning action. Once deeply embedded, the arrowhead would be held tightly by its twin barbs. Without thought, their bare feet followed a well-known trail.

As they climbed higher, the carpet of dead leaves and dried moss grew thicker, until even the greatest care failed to prevent a slight crunching sound with every step. A gentle breeze tickled the forest canopy lacing the air around them with a ballet of sunlight and shadow.

From the time they were small boys playing at mighty hunters, these young men grew up with bows and arrows. Both had spent long hours making their prize hunting bows, and special iron tipped hunting arrows. Arrows designed so that once embedded in a target the arrowhead quickly detaches from the shaft.

On their coming of age, each boy had diligently performed the secret ceremonies, known only to the men of the island, so that their weapons would be blessed and their hunting always successful.

Arno was 18 years old, and slightly taller than his friend Pilli, who was a year younger. Both shared the typical black hair and dark brown eyes of islanders. In the peak of health, their young muscles rippled under a sheen of sweat as they silently stalked through the jungle. Their well-formed bodies had been work hardened by a life spent roaming the steep sides of a volcano, diving for lobster in the lagoon, or rowing the heavy dugout canoes the islanders used for fishing. Although not an easy existence, life on their remote island was healthy, and the people content.

From high on the volcano, Arno had an unparalleled view of the surrounding ocean. There were no ships in sight, only the deep blue of the open ocean, not that this surprised him. In his entire life, no ship had ever stopped at the island. The old people said no outsiders had visited Nila since the government recalled the health worker, teacher, and priest in 1978. Since then the islanders had been on their own, completely isolated from the outside world.

For Arno and Pilli their entire world consisted of a small island barely 3 kilometers from north to south and 2 kilometers from east to west, most of that, the precipitous flanks of a semi active volcano. A world where everyone is related and the most exciting events were a giant fish caught by uncle Jaap last year, or the squabble between Ma Rosa and Ma Lala. A scandalous feud that had been going on for so long now, no one was quite sure how it had started.

Quietly stalking elusive wild boar on a steep volcano covered with lush tropical jungle is difficult work. Therefore, it was not surprising when later that morning Pilli, always considered the lazier of the two, decided to have a rest. Pilli would wait in the shade while Arno climbed a near bye clove tree. From that lofty, well hidden, vantage point Arno would keep watch for any boar that might wonder along. It was a perfect plan. Since wild pigs have no predators from the sky, they rarely look up when moving through the forest.

As morning progressed into another lethargic tropical afternoon Pilli soon found an agreeable niche and promptly fell asleep, while his friend Arno made himself comfortable among the branches of a nearby tree. Lulled by the cool breeze, the pungent aroma of clove flowers, and the incessant song of tropical birds the day progressed in leisurely island fashion. With Pilli deeply asleep, Arno diligently scanned the surrounding forest for the slightest sign of a wild hog.

The air was hot and humid. Insects chittered and buzzed. Streaming through the trees, a constantly wavering pattern of sunlight dappled the forest floor while perched high above the jungle Arno drifted in a hypnotic daze.

Suddenly he came fully alert, a slight discordance in the sound of the jungle attracting his attention. Scanning the forest his keen young eyes spotted stealthy movement in a tall stand of bamboo. Some of those stately bamboo stalks were twitching their bright green heads in a manner that had nothing to do with the prevailing breeze. He shifted his weight slightly, the rough tree bark abrading his right leg. Ever so slowly, he reached behind his neck flicking away a large insect. With the infinite patience of an accomplished hunter he waited.

As he watched, the wavering stalks of bamboo indicated purposeful movement slowly advancing his way. It had to be a wild boar, and a big one, no other animal on the island could move through such a thick stand of bamboo. The excitement mounted. Like all island boys, Arno often talked about killing a wild boar. In reality, few wild hogs remained on the island and those few were wily old creatures well versed in the arts of avoiding people. The chances of discovering and killing one were extremely rare.

Arno's concentration sharpened at the thought of what bringing back such a prize might mean for his future. Glancing down, he saw Pilli was closer to where the boar would exit the bush. Yet, Pilli was soundly asleep. Arno freverently prayed his friend would not start snoring; a dubious talent for which was Pilli renowned. Should Pilli make the slightest sound that boar, which represented a potentially wonderful dinner for the whole family, and praise from the village for Arno's prowess as a hunter, would quickly disappear into the depths of the forest.

Returning home with a large wild pig would make him a village hero. It would also make him a champion in the eyes of a certain young woman named Rosa, whose attention Arno dearly coveted. Rosa was the most beautiful girl Arno had ever seen. For years, he had dreamed of marrying her, although for the moment just getting her attention would be an important step forward.

From his elevated position, Arno carefully studied the ground. If the boar continued its current route, it would be exposed and vulnerable as it crossed an open space between two large stands of bamboo. When it emerged, Arno knew the hog would pause for several seconds sniffing the air and carefully listening for any sign of danger, before plunging back into the relative safety of the bamboo forest.

That was when he must strike. Those critical seconds would see him either basking in glory, as a successful hunter, or not. There would be only one opportunity. A single arrow would define his future. Reaching into his quiver, Arno carefully selected his lucky arrow. Touching his forehead with the arrowhead, with a traditional hunter's prayer he silently sought the support of his ancestors.

By leaning around the tree, he should be able to draw his bow, and make the shot. It would be difficult at that angle, but he was confident he could do it. Then of course, they would dress the boar and carry it back to the village where he could tease his friends, and play the mighty hunter in front of Rosa. He could almost taste the best pieces of meat that would be his by right, either to enjoy, or share.

With fantasies of a glowing future rampaging through his mind, Arno waited motionlessly, barely breathing for what seemed like ages. He feared opening his mouth, least the boar hear the heart beat thundering in his chest. His entire being focused passionately on a slight opening where the bamboo stopped and the clearing began.

First, a small bamboo shoot twitched, then a large snout came into view, questing between the bamboo plants; cautiously sniffing the air for signs of danger before fully emerging. As the boars head slowly came into view, Arno held his breath. This was no ordinary boar. It was enormous. There, only a few meters away stood the great grandmother of all wild pigs.

After what seemed an eternity, the gigantic beast cautiously nosed its way into the clearing, and then stopped. Arno swallowed hard. He could not believe his luck. There in the open stood an immense sow, within seconds; several small piglets came scampering out of the bamboo to join their mother. This was a fabulous treasure, straight from his wildest dreams of wealth and riches.

His mouth became dry as a desert. If he succeeded in killing the sow, the piglets would be easy to capture. Taken home, and raised by his family, those piglets would represent an enormous wealth. It might even be enough for him to ask for Rosa's hand in marriage.

After all, two of those piglets would set them up nicely with a house and a fishing canoe. Another two small pigs should satisfy even her greedy old father. The remainder would go to his own family, winning him enormous prestige in their eyes and the eyes of the community. The whole island would talk about this exploit for years to come. He would be famous; fathers would hold him up as a shining example for their sons.

His body tingled with excitement, as he slowly breathed; his well-toned muscles rippled, smoothly drawing the bow to its fullest extension. The arrow touched his cheek. Adrenaline coursed through his body. His heart quickened as he carefully aimed one finger width behind the pigs left shoulder. An arrow striking deeply there had every chance of piercing the boar's mighty heart, instantly dropping her where she stood.

Then with another small prayer for luck he spoke Rosa's name. As he released his breath, he also released the long iron tipped arrow. The bowstring twanged. Arno's spirits surged, as he watched the arrow he had worked so hard to make fly straight and true, directly toward its intended target. That is, it flew straight and true until a tree branch, suddenly shifting in the breeze, deflected it.

As Arno watched in slow motion horror, his deadly arrow wobbled away on a new trajectory, directly toward his sleeping companion. There was no time to call out or even to blink. With a dull wet sounding thump, the arrow imbedded itself deeply into his sleeping friend's side.

Startled, the wild pig squealed, bolting back into the bamboo forest, the piglets following her in confused panic. Within seconds Pilli's shriek of mortal agony echoed through the forest. Arno's moment of triumph had become a deadly disaster.

Chapter 27
The Finger of Fate

Alone figure, dressed in ragged kaki shorts and a faded blue "T" shirt, strolled along the shoreline, occasionally looking out to sea. He had been born on this island over fifty years ago; back in the days when the island still had a government health worker, an official teacher, and of course the preacher; a man whose main vocation had been to polish souls, in between marrying, and burying the islanders. A job made difficult by his steadfast refusal to respect the ancient island traditions. All three men were gone now. Recalled in a fit of economy 35 years before, by a government that scarcely knew this island even existed.

A man of medium height, with broad shoulders hardened from a lifetime of fishing and working his garden, he carried himself with dignity. His rugged features accented a face formed by years of experience, and the confident acceptance of responsibility. Streaks of gray highlighted his curly black hair. That evening, Pa Eki was in a pensive mood, reflecting on his life with its many successes and failures.

As a small boy, he played on this beach chasing crabs, or helping with the fishing canoes. The small cave where he and his friends had shared their secrets was still there, only a stone throw from where he stood. Even then, he had been a leader, chosen by the other boys to be their headman. Now, he was headman of the island, and his people's only source of medical care.

Seating himself on an old rough-hewn palm log bench, he watched the sky dim through various shades of evening. Deep in thought, he failed to notice the myriad stars as they appeared, stark against the velvet background of night, the Milky Way spreading a faintly luminescent cloud across the sky. He was more than 30 years away, on a day long ago when the island health worker had offered him a job as his assistant. Back then, there had been a ferry, a boat whose monthly visits everyone on the island anxiously anticipated.

The first health worker had been a cold reserved man from Jakarta. Frequently passed over for promotion, he was deeply unhappy. His posting to such a remote island only served to make him even more resentful and bitter. He was an incompetent, deeply frustrated, alcoholic who remained an outsider among the villagers until the day he left. Under him, Pa Eki had learned little, other than how to sweep and mop the health post, run errands, mix hang over cures, clean up vomit, and meekly be yelled at. When that man left, the entire island breathed a sigh of relief.

The next health worker was completely different. He liked the island, and its people. Quick to make friends, he worked hard to earn their respect through his dedication to their well-being, and his honest respect for their traditions. Discovering in his young assistant an inquisitive willing student, he began teaching Pa Eki the basics of health care. For Pa Eki these practical lessons were a revelation. As time passed, his knowledge and experience grew. Then, with a single radio message from Jakarta, his whole life changed.

Remembering that day Pa Eki shifted his position on the log bench. Flexing his toes in the warm white sand, he could still envision the sorrowful look on the health workers face when he broke the news. The government would no longer support Nila. The next ferry would be the last; and he, along with the teacher, and the preacher, had been ordered to leave on it.

Getting to his feet Pa Eki turned onto the path leading to his house. It was almost suppertime. His wife, Ma Lala, would not appreciate it if he were late. As he climbed the path, he envisioned that final morning.

With the ferry waiting off shore, the three government officials boarded the ship's launch with all their possessions and departed. Having spent the previous night drinking themselves into a stupor of celebration the teacher and preacher never looked back.

The health worker kept his eyes firmly fixed on his friends ashore, frequently waving goodbye. The night before, he had given Pa Eki the keys to the health post and the medical supply room, with its modest stock of bandages, sutures, and a few medicines. With a tear in his eye, he implored Pa Eki, use those supplies to care for the people. That night Pa Eki had cried himself to sleep, the health post keys held tightly in his hand.

The morning after the ferry departed, Ekus the boat maker managed to cut his foot rather badly while digging out a new canoe. His friends naturally brought him to the house of Pa Eki, who sewed up his cut and bandaged the wound. From then on there was no turning back. With no official training, a cheerful young man suddenly found himself thrust into a succession of life or death situations simply because there was no one else to do the job. Pa Eki had become the island health worker.

Over the next 35 years, Pa Eki matured. He married his childhood sweetheart, Ma Lala, and became headman of the island. He also struggled to keep his community healthy. A difficult battle, one he fought without drugs or other medical supplies. Today the islanders call him "The Needleman" and firmly believe that if a person has not completely passed over into the land of their ancestors then Pa Eki can save them.

Now you know how a young man who had been the unpaid assistant to Nila's last official health worker became the sole source of health care for the island.

Coming from countries where medical care is often taken for granted, we can only imagine what it must have been like for him as he faced the ailments and traumas of a small remote community. He did it all alone, with no medical supplies, and no one to consult with.

Chapter 28
A Cargo of Hope

Another ripe coconut fell. It hit the sand with a solid ka-thunk, another vivid reminder never to sit under trees with coconuts on them. Laugh all you want, but "a coconut falling from height can do some seriously damage, no matter where it hits you. Granted a hammock stretched between two gently swaying coconut palms may look enticing in a beach resort brochure, then again everything looks good in those brochures – even the food. What they do not tell you is how aggressive palm trees can be when agitated. If you really must park yourself under one, always scrutinize it closely to determine if it is armed". *Extracted from: A Dummies Guide to Surviving the Tropics.*

Several years after surviving the great tsunami, and our adventures along the west coast of Sumatra, we were busy gathering and delivering donated educational and medical supplies to small remote island communities in Eastern Indonesia. Out of the aftermath from that devastating tsunami had emerged a productive occupation for ourselves, and *Vega*. Honest employment that not only kept Meggi and I off the streets and out of the bars, but also seemed to be helping quite a few people living on remote islands to enjoy a better life.

On this particular day, Meggi and I were investigating an island we had not visited before, an island so remote we were the first boat to stop there in ages. It still amazes me how lovely pieces of paradise like this continue to exist. Here were communities living exactly as their ancestors had, completely free from the civilizing effect of outside influences, lucky devils.

There we were, enjoying one of those days straight out of a fantasy adventure novel where a gentle tropical breeze ruffles the local palm trees while a few errant fluffs of cloud drift across a cobalt blue sky. The only sound was a slight susurration of surf washing along the beach and the rustling of palm fronds overhead. Several of the village children were noisily playing in a small canoe. Fishermen had stretched a fishing net, hand woven from coconut fiber, across one side of the lagoon. *Vega* seemed content enough, resting about a hundred meters offshore, gently tugging at her anchor.

Meggi was off somewhere nattering away twenty to the dozen with the local ladies sewing circle, most likely discussing the latest in island fashion or the price of bananas in Singapore. Judging from the boisterous peals of laughter that erupted from that direction every few minutes, they were enjoying themselves immensely.

I was sitting on a raised bamboo platform, roofed over with a thatch of split palm leaves playing at politics. I was also marveling at my current predicament, and feeling generally sorry for all the people stuck in big cities who will never in their lives know such perfect peace and tranquility.

For sure, there must be a better way to pass your time than sitting on a tropical island, hundreds of miles from the next landfall, but if there is I have yet to find it. I was talking with a man who had never left this little paradise about how to help his village prosper. I am sure he thought quite a few of his prayers had just been answered. Then again, you never know with some people. He could have been sitting there doubting my very existence; thinking it was all a dream brought on by a mixture of palm wine and mystical local herbs.

After all, we were the first outsiders to stop at his lovely little island in over 12 years. To top it off, we arrived on a 100-year-old sailing ship bearing gifts of donated medical and educational supplies, as well as an assortment of knives, rope, fishing gear, and vegetable seeds we were willing to trade for spices. We even had a few good quality pots and pans with us that year. Which, judging from the occasional clatter of metal and squeals of delight, were going over a treat with Meggi's group.

To appreciate what our arrival meant to those people, just imagine a place where no goods at all arrive from the outside world. They had to be completely self-sufficient in everything. No nails, fishhooks, fishing line, knives, axes, cooking pots, cloth, or even matches had come to the island in over a decade. Medical supplies were a distant dream. School supplies were non-existent.

I must admit, Trader Meggi's Traveling Emporium was one of her better ideas. To be sure, an unexpected chance to go shopping was always extremely popular with the local island ladies. What with there being no other source of everyday kitchen utensils, sewing supplies, or other domestic knick-knacks she was providing a much needed service. The idea was not to make a profit, it was to supply a need.

Since randomly donating such treasured items to some of the villagers and not to others was a sure formula for animosity, and what with cash money being almost unknown on those islands, Meggi hit on the use of local foodstuffs, handicrafts, and locally collected spices as a form of barter currency.

Being an artist from the hair on her head to the tips of her toes Meggi can be worse than a magpie when it comes to collecting island handicrafts and art work. I usually go along with her artistic quirks, if for no other reason than to maintain domestic harmony. I did draw the line at a carved wooden statue of some local chap who looked to me like he was either severely constipated, or would soon be in dire need of some toilet paper. The thing was almost as big as I am. Well, you try finding a place for something like that on a boat. In any case, Meggi's General Store gives her a wonderful chance to get to know the village ladies and collect all the local gossip while they haggle.

You may laugh, but that gossip is our best source of information about what each island needs and how best we can help. The funny part is that to this day neither Meggi nor I speak Bahasa, other than the few polite phrases one needs to scrape along. Mind you, Meggi has become quite proficient with numbers and what she needs for shopping.

* * *

Being the most exciting event in their young lives most of the village children had gathered at a respectable distance around the meeting platform where I sat with the island headman. They behaved well those children, sitting quietly, watching intently. Whispering between themselves, their large dark brown eyes took in my every gesture. Their occasional giggles drew stern looks from the man sitting across from me.

At his call, a lovely young girl came running from one of the near bye houses. Her long black hair flowed from side to side as she skipped bare foot across the clearing. Hair so full and lustrous it would have made a shampoo company advertising agent cry. Her lithe young body clad only in a short wrap-around, and a bright yellow frangipani flower behind one ear. The happy smile on her face was warm enough to melt polar ice caps.

If you read this far, you have a pretty good idea my usual response to a very attractive, lightly clad, young woman is not what one would call paternal. Yet there are times when the situation is different. That lovely nymph of nature fit into her surroundings so perfectly, I could not imagine things being any different. All I can say is those island lads do not know how lucky they are, or maybe the fact they do is why they stay on the island. iPhones and taxes be damned.

At a gentle request from the headman, she danced away toward one of the houses that set on a slight raise well back from the beach. Moments later, looking for all the world like a golden hued goddess from some ancient Greek vase, she returned with a woven tray elegantly balanced on her head. Her tray held two opened coconuts, both well laced with local rotgut. I swear, that girl had an unpretentious walk on her that could bring a plaster saint down off its perch, drooling and gibbering.

Sipping my drink, I studied the man sitting across from me. He was as proud and dignified as a Spanish duke. Over the next 7 years, I would develop a lot of respect for that man, and a strong friendship. Pa Eki was the island headman and ad hoc health worker, a position he had occupied for over 30 years. Together we talked long into the night about the problems his island faced, and how he saw the possibilities to improve life for his people. In the end, I had a long list of items he felt were needed, and a very good idea of life on a remote island far from any infestation of what we call civilization.

Chapter 29
A Trail of Tears

As Pilli's screams of mortal agony tore at his soul, Arno dropped his bow and arrows. Half scrambling, half falling, he slid to the ground ignoring the clove tree's coarse bark ripping at his hands and feet. All he could hear were Pilli's shrieks of anguish. All he could see was thick red blood oozing from around the arrow.

With tears welling up in his eyes, Arno scrambled on all four to his friends side. Words of apology tumbled from his lips. His mouth was suddenly dry, as trembling with shock, he saw what he feared most; the meter long arrow was deeply embedded in the side of his friend's belly. Everyone knew that belly wounds were always fatal, a long slow painful death.

Panic set in. Through streaming tears, Arno begged Pilli not to die. Then with fumbling hands, he reached to pull the arrow out. No sooner had he touched it than Pilli's agonized scream stopped him. Sitting back on his haunches, Arno wiped the tears from his eyes and tried to think.

There was only one hope. They must go back down the volcano's steep side to their village. Once in the village Pa Eki, "the Needleman", would know what to do. Pa Eki always knew what to do. Struggling to his feet, he called on God and all his ancestors for help, then explained his plan to Pilli.

With Pilli leaning heavily against him, they started the long difficult decent to the village. As they stumbled along, the blood stained arrow shaft came loose from its head. Neither of the boys noticed when it fell to the ground. Nor did they notice the distance they slowly covered. Both were lost in their thoughts, and fears. For Pilli, it was the constant agonizing pain, and fear of dying. For Arno, the repeated image of his arrows flight and the sickening wet thunk as it drove deep into Pilli's side.

Twice during that seemingly endless journey, Pilli lost consciousness. Without warning, there would be a whimper, and then his knees would turn to rubber. Both times, as he carefully lowered Pilli to the ground, Arno was certain his lifelong friend had died.

Only the occasional whimper of pain, and Pilli's rapidly fluttering eyelids, indicated he was still alive. Arno pleaded with his friend not to die, promising him his best fishing line, and even his favorite bush knife, if only he would live. He also prayed. His prayers filled with promises never to drink sopi again, and go to church every Sunday, if only God would spare the life of his friend.

Each time, as Pilli slowly returned to consciousness, he was confused and in pain. Each time Arno gently helped him to stand. As they slowly made their way down the mountain, Arno pointed out landmarks, reminding Pilli that they were getting closer with every step.

Arno did his best to distract Pilli from his misery by telling stories about the good times they had enjoyed together; he even tried to sing a song, until Pilli told him to shut up, commenting between clinched teeth that one painful experience was more than enough. When Pilli faltered, Arno would coax him onward, a single step at a time, anything to bring them another step closer to their village and Pa Eki's house.

It took four interminable hours for the two boys to make their way down that tortuous mountain path. Arriving at an outlying area of the village, neighbors soon answered their anguished calls. Friends and family came rushing to their aid. On seeing her son covered in blood, Pilli's mother began to cry out and tear at her hair in grief. A stretcher was quickly fashioned for Pilli. Four strong men solemnly carried it in the direction of Pa Eki's house. Children were sent racing away in search of "The Needleman".

Exhausted from the effort and stress, Arno fell to the ground gasping. Pulling his knees up against his chest, he wrapped his arms around them letting his head come to rest in the cradle they formed. He was parched, he needed rest, but most of all he needed to know Pilli would live. He had never felt so helplessly alone in his life.

A hand touched Arnos shoulder. At first, he wanted to shrug it off, but when he opened his eyes, it was Rosa. He tried to smile; she passed him a gourd of water. Kneeling beside him, without a word she took him in her arms, holding him tightly, rocking him like a baby. Somewhere deep inside a dam broke. Shaking and sobbing in his grief, Arno's tears drenched her shoulder.

As news of the disaster rapidly spread through the village, a barely conscious Pilli arrived at Pa Eki's house. There they gently laid him out on a rough-hewn wooden table under the shelter of a traditional grass thatched roof. Little more than a single wall with a sloping roof constructed from bamboo and palm thatch, it was the village clinic. Quickly, more children raced away in search of Pa Eki. While Ma Lala began to boil water, someone began to ring the meetinghouse bell, others began banging out the news on the islands bamboo jungle drums. Within minutes the entire islands was aware there was an emergency.

*　*　*

Pa Eki was tending his garden when the turmoil began. Excited children, calling his name, soon followed the initial shouting. The meetinghouse bell began to ring with a slow somber rhythm. From long experience, he knew something was very wrong. One of his neighbors was badly injured and needed help. Resting his shovel against a tree, he wiped his hands.

With a worried expression on his naturally cheerful face, Pa Eki settled his wide brimmed hat firmly on his head then stepped out quickly along the path to his house.

For almost 35 years, Pa Eki had done his best to care for the villagers. He was always there to bandage their wounds with scraps of cloth, and help the best he could with traditional medications when they were sick. He had cut out so many fishhooks, sewed up so many cuts, and set so many broken bones, he no longer kept count. Yet, when he saw the Pilli lying on the table, an arrow protruding from his belly, he knew this was different.

Even though more often than not he was successful in his efforts, to Pa Eki that was only a matter of luck. Deep inside, he felt he did not deserve the people's faith in him, or his vastly exaggerated powers as their healer. He was not a trained health worker. In fact, his only qualifications stemmed from the fact he had once been an assistant to the last official health worker.

Blinking away those memories, he knew Pilli's life teetered on an unseen knife-edge. Like it or not, that boys life, a life he had helped bring into this world, had been placed in his hands. He shook his head. He had none of the supplies, training, or even equipment needed to treat this kind of wound. As Pa Eki looked down at the injured boy one thing was certain, this case would test his paltry medical skills to their very limits.

Chapter 30
Another Island, Another World

A few days sail away from Pa Eki's island is another little slice of paradise, remote and unspoiled. The inhabitants of that island had also been cast adrift by their government during the budget cuts of 1978. As the years rolled by life on that island continued much as it would have been hundreds of years before.

Until *Vega* arrived, many of the islanders were only vaguely aware an outside world even existed. Although the elders told stories of great ships that belched fire from deep in their bellies, to the younger islanders those tales seemed like mystical legends. The few who had set out in their canoes searching for that illusive outside world had never returned.

Lela stood alone in the doorway of a bamboo and thatch house. The light from an ancient oil lamp cast her in silhouette against its deep orange glow. Never intended to burn coconut oil, the lamp sputtered and smoked no matter how she adjusted its homemade wick. The chimney glass had broken long ago which only made it smoke worse. She hated that lamp, yet it was all she had.

The clatter of a shovel laboring against the stony volcanic soil disturbed the night. By the light of a waning quarter moon, she sensed the man's presence, a darker shadow against the night. He was dolefully digging a small shallow grave. A faint sob told her he was crying. Taking a deep breath Lela turned, looking back into the dimly lit palm leaf and bamboo house. A woman lay on the only bed. A bed covered in blood. The man's suffering was still far from over.

Close bye, she could hear the rippling sound of surf, and a soft breeze rustling the palm leaves; her island was once again peaceful. That peace was welcome. It stood in stark contrast to the agonized screams of a woman tormented by childbirth. A woman who, sweating, panting, and gasping, had bravely fought against the pain, struggling to bring forth her baby, trusting Lela's skill as the island midwife to bring them safely through the ordeal.

It had been a long hard delivery. Even so, the baby died in Lela's arms before taking its first breath. Now her main concern was saving the mother. The woman was bleeding badly. There was nothing Lela could do for her. She hung her head, a strand of loose hair fell across her eyes. Her birthing kit consisted of a sharp knife and a piece of string made from coconut fiber. It was exactly the same kit her great, great, grandmother would have used.

Turning away from the door Lela brushed the errant strand of hair from her eyes and stepped back into the single room house. She pulled a rough-hewn wooden stool closer to the bed. Sitting awkwardly on the small stool, she gently took the woman's hand in hers. She felt a slight pressure as the woman tried to squeeze, an indication she was fighting back. That was always a good sign. If only Lela could stop the bleeding, this woman would live.

Rhythmically patting the woman's hand, Lela let her mind drift. This was not the first, nor would it be the last, time she sat like this watching a woman struggle for life. Lala felt helpless, unable to do more than provide encouragement. A bowl of fresh water sat beside the bed. Lela dipped a rag into the water, and then wiped the woman's forehead.

For as long as could be remembered, Lela's family had provided the island midwife. A tradition passed along from mother to first-born daughter for countless generations. Fortunately, for Lela, her older sister had shown neither the interest nor ability to become a midwife. She still clearly remembered the day her mother ask if Lela would like to become a midwife.

Lela was proud of her position in the community. She had worked hard at her mother's side to learn all she could about the art of bringing new life into this world. Yet, deep in her heart, she knew there was much she did not know. The mysterious ways doctors had of saving lives, was knowledge denied to her. Lela bowed her head, taking several deep breaths in silence while splaying the fingers of her free hand across her forehead.

Drops of water boiled over from the old cast iron kettle. They hissed as they hit the fire, bringing her back to the present. She crushed a selection of medicinal herbs into an ancient chipped enamel mug then poured the boiling water over them. Stirring the infusion with a twig, she sat back, blowing gently into the mug to help the mixture cool.

The woman stirred ever so slightly. Lela reached out, pushing back a loose strand of hair from her friend's forehead. Supporting the woman's head with one hand, Lela held the still warm mug of medicine to the lips of her patient. With luck, the herbs would help stop the bleeding. A faint smile from the exhausted woman was her reward.

Ponderously getting to her feet, for Lela was not a small woman, she removed the bundle of rags resting between the woman's legs. They were soaked with blood, yet it seemed there was much less now than when she last checked. Either the bleeding was slowing, or the woman would soon be dead. Stepping once again to the door she immersed the bloodstained rags in a wooden bucket filled with cold water. She would wash them out in the morning, after all real cloth was a rare commodity on the island.

Faintly from the village meetinghouse, she could hear her neighbors singing hymns. At times like these, the village always gathered in support, imploring heaven to spare one of their own. Lela silently added her prayer to those of her neighbors.

* * *

It is difficult for us to imagine the difficulties faced by traditional midwives in isolated surroundings. Poorly trained, with only the most basic equipment, they struggle to care for the women of their villages. Often, because of their basic understanding of health care, a midwife is also the informal village nurse.

You want to know what I think. No one will ever understand the needs and priorities of a community better than the inhabitants of that community. It always amazes me when some big aid agency sends out Dr. Sniffle P. Muggins, PhD, et al, to waste a few trees writing another sociological report on the development requirements of some rural village located out in the back of beyond.

Think about it for a minute. For ages, those people have been surviving, raising their families, and even finding time for a bit of fun. They do that in conditions where, left to his own devices, the good Dr. Muggins would not last a single day.

The problems are clear, every year millions of children under the age of five and women giving birth die from easily preventable causes. Almost 85% of all infant death is attributable to five easily treated or prevented conditions. Here is the list, neonatal causes, pneumonia, diarrhea, malaria, and measles.

The most basic of training, medical implements, and drugs can easily save most women who die giving birth. So if we want to start reducing fatalities right at the beginning of the chain, then we need to get basic supplies and equipment, along with practical training, to the people delivering the babies; the ones who care for those babies and their mothers.

In the vast majority of cases, at least where we work, those are traditional village midwives; a dedicated group with more practical experience than you can imagine. When we asked what they needed to do their job every one of them said, 'training and supplies'.

So now, you know where the idea for our traditional midwife kits and training workshops came from. Later we added medications for pneumonia, diarrhea, and malaria. Measles is something you need to vaccinate for, so that is a bit past our capacity. Minus the measles, what we do is proving successful.

People like Dr. Aida, Dr. Hendra, and Dr. Dan, who are constantly out in the bushes treating cases and solving problems, estimate that those Midwife and Health Worker kits have reduced maternal and infant mortality by as much as 40%,. In some places, even more. Not at all a bad day's work, for a 125-year-old boat and a few lost souls out here trying our best to be helpful. And, when you figure we do it with almost non-existent budgets, well, not bad at all, really.

Chapter 31

A Star to Steer By

Everyone knows that poem by John Masefield, *A Star to Steer By*. I just wonder how many have tried it, and found that steering by the stars can be more difficult than it sounds?

Steering by the stars is one of a sailor's oldest tricks. You pick a star more or less directly in front of you then head for it. Align your star with a stay, shroud, or other convenient reference point then by careful steering, keep them aligned that way.

It is a great way to steer at night. Even the smallest deviation from your course, is noted by your star's movement faster than by the compass. When you really must "steer small" at night, this is the way to do it. However, that old trick is fraught with dangers for the unwary.

First, the star you choose should not be too high in the sky. Any star more than about 45 degrees above the horizon is difficult to use. The higher the star, the harder it is to notice deviations from your course. A star right over your head would appear not to move at all, no matter what course you steered. On the other hand, a star just above the horizon will apparently respond to the slightest change in heading. So, me hardies, lying on your back looking up at the stars while steering, is completely out. Laugh all you want, I have seen newbies actually try to do it that way.

When steering by the stars your intended heading has a lot to do with how accurate your star will be for steering. If you are going East or West then all you need consider is how long before your star sets or gets too high to be useful.

If you are heading North or South – and not using the pole star or Southern Cross- the stars appear to move from East to West as the night progresses. This means that over 4 hours you can see up to 60 degrees of shift. I think there are still 15 degrees to an hour. One can never be sure in this fast passed age of electronics, pocket calculators, and modern math.

In any case, the drift can be up to 5 degrees every 20 -30 minutes. More than enough to put the skipper in an arm waving, hornpipe dancing, passion after a 4-hour watch, just when you thought you were doing so well.

How you compensate for your stars movement is up to you. Some pick a star on an East or West heading, something more or less off the beam and use that. To do that takes a bit of practice, but it works just fine. Others are more exact and demand a new star every time the course appears to shift by 5-10 degrees.

Being a typical lazy sailor, I just shift my bottom a bit to compensate for the stars movement as I see the coarse drifting on the compass. Bring the boat back on the proper heading, and then scoot your butt over a bit until your star seems to move back where you want it to be. That highly scientific method saves me a lot of headache, and provides a good excuse to move around a bit on watch.

Chapter 32
With a Razor Blade and a Prayer

With a sharp knife Pa Eki slashed away the boys blood soaked shirt. Laying bare Pilli's stomach, he exposed the dreadful wound. Bending close he sniffed. There was the sharp metallic sent of blood, but no smell of feces to indicate the intestines were punctured. Looking closer, he could see the arrow had entered at a sharp angle. As his examination progressed, Pa Eki began to feel a glimmer of hope.

If the intestines were pierced, without antibiotics and special sutures, of which he had none, the boy would die. Even if he successfully removed the arrow, there would still be the threat of deadly infection. Pa Eki had no medications, no surgical supplies, and no painkillers, yet he was facing a major surgical intervention, one with little hope of success.

For Pa Eki, there was no choice. Doing nothing was not an option. If he did not intervene, the boy would die. If he tried and failed, the result would be the same. Nevertheless, if he was very careful, and extremely lucky, there was a small chance Pilli might live. So it was, that while the meetinghouse bell rang, calling the village to pray for Pilli's life, Pa Eki prepared himself, and the few paltry tools at his disposal, for major surgery.

Those tools consisted of five old style double-sided razor blades, a pair of scissors, and some bandages made from rags. To close the wound, he had a sewing needle and cotton thread. He knew the stiches would be a problem later, yet that was all he had. Fortunately, he also had a good supply of a local drink called *sopi*. Being almost pure alcohol, *sopi* makes an amazingly effective disinfectant.

Sopi is a powerful concoction the islanders distill from palm wine. Some say it is almost pure alcohol; others call it pure radiator cleaner. I call it pure rotgut.

While Pilli's father applied liberal doses of sopi as a painkiller, Pa Eki used it to sterilize his hands, scissors, and razor blades. By the time they were ready to start, night had fallen. Without a word, people brought every coconut oil lamp and homemade candle in the village to the small health post, so that Pa Eki would have light to work bye.

After a fervent prayer of his own, against a backdrop of hymns from the small village church, Pa Eki began an operation that lasted for over five stress-filled hours.

When the arrow struck, Pilli must have been laying on his side. Pa Eki could see it had pierced his side, and been defected along the inside of the boys ribs. The arrow was resting precisely between intestines and muscle.

It soon became clear he would not be able to remove the arrow by cutting around it then pulling it out. The sharp barb would surely rip open an intestine. His only hope would be slowly working the sharp arrowhead through the layer of muscle, then remove it from the back. Centimeter by centimeter Pa Eki slowly and carefully negotiated a way past the boys intestines, with the constant danger a razor sharp barb might rupture one of those delicate tubes, condemning the young boy he had helped bring into this world to a slow lingering death from infection.

He used tablespoons, carefully sterilized with sopi and fire, to protect the boy's intestines from the arrowhead. He also used the spoons to surround the arrows lethal head while easing it ever further through the boy's body gently guiding it towards a point on the boy's side where it would be safe to push it through.

The tension would have been unbearable, were he not concentrating so intensely on the work at hand. He was not even aware of Ma Lila wiping the sweat from his brow, or Ma Rosa, the island midwife, passing him his few tools and sponging away blood as it pooled around the wound. Hours of passionate attention simply faded into the past unnoticed. Fortunately, in his now drunken state of shock, Pilli spent most of that time passed out from the pain, and liberal doses of sopi.

It was well past midnight, when Pa Eki finally eased the arrow head between two muscles and gently pushed it out through the boy's side. Holding the bloody arrow head in the dim lamp light, he breathed a sigh of relief. There appeared to be no damage to the boy's intestines. So after carefully closing the wound, using a common sewing needle and thread, they left Pilli under the watchful eye of Arno, who had remained by his side throughout the operation. All that night prayers and hymns filled the air, as the whole community gathered in their small meetinghouse, beseeching their God to spare Pilli's life.

The next few days were nerve racking. Several times Pilli ran a high fever. Each time the fever abated after only a few hours. Thankfully, there were no signs of virulent deep-seated infection. It was on the twelfth day when Pa Eki finally began to admit there was hope. A few days later, it was all they could do to keep Pilli in bed.

Until this day, Pilli has a nasty scar, replete with stitch marks that would have most doctors unceremoniously ejected from the profession. Nevertheless, he is alive. He is also still best friends with the man who accidently shot him. Arno finally married the girl of his dreams. He and Rosa have three lovely children; one of them named Pilli.

Several years ago, *Vega* slowly entered the bay in front of that small village. Turning into the wind, we dropped anchor. We were the first boat to anchor off the island since 1997. On board we carried a full health worker kit, and a complete traditional midwife kit, along with school supplies.

We did not know the arrow story when we presented Pa Eki with his first health worker kit. That kit was complete with antibiotics, painkillers, minor surgical implements, and other important tools for community health care. What I did see were tears in a proud man's eyes as he unpacked those two kits, carefully examining every item. When he came to the book, "Where there is no Doctor", in Bahasa, he clutched it to his heart. Looking up he said, "I have needed something like this for 35 years, thank you."

Sometime back, I read where a famous philosopher once said, 'The things we do for ourselves will die with us, The things we do for others are our chance at immortality"...or some such gibberish. In any case, I like to think he was right.

Chapter 33
The Wind of Change

For Lela, change came in the form of a small sailing ship. It silently appeared one morning then anchored close to her village. The appearance of a vessel from the outside, the first many of the islanders had ever seen, frightened some of them so badly they hide in the forest. Some of the men took up their hunting bows and arrows, or fishing spears determined to defend their homes and families. The longer the boat sat there peacefully riding to its anchor, the more intrigued the islanders became.

Clearly, something had to be done. As the day wore on five people were seen moving around on the deck of that strange vessel, including several women. At last it was decided the island headman with a delegation of island notables should investigate. After all, the elders always said the people who once came from outside were friendly. It was also decided that perhaps a few invigorating cups of sopi were in order before undertaking such a dubious mission.

While the village leaders were busy fortifying themselves with sopi, several of the island children took matters into their own hands. Having drifted back from their hiding places in the forest they were soon speculating on what treasures such a strange vessel might hold. When someone was seen out on the mystery vessels deck the children called out greetings and waved. When people on the boat waved back in a friendly manner, several of the more adventurous youngsters promptly dove into the water fully intent on exploring something new and potentially exciting. Worried parents calling them back were promptly ignored.

While the children were swimming out someone lowered the ships dingy. By the time they arrived it was tied alongside. Children being children, they launched themselves like little otters right over the side and into the dingy. A woman on the boat welcomed them in their own language and soon the air was filled with excited squeals and a thousand questions. Then wonder of wonders the woman gave each of them a piece of hard candy, something they had never seen before.

By then the more than slightly inebriated village notables, found themselves being heckled by some of the older women who laughingly teased them about their bravery. With no other choice, and seeing the children seemed to be enjoying themselves immensely, a canoe was launched and the tipsy delegation of island grandees set out to greet the newly arrived visitors. A meeting that went extremely well for all concerned. It was soon agreed that since they were all tired from days at sea the boats crew would come ashore early the following day.

* * *

Early the next morning, when the sun was about two hands above the horizon, four of the ship's crew boarded their small boat and came ashore. Among them, was an Indonesian doctor. Never before had a real doctor visited the island. On hearing that the woman was a doctor, Lela timidly introduced herself as the island midwife and nurse, fully expecting that a full doctor would look down on her and her uneducated ways. Yet, the friendly lady doctor had smiled with those gentle brown eyes and taken her hand.

Lela was truly shocked when the doctor not only offered to hold clinic on the island, but also insisted that Lela assist. Within minutes, the ice was broken and the two women were deeply engrossed in various technical aspects of their profession.

Three hours later, she was dazed from the wealth of information her simple questions had brought forth. She still had no idea how a pulse oxymeter worked or even what one was, but at least now, she was ignorant in much greater detail than ever before.

For the next two days, Lela eagerly absorbed new medical techniques and knowledge from the doctor. Those were exciting times for Lela. Every morning she would sit on the beach anxiously waiting for the doctor to come ashore. Every night she would sit up late reviewing in her mind's eye each precious new gem of knowledge.

Far from treating her as uneducated, Lela could read and was extremely proud of the fact, the doctor spent long hours every day freely sharing her knowledge and skills. Yet, as the doctor frequently pointed out, skill and knowledge alone were not enough. To be a fully effective midwife and nurse Lela would need the proper drugs and equipment; she would also need to understand how to use those drugs and equipment.

For Lela, living on a small remote island far out in the Banda Sea, the prospect of finding those drugs and equipment seemed a depressingly impossible task, yet without them women and babies would continue to die. The more she learned, the more frustrated she became. She could be saving lives using simple techniques, but those techniques required materials she could never dream of possessing.

Then came the most magnificent day in Lela's life, a day she would never forget. It was a day that changed the lives of every person on her island. Stepping gingerly ashore the doctor reached back into the boat and tried to lift out a heavy black bag. From where she stood, Lela could see a slightly smaller black bag sitting beside it.

Looking around the doctor called Lela to come help carry the bags, something she would be happy to do. Then again, was that not what children are for? Using her authority she soon had two boys scampering down the beach toward her house, a black bag balanced on the head of each. As they ran along, they played with a football someone on the ship had given them.

Beside Lela's house stands a raised bamboo platform, carpeted with a mat woven from palm fronds. It is a place where she, her family, and friends frequently sit enjoying the cool shade and gentle breeze. The palm leaf roof is more for the cool shade it creates, than protection against rain.

Lifting one of the bags from the sand where the boys had left them the doctor placed it on the platform, motioning for Lela to do the same with the other bag. Lifting her bag, she noticed it was small, yet quite heavy. Lela marveled at the two stoutly made black ballistic nylon bags with their heavy plastic zippers and various snap pockets. More than a little envious, she wished for even a small bag like that.

For the next few minutes, the two women sat together comfortably sipping herbal tea, enjoying the cool breeze and each other's company. The black bags rested innocently between them. Lela noted the bags were tightly packed, and wondered what they contained. She was so curious she could hardly restrain herself, yet her inherent dignity prevailed. The doctor's face wore an enigmatic smile. As they talked, their conversation naturally drifted to medical matters.

Pulling the smaller of the bags closer to herself, the doctor unsnapped one of the side pockets. Reaching in, she extracted a medium size paperback book. At first, Lela thought it was in English, a language she did not understand. Then she noticed the title was in Bahasa. As she read the title, her heart leaped; the book was, "A Guide for Rural Midwives".

As the doctor passed that precious book to Lela, she explained some of its contents. Everything Lela had always wanted to know was there between those covers. Caressing the book, Lela clasped it to her ample breast. Then the doctor opened the opposite end of the smaller bag easily extracting another book. In silence, yet with a little smile she could not hide, she passed this new book to Lela.

The second book made Lela's heart beat even faster; her emotions overwhelmed her, unbidden tears came to her eyes. The title of that book is *Where There is No Doctor*. Opening a page at random, she saw this was no deeply complicated medical tome, but a simply worded book intended for people like her, and it was in her language.

Her breath caught in her throat. Without thinking, she leaned across the bags hugging the doctor tightly, all the time thanking and blessing her profusely. Time ceased to have meaning for the university trained medical doctor and the traditional island midwife. Each of them overwhelmed by their private thoughts and emotions.

Finally breaking the spell, the doctor encouraged Lela to open the two bags and explore their contents. With trembling hands, Lela unzipped the larger bag. It was packed tightly with bandages and drugs. Piece by piece, the two women emptied the bag, the doctor carefully explaining each item and its proper use. Lela was stunned. All she could do was nod her head as she gapped in awe at the magnificent treasure trove of supplies as each new item emerged.

Turning to the second, smaller, bag the doctor slid open the zipper. There on the top of that bags contents was a carefully folded black ballistic nylon shoulder bag. The doctor quickly explained how that bag was to become Lela's "carry out bag". Grinning like a little girl, Lela simply could not resist getting to her feet and strutting up and down a few times with the new black bag on her shoulder.

The second bag seemed to be packed with small boxes. One by one, the women extracted each box, carefully opening it to reveal the medical equipment contained within. Blood pressure cuff, Doppler fetal heart beat monitor, stethoscope, surgical implements, a natal resuscitator, a suction device, syringes, and sutures, even a stainless steel kidney dish.

One at a time, these treasures emerged. Like little children with new toys, they removed each from its box to assemble it, the doctor explaining its use. There was even a small solar panel to recharge batteries for some of the equipment.

When the doctor opened a small blue box, Lela's mouth fell open. It contained a stainless steel nurse's watch. Lela had never seen a watch before, much less even dreamed of owning one. It was the only watch on the island. Holding it in her hand Lela fumbled with the clasp, until the doctor showed her its secrets, explaining the watch was an important tool for timing contractions. Thirty exciting minutes later, Lela had more or less mastered the mystery of clocks.

As they worked, the doctor warned Lela that the next few days would be intense. There was much to learn and little time to teach. In her awed state, in between surreptitious glances at her new watch, Lela could do little more than nod her head, often forgetting to keep her mouth closed.

The next few days were strenuous. They were also magical. Lela discovered the mysteries of blood pressure, how to prepare and give injections, how to clear a new babies breathing passage, and how to use the natal resuscitator, even how to sterilize her surgical implements to avoid infection. At first, the fetal heart beat monitor mystified her, until a sudden inspiration brought understanding.

It was a pleasant surprise when the doctor suggested using sopi as a readily available antiseptic. Just when Lela thought her head was going to explode, they began with drugs and their proper use.

Lela was relieved to discover the drugs in her bag corresponded precisely to the ones mentioned in her new books. When a book suggested a drug, she knew it was there in her bag to use. More than once, the doctor warned that she should not waste the drugs, admonishing her to use them only when she was certain they were needed.

All too soon, it was time for the doctor to leave. As she explained, the old sailing ship she arrived on would be visiting other islands to train and equip more midwives like Lela, but with luck, they would return next year to resupply Lela's kit, provide her with more training, and help with other village projects. Lela had been so intent on learning; she had scarcely noticed what others from the ship were doing. Later, she discovered they had also been busy.

The next morning, as silently as it arrived, the old ship pulled up its anchor and sailed away. The whole village was gathered on the beach to wave them good-bye.

At sunset that evening, Lela visited a small grave beside the house of her friend. Some years ago, the woman had almost died in childbirth, her baby had not survived. Kneeling beside the small grave, Lela placed her precious new books on each side of the small mound. Deep in prayer, she gave thanks for what she had learned over the past few days. Now she had the skills and equipment to save babies like this one. As a single tear ran down her cheek, she swore that never again, would a baby die like this one had, or a mother bleed to death.

Chapter 34

Welcome to Paradise

It was early morning, when we hove to off a remote island in the Banda Sea. A light scattering of crisp white clouds streamed from the volcano's peak, highlighting intensely green tropical foliage. In the lee of this lovely island the seas were calm, the wind a gentle zephyr laden with the exotic fragrance of a tropical landfall. In contrast, the bedraggled crew of *Vega* was still rather well shaken up and green around the gills from the previous night's adventure.

Not wishing to arrive in the dark, we had spent the previous night plodding along at 3 knots. Unable to come to terms with waves from several directions, and with only a few small sails to stabilize her, *Vega* could not settle into her usual gliding rhythm. That was a miserable time, a long hard slog through turbulent seas, constantly pitching and rolling. The kind of night where the whole crew hardily wished they were somewhere else. Inspecting the Great Wall of China was one of my favorites, the bit that crosses the Mongolian desert, that is.

This small island, formed by a single volcano, is only the tip of an ancient tectonic ridge running from southwest to northeast. Ascending almost 5,000 meters from the ocean floor before broaching the surface this massive fault line, formed by two of the earth's most active tectonic plates, supports only a few widely scattered islands. These islands are the craters of semi-active volcanoes. They rise for another 600 or so meters above sea level. Basking lazily in the tropical sun, those small islands support some of our planet's most remote communities.

For most of us, imagining life with no electricity, internet, telephone, or radio is almost as difficult as imagining life where money has no meaning, there being no shops to spend it in. Being far from wealthy, I personally find the lack of money part quite refreshing. The islanders just take it in stride, and look at you in an odd way if you talk about the importance of money.

Isolated and alone, people on these islands live in a time warp, blissfully unaware of the outside world. For us, arriving is like a mystical sojourn, illuminating an idyllic tranquility where the concept of time takes on new meaning. Like Eden before the fall, there is morning, midday, afternoon, and evening. Each roughly demarcated by the suns passage. Rainy and dry seasons replace months, while the moon tells the weeks and days. We jokingly say they have their own time zone, IMT. That stands for "Island Maybe Time", by the way.

Once in the lee of the land we all breathed a sigh of relief, before heaving to in preparation for anchoring. It was not long before every available canoe on the north side of the island was scurrying in our direction. Every one of them loaded to the tipping point with friends and well-wishers, all waving and in some cases singing.

First up the side was the headman of the island, our friend Pa Eki, with his wonderful sense of humor, and more dignity than a bus full of bishops. Soon our deck resembled a tramp inter-island ferry, covered with smiling faces and the cheerful banter of excited people.

Over the next hour or so, that many visitors did serious damage to our meager store of concentrated fruit juice and biscuits. Not that we mind, it all being shared among friends whom we are heartily glad to see again. Even the island drunk managed to make it on board, where he took one look around, yelled something like "Yippee", and proceeded to pass out under the aft awning.

For the island of Nila, *Vega*'s annual arrival is an important event. When you consider we are the only outside faces they see from one year to the next, you can easily imagine what it means for a community where excitement consists of catching a big fish, or getting drunk on the local hooch and watching palm trees grow.

Lucky for us, one of the first to climb on board was our friend Pak Jak, the best reef guide on the island. Having him to guide me safely through their nightmare tangle of reefs and into the anchorage is always welcome. Mind you, I find him better than a double dose of Valium or a tot of rum as we slowly make our way into that anchorage.

The entrance to Nila's anchorage is full of sharp-toothed coral traps, just waiting to rip the bottom out of any unwary vessel. The main entrance is a twisted channel between coral reefs that leads into a small lagoon. Nila is one of those places where even with four anchors out behind coral heads, I still worry about the anchors dragging. The thing is, once inside if the anchors do start to drag there is only one place to go, and that place is the stuff of every sailor's worst nightmares.

On Nila we supply 3 communities with educational and medical supplies, as well as other important items such as tools, vegetable seeds, spare parts, fishing gear, nails, nuts , bolts, screws, thread, sewing needles, you name it. You see, we are their only contact with the outside world, and their only source for these important supplies. No wonder they are so happy to see us every year. How would you feel with a hole in your knickers and no thread to fix it?

When we arrived, the tide was falling rapidly. Therefore, I decided to wait until it turned before making our entrance. Even with the guidance of someone like Pak Jak, I always prefer to enter tricky places on a rising tide. That way if we run ground – again – there is every chance the tide will quickly lift us off.

You may have noticed that being a sailor is often an exercise in wariness. The reason for that is simple, at sea anything that can go wrong, will go wrong, eventually. Yet frequently even a healthy measure of paranoia is not enough. Which constantly has me wondering, "am I being paranoid enough?" As one of my mentors once said, "The emergency you prepare for never happens". Mind you, he also said, "It's your job to worry about everything that can go wrong, then once you've done that, start worrying about the things you forgot to worry about in the first place."

Waiting for the tide to change, we filled our time with general gossip from the island, new babies born, canoes launched, fish caught, the myriad things people on a small island find important. Strange how their news was all about real things that have an effect people's daily lives. Makes you wonder about all the various "crises" the rest of us call news. Most of it is media rubbish, which has little or no effect on people at all – other than keeping journalists employed busily causing more stress and worry among the general population. Little wonder we never watch television.

Several hours later, we slowly worked our way in through the coral infested entrance. Even with Pak Jak guiding us, I had one of our crew up in the main tops with a hand held radio watching out, while Meggi was out on the bow sprite doing the same. Slowly. Very slowly. We picked our way into the anchorage. I admit, I chewed my mustache the whole way, and added a few more gray hairs, while twisting and contorting *Vega* through that narrow channel.

The final turn, where the channel disgorges into the lagoon, is so tight I can only make it by backing and filling, judiciously using *Vega's* notorious prop walk to twist her around the bend. All this, in a channel that may have been as broad as the Suez Canal, but from my position at the wheel seemed only slightly wider than *Vega*.

Getting our anchors down, and safely lodged behind large coral heads, seemed to be an unspoken cue for the wind to pick up. For the next two days, the wind blew hard, making it impossible for our small boat to land on the beach.

Fortunately, the main reef extends almost a mile out to sea, effectively protecting the shallow northern anchorage from the massive swells we could see breaking with astonishing force along the reefs outer face. Unable to go ashore, we waited, fixing a few things, and cleaning up the boat, happy to have arrived safely and excited about our upcoming adventures ashore.

Chapter 35
The Wonders of Coffee

For years we have been roasting our own coffee, then hand grinding it each morning in a 75-year-old cast iron Sponge coffee grinder. Meggi and I found that coffee grinder many years ago in Durban, South Africa. I still say, that thing was one of the best investments we ever made, even if it did cost half the national debt.

Meggi and I have always enjoyed coffee. After living in so many places where the world's finest coffee is grown, we finally broke down and started grinding our own.

We began that tradition just after visiting a coffee plantation in Tanzania. Over coffee – what else on a coffee plantation – the owner explained the intricacies of storing, transporting, roasting, and grinding coffee. His expert enlightenment was a revelation for us both. With lovely aromatic cups of coffee in hand, we learned coffee beans could safely be stored for years, with only a slight loss in flavor. The trick is to keep them dry in well-ventilated bags.

His second revelation concerned the roasting process. Roasting is how all the hidden flavor is released from coffee. He explained that roasted beans would last quite some time, retaining most of their flavor. Yet, to get the finest aroma, and savor you needed to re-roast the beans shortly before grinding them.

He happily rambled on in detail, as experts with a captive audience tend to do, about proteins, and peptides, and other pollyputheketleon molecular gibberish he seemed to think was important. After the first few minutes, Meggi and I sat there politely sipping our coffee with glazed expressions plastered across our faces. The up-shot of his dissertation was that the beans needed a good re-roasting within a day or so of use to bring out the flavor.

Then he explained another key element in the preparation of great coffee, the grinding of the beans. If the beans become too hot while grinding, you lose delicate volatile oils responsible for aroma and flavor. Taking us into the kitchen, he introduced us to a marvel in cast iron that was solidly mounted on the wall. It was the first wall mounted turn the crank Spong coffee grinder we had ever seen. That coffee grinder, he explained, had been in his family for almost 100 years, and was still going strong. As you easily can imagine, Meggi and I fell in love with it.

You may have seen small ornamental coffee grinders in specialty shops. Charming little things, made in China, designed to sit on a shelf in the kitchen looking pretty, and doing nothing. When you attempt to use them, trying to grind enough coffee for a single cup can drive you nuts. That is until about the fifth or sixth use when they inevitably self-destruct.

The Spong is about as far from those cheap imitations as chalk from cheese. In fact the Spong is what most of them are trying to imitate.

So, now you know how we started grinding fresh coffee every morning. Over the years, we owned a plethora of coffee grinders, mostly electric. Then one fine day in Durbin two things happened that led us to our very own Spong coffee grinder.

The first incident was due to a catastrophic failure in the motor of our latest coffee grinder. A failure that soon had me casting about in a frantic attempt to produce some semblance of ground coffee for our morning caffeine fix. An effort that involved dismantling the little monster and mounting the top part of it on an electric drill.

Trust me that scheme may have amused the neighbors immensely, but it did not work as planned. The drill turned too slowly for one thing. We also had the devil's own time keeping the grinder joined to the drill while holding the top on the grinder long enough to grind a few beans. One of those jobs that needs three hands when you only have two available.

They say "desperation is the mother of invention", or, should that be, "desperation without coffee in the morning is a mother"? In any case, after a lot of effort we managed to produce a sad brown liquid that vaguely resembled coffee. And so, suffering from a dismal lack of caffeine, that fateful day began.

* * *

Later that morning Meggi and I set out to purchase some electrical parts and a new coffee grinder. As fate would have it, we happened to pass in front of an antique shop.

Before I go any further, it might help if I explain that for Meggi and I antique shops were, and still are, places we exploit as miniature museums without an entrance fee. Places where we can freely nick ideas and get to see how things were done in "the good old days".

Neither one of us ever spent a penny in an antique shop, and did not plan to change that economically healthy lifelong habit anytime soon. The problem was this particular shop had a wall mounted Spong turn the crank coffee grinder prominently displayed in the window. After a few moments of wistful dreaming, longing looks, and comments about exactly where in the galley it could be mounted, we wondered off to purchase our electrical parts.

I imagine things would have turned out quite differently had our return route not taken us past the same shop. Of course, we duly stopped in front of the window for another meditative bit of coffee grinder reverie. If we had foreseen the fleecing we were in for, both of us would have scampered down the street, so fast there would have been a vacuum clap where we had been standing.

You can say one thing for antique dealers. They are an astute lot. Not at all the type to let a potential sale slip through their ring covered fingers. In an instant, out swished the owner under the pretense of polishing the shop window. More than likely, he was already on his way out in any case to wipe away the palm and nose prints from our last visit.

The next thing we knew we were being ushered into the shop accompanied by the obligatory flapping of wrists and blatant patronization one expects in such places.

While the owner, now joined by his partner, busied himself or herself with some useless task, I took a casual squint around the place. Funny how I remember reflecting; it was even odds the two of them had sold their hair dressing salon so they could retire to running this quaint little antique shop. Odds on, they lived in a cozy little apartment over the shop, had a poodle named Poopsie, and a lifetime subscription to *Playgirl* magazine.

Meanwhile Meggi was wondering around the place sniffing out interesting items, leaving fingerprints on the brass, poking into dusty corners, and in general doing her best to appear uninterested in coffee grinders.

Before the morning was out that shop had turned into an Afghan bazar stall, complete with a serving of coffee ground in the old Spong grinder, and the lot. All that was missing as we haggled and bargained were the rug to sit on, the water pipe, and a few camels braying in the background.

My God! That shop owner must have been a cross between a Jewish pawnbroker and a Gujarati rug merchant. Good thing there were no Chinese in his background or we might have left the place stark naked.

As the morning progressed so did the vicissitudes in the negotiations, at one point I remember the owner was swearing the grinder had belonged to his sainted old grandmother having belonged to her mother who passed it on as a family heirloom to her granddaughter on her wedding day. At one point, the owner swore that his wife would murder him if he let such a valuable treasure slip away for so little money, at which the other one muttered "damn right I would".

When eventually we staggered out of the place, I had the Spong under my arm and Meggi was carrying a kilo of espresso coffee beans she had somehow wrangled into the deal. I found it rather endearing how the owner's partner had flounced out of the shop, with a wiggling of hips that should have dislocated several pelvic bones, to find that bag of coffee beans. I did notice when he returned the bag had a half torn shop sticker on it. Looking closely, I could just make out "Reduced for Clearance".

Standing in the doorway waving, the owner's partner seemed on the verge of tears – good actor that one was. The owner was following the age-old ritual industriously calling after us that we had robbed the food out of his children's mouths. As if, there was any danger of those two producing offspring.

Overall, it had been an interesting, if somewhat expensive morning. On the other hand, we were now the proud owners of an original Spong turn the crank wall mounted coffee grinder. As I said, one of the best investments we ever made.

Chapter 36
The Sighting of Komba

Outward bound on our delivery route one morning, we were sailing along just a few miles north of Kawula Island when I spotted a strange looking cloud almost due north of us. Nature is not exactly noted for symmetrically shaped clouds, yet there on the horizon was an almost perfectly round cloud raising up into the sky. Being the curious type, and bored to thumb twiddling distraction, I watched it for a few minutes then lost interest until a few minutes later I spotted another perfectly round cloud rising into the clear morning air from roughly the same position.

Since these were practically the only clouds in the sky that morning I started to watch more carefully. Within minutes, my careful observation was rewarded with another round cloud. At that point, what had only been a curious event suddenly became a mystery. If there is one thing Meggi and I dearly love, it is a mysterious place in need of exploration.

Clouds do not simply form themselves at ground level and rapidly rise up into the sky unaided. So, carefully taking a bearing on my mystery clouds with the hand compass, I went below to consult the chart. Sure enough, about nine miles from our position, on precisely the bearing I had just taken, the chart showed a small island by the name of Komba.

What made it even more interesting was the notation alongside the island. It read, "Volcano - erupting".

Hummmm thinks I, my mystery clouds are coming from an active volcano. I quickly called Meggi and Jo to share my great discovery. Together we watched as roughly every 12 minutes another round cloud would form and slowly drift up into the morning sky.

Then and there, we decided to visit that little island, if for no other reason than to watch it pop it's top every few minutes. The problem was that we were short on fuel, as always, and had a volunteer crewmember hopping from foot to foot worried he would miss his flight from Dili back to Singapore in a few days' time. Why people insist on booking their flights so far in advance is a mystery to me. We do tell them *Vega* is a sailing boat and not the Lisbon Packet. I never give exact arrival dates, simply because we never know what the wind or seas will send us.

For the moment all we could do was give the island clouds a few long looks and dream of what it would be like to approach an active volcano while it thundered and roared. With a glance between us, Meggi and I decided a visit to Komba on our return trip was a must. That was a promise we kept several months later, when our deliveries finished and we sailed across the Banda Sea on our way to Jakarta.

* * *

Waving away the flies with his broad brimmed hat, Hendra sat in the shade on a large flat rock watching his ponies graze. He did not begrudge them these few moments of rest after the long hard climb they had just accomplished, even though it might mean reaching his village after sun down. Hendra loved these mountains, they were his home, and their majestic natural beauty never failed to captivate him.

With an unconscious motion born from years of habit Hendra jammed his hat back in place, pulling the wide brim down low over his eyes. Taking out his soft leather tobacco pouch he began to roll himself a cigarette. With his fingers rolling more or less on autopilot he gazed out over the valley. A few miles further on, and roughly one thousand feet below where he sat, a little village was nestled into the precipitous shoulder of this scenic valley. Squinting against the glare of the sun, he could just make out the red tile roof of his house.

This is a harsh land, his father had often told him, but fertile enough for those willing to accept its caprices and work its rich soil.

For half of every year the land lay desiccated, thirsting for rains that never came, while for the other half of the year it would be a daily regime of torrential rains. When the rains came, that dry riverbed snaking along the valley floor became an impassable raging torrent, completely isolating his half of the valley from any contact with the outside world. Then the hills surrounding this dry brown landscape would turn a luxurious green so deep and rich it almost glowed. For now the air smelled of dust, there would be no rain for months to come.

Shoving the newly rolled cigarette between his lips, he scratched a strike anywhere match on the stone where he sat and lit up his smoke. He could still remember the first time his father brought him along this path, one of the few connecting his village to the outside world. Hendra had been about 10 years old. Just old enough to help lead their string of tough little mountain ponies from the village through this high pass to Ermera, where an elderly Portuguese merchant would buy the coffee beans his family had so diligently harvested.

Slowly exhaling a puff of smoke Hendra studied his string of horses. His ponies might not be big, but they are sturdy creatures and as sure footed as mountain goats. He knew from long experience they could easily carry two 50-kilo bags of coffee beans all day without tiring.

Lali came over came to where he sat resting her soft muzzle on his shoulder. Her warm breath like a velvety caress, her strong smell of horse was both familiar and comforting. She had decided it was time for them to push on. Hendra agreed. He had no wish to be on the trail after dark when the path would all but disappear and the temperature plummet. Slowing getting to his feet, he dusted himself off.

Reaching out he picked up Lali's reins, then smoothly swung himself onto his new saddle. He had made that saddle during last rainy season, and was rather pleased with it. Adjusting his wide brimmed hat, he looked out across the valley. Nudging Lali toward the trail he whistled to the lead pack horse. In a few more hours, he would be home.

The old people claimed there were once roads through these mountains wide enough for carts, rather than narrow trails like the one he was following. According to them on one occasion, an automobile actually came as far as the village.

If they ever really existed those roads were long gone, most likely washed away by the yearly torrential rains. Everyone knew the only practical way to travel between villages in these mountains was by horse, or on foot. Of course he also knew you had to be careful believing old people, they claimed just about everything had been better back then. The way Hendra saw it, of course everything was better when you were young, anything was better than being old and worn out.

When Hendra was young, there had been a school down in the valley, with a real teacher. She was a pretty woman from Dili who patiently taught him to read, write, and do sums. He grudging admitted the time spent scratching his head had been well worth the effort. In his village, he was one of only three who had those skills. Thanks to those abilities, he was now considered one of the village elders and a man to be respected. Those same skills had also earned him the post of volunteer teacher at the new school.

Collecting his string of ponies, he urged Lila forward onto the well-worn path. A path she had walked many times. Settling into his saddle, Hendra felt proud as he looked across the valley to where the new school building stood. That small structure had taken the village 3 years to build. They had done it using local materials and volunteer labor. Even the tables and benches for the students to sit at were village made. The object was simple, provide their children with an education, or at least the start of one, an opportunity most of the other villagers had been denied.

Lured by the dream of a brighter future for their children, they now had a school building. What they did not have, were the things that only money could buy. Things like exercise books, pencils, pens, or even chalk for the chalkboard.

The village was poor. Most families existed on less than one dollar a day, so money to buy school supplies was hard to come by. Currently he was teaching the children by repetition. Letters and numbers they learned outside on the playground where his students would squat in small groups scratching those numbers and letters in the dirt with sharp sticks. Hendra knew that was not the best system for learning, but it was the only thing he could think of.

He clearly remembered the first day they officially opened the new school. The whole village had turned out dressed in their finest clothes for that long awaited event. Oh, how they had cheered to see their children going into the school. It was a very special occasion, one that made every member of the community proud of what they had accomplished.

Now several months later, being the head master, and only teacher, for a school with thirty students ranging in age from seven until fourteen was proving quite a challenge. Taking off his hat, Hendra wiped his brow on his sleeve. As much as he did not wish to admit it, in his heart Hendra felt he was failing. The village had done all they could with their meager resources. He was doing all he could, but it was simply not enough. Their school was going to fail.

Chapter 31

Why Dolphins Are so Playful

Monsoon wind poured across *Vega's* stern quarter, a great river of air thrusting against taught red sails. *Vega* danced along her intended route as if running on rails, broad reaching across calm seas. The decks heeling slightly, a gentle roll accented the boat's tendency to give a dainty little wiggle of her stern each time a wave passed under the keel. Her passage through the water at a consistent 7 knots trailed an arrow straight wake behind. The only thing missing were a few seagulls wheeling around the masthead, keening in time to the rhythmic creak of lines running through wooden blocks.

Having the watch, I decided to pass the time catching up on my rope work. Touching up whippings and making a few new working lines are menial tasks for a sailor, but enjoyable all the same. I had my tools arrayed around where I sat, electrical tape, waxed string, gas burner, small Swedish fid, and of course, my seaman's knife honed to a razor edge.

I had just pulled the whipping tight when a flicker of light gray followed by a slight splash caught my attention. Looking that way, I saw a dolphin gracefully roll on the swell, then race toward our bow. As always, I yelled down the hatch to say we had dolphins around. As a crew, we never tire of watching those highly intelligent creatures frolic around the boat.

We often see dolphins playing around the bow. However, do you know why they do it? I was amazed when I first heard this tidbit of dolphin lore, and more than a little skeptical. Now, after years of close observation, I know it for fact.

Next time a group of dolphins comes to play around your boat watch them closely. Notice how they pass close to your bow, then turn and swim off in a specific direction. No matter which side of the hull they run down they will always, without fail, turn away on the same heading. Their objective is to tease your boat into chasing them in that direction.

The dolphins doing the teasing are designated guards for the main group. Their job is to protect the main pod, warn of approaching danger, kill sharks, and amuse passing sailors. If you look in the opposite direction to the one they want you to take, you will find the main pod either happily feeding or traveling along in formation.

The way a dolphin sees it, they are imitating a tasty morsel passing close in front of a mouth full of danger at speeds that make them appear an easy catch. In reality, they are swimming ridiculously slow, for a dolphin that is. With a flick of the tail, they can accelerate to speeds few other ocean dwellers would be able to match.

Think of it as the dolphin way of swimming up to the school bully thumbing its nose while blurting out a rude raspberry, then running like mad to avoid a swat. The fact they can swim 5 times faster than your boat, makes it even more fun. No wonder they always look so smugly happy when they play that game.

* * *

I was not the only crewmember enjoying that lovely morning. When I came back to my place at the helm, Scourge, the ships cat, was luxuriating in the early morning sun, adapting the gentle rolling motion to her esoteric feline requirements. As the boat rolled to port, she would roll with it waving all four paws happily in the air until with a flop she would land on her side, squirming away to rub her back on the deck. Then as the boat rolled back to starboard, she repeated the exercise. Watching her playful antics, I remembered the first time I saw her. It was in Singapore, where we were doing some work on the boat. I was in the midst of a complicated long splice that day when Meggi came bouncing down the pier.

Beaming from ear to ear Meggi looked happier than a mouse in a cheese factory. She had her hands cupped together in front of her, as she made her way on board. No sooner was she on the boat than she rushed up to me babbling, "Look what I found! Look what I found!"

Holding up her hands, she spread them slightly. Resting between her palms, I could just make out a small ball of fur highlighted by two tiny black eyes peering timidly up at me. It was a kitten, a diminutive one at that. Reaching out a single finger, I caressed the kitten's head. My reward for that effort was a lick from its miniature pink tongue.

Meggi had been rummaging around the boat yard when she came upon the night watchman's shed. Inside, carefully arranged along one wall, she discovered seven sets of feline dinnerware, each with its own water and food bowl. Clearly, the night guard spent a lot of time with his cat, who had recently brought off a litter of kittens. Meggi had gone back that afternoon and ask the guard if she could have one of the kittens for our boat. With his consent, she proceeded to choose one.

This little bundle of fur, with two tiny sparkling eyes and a bright pink nose, had emerged the lucky winner. In the end, Meggi picked the smallest of the litter, rationalizing that the runt would need all the help it could get in life…the way I see it, if we were Chinese, we would have named her "One Lucky Cat" or "lucky" for short. Then again, "Two Lucky Cat" might be a better play on words.

That cat now lives a life of luxury, with on demand scratches, self-replenishing water and food bowls, and a self-cleaning litter box. In any case, that was the day we signed-on another full time member of *Vega*'s crew. I must admit she takes her duties seriously. Scourge is always ready for a good scratching, to play, or just to snuggle up beside whoever has the watch. She even caught a rat, once.

I finished the eye splice I was working on with a taper then applied a Cornish whipping to the other end. Amazing how daydreaming makes a job go faster. Burning off the ends, I tossed the newly made working line onto the small pile growing at my feet. Remembering how the starboard main cap shroud dead eye needed a new lanyard, I selected a larger piece of line and began working a Mathew Walker knot onto it.

Off our bow, the dull gray shadow of land slowly crept over the horizon. Resisting the impulse to yell out "Laaaaaaand Hooooo, Haarrrrrrd on the Starrrrrborrrd Boooow"" – like I said, it was one of those days straight out of the golden age of sail - I went down and checked the chart; 90% certain I was seeing the mountains of East Timor. In the crisp clean air, they looked so close, yet I knew it would be half a day or more before we arrived. With any luck, it would be anchors down in Dili harbor by sunset.

Chapter 38
A Successful Failure

B riskly she closed her lecture notes. In front of her sat six women. For the past few hours, they had diligently assimilated her every word. Watching intently, absorbing her lessons as only people who depend on their memory rather than the written word can. She knew that years from now any one of these women could easily recall the gist of her lecture almost verbatim.

This was their final session. The end of three intense months of training during which these women had gone from being traditional rural birthing assistants, to possessing all the skills and knowledge of clinically trained midwives. The change was nothing short of spectacular. It was a moment Aida had dreamed of for years.

Leaving her notebook on the crudely made wooden lectern, Dr. Aida Gonzales stepped out to mingle with her students. Her lecture hall was a small windowless room at the back of Dili's free Bario Pite Clinic. Her students sat on an odd assortment of chairs ranging from an old office swivel chair with a missing wheel to a bright pink plastic lawn chair. One particular woman caused Aida to smile. The woman's expansive bottom seemed to swallow the birthing stool she was sitting on. It was easy to imagine her standing up and taking the stool with her.

As usual, after class the women gathered in the center of the room to discuss the day's topics, the most important being their impending graduation. Looking around the room, Aida felt proud of these women and what they would go on to accomplish for their remote villages. She had not felt such pride since the day she graduated medical school.

No one would ever accuse Dr. Aida of being tall, although some might effortlessly accuse her of being highly intelligent and attractive. Even her detractors would willingly admit what Aida lacked in centimeters she easily made up for in kilowatts of energy.

With her dark eyes framed by intensely black hair, she was a naturally cheerful person, yet woe to anyone who crossed her when she was in what her friends called "Doctor Mode". Those highly intense moments when she was in perfect control or when arms crossed and foot tapping, lips pursed to a pencil thin line, her eyes would flash like black diamonds; moments when the hospital staff and her smarter interns suddenly had other places they urgently needed to be.

Stepping out of her dimly lit little lecture room, she was greeted by bright tropical sunshine. Although swelling with pride in what she had accomplished, a depressing fact was over shadowing her moment of triumph. She had trained this first group of students well. Returning to their villages, they would be ready to save lives. Yet in one respect, she had seriously failed them.

Passing close to a small tree, she gave it a passionate kick only to realize why tree kicking is not a good idea while wearing sandals. After holding her foot and dancing around for a few seconds, she hobbled away toward her office, cursing profusely.

The problem was not one of knowledge; it was one of equipment and supplies. Tomorrow she would be sending these dedicated women home to their villages full of knowledge, but with empty hands. Without equipment and drugs to work with, they would be precisely like factory-trained mechanics without tools and spare parts.

Failure was not a concept Dr. Aida accepted easily, but as she threw herself into her office chair, she knew that failure was starring her in the face and laughing. One of her interns chose that moment to open the door, fully intent on asking Dr. Aida a question about one of their patients. After a single look at her scowling face he quietly closed the door and beat a hasty retreat.

Chapter 39
A Change of Heart

I spent the greater part of my school career either bored to distraction, or plotting my escape. Mind you, I am sure my teachers were happiest when my escape plans succeeded. Looking back, I clearly see how the turbines of boredom were the motivating power behind my enforced scholastic servitude. There I sat, squirming and scratching, as those mighty turbines hummed away in the background, tidihum-drum-hum-drum.

For me, school was a form of purgatory, so it never ceases to amaze how excited children in remote villages become about going to school. Maybe something in all that fresh mountain air makes them a little strange. Whatever it is, they actually look forward to confinement in a stuffy classroom, repeating the same stuff over and over. I say repeating, because pencils, pens, and paper, are hard to come by for most of those schools. Even chalk is a commodity employed with the greatest of care. The reason for that is poverty.

When you are trying to support a large family on the equal of one US dollar a day – or less – there is precious little surplus to purchase school supplies for the children, much less for the school. In most cases, it is all those families can do to feed themselves and keep the older children in what passes for clothes. Mind you what passes for clothing is often a thread bare collection of holes held together by wishful thinking.

Imagine a farming family so poor they lack the basic tools to work their farm, or even seeds for planting. Imagine a school with one volunteer teacher and 30 students - no chalk, no pencils, no exercise books, and few if any textbooks. On the other hand, imagine a community health post that has no medications at all, not even aspirin, or bandages.

These are places so poor midwives deliver babies by candlelight, equipped with only a sharp knife and a piece of string. Every year hundreds, maybe even thousands, of children die. Most of them succumb to easily cured illnesses, while the number of women who needlessly die in childbirth is appalling.

Even the smallest infection can be life threatening when there are no drugs available to treat it. The majority of villages do not have a first aid kit, much less a health post. It may seem incredible to you, but for most of the people we assist, those are the sad realities of their existence. Even a basic education is seen as one way to escape that grinding poverty, and in a way it is. When we provide a child with the tools to learn, we help provide them with a brighter future. Their little faces glow with happiness and I wonder, Will one of these children change the world? Which is why we try our best to support so many village schools in small villages.

Well you may ask, what happened to make me forget all the torture and torment my teachers inflicted upon me, although I fancy I managed to give as good as I got on that count. Well, the answer is simple. You might say, I saw the light and became a devout supporter of education for others. This sudden about face does not stem from some latent streak of sadism on my part, but rather from an experience, Meggi and I shared in East Timor.

It was several years ago when we visited a remote village high up in the mountains. It took several hours of arduous travel to reach the place; the return trip would take even longer.

Chapter 40

A Stroll Through the Jungle

With dawn's first light painting the mountaintops a golden hue, the bluish mist of night began to lift from a remote valley. The coming of dawn revealed a stark lunar landscape of rugged mountains. Soon, much against my better judgment, I would be ascending on foot to a small village located high in those mountains.

Draining my morning mug of coffee to the dregs, I returned the cup to our open-air kitchen. Stretching and yawning, I ran my eye over our little expedition. A group of children lounged around the compound laughing and joking with each other. I envied them their seemingly boundless energy. Having arrived during the night, they would be the porters for our mission.

This was not some televised adventure in a can, or even a wild dream; we were about to set out along a narrow, often precipitous, path, hiking beside a river that cascades down through high mountain jungles on another mission of mercy. The objective of our mission; deliver educational, medical, and farming supplies to a remote village high in the hinterlands of East Timor.

Clapping my hands to get everyone's attention, I gestured toward the small hill of boxes and bags we would be transporting. With that simple gesture, our adventure began.

Amid laughter and good-natured banter, the children divided our cargo of school bags, and other supplies into easily carried bundles. There was none of the surliness you would expect from modern city children when faced with long hard physical effort, only happy young people cheerfully doing something to help improve their community. In this case, their community was a remote village accessible only by horse or on foot.

The first stage of our journey followed a rural dirt road, before suddenly veering off across an open field. Soon our route became a small track heading straight up into the highlands. Although not very wide, this was a well-used trail leading toward an isolated stand of trees. There we discovered the beginning of another path branching off into the mountains, a trail which soon became more rugged. The real ascent had begun.

In single file, with packages gracefully balanced on their heads or cradled in their arms the children formed a line snaking off along the path, a footpath that soon led into a verdant tropical jungle. The heavier boxes they suspended from bamboo poles. The stronger boys shared those loads by resting the pole on their shoulders. The ends of those poles were soon wrapped in large dry teak tree leaves to help cushion the load. It seemed only moments, before we found ourselves ascending alongside a swift flowing jungle river.

Our little caravan soon entered a tunnel of lush green foliage. Over the ages, vines and trees had grown together into an overhead vault enclosing our trail more effectively than any man made fence. Accustomed to wide-open spaces and life at sea, this dodging around massive boulders as big as buses, or plunging through tunnels of dense jungle was an unusual experience.

Making our way through the stark contrast provided by this wondrous landscape was hot work. The stillness of the air was oppressive, almost claustrophobic under that dense forest of interwoven greenery, yet the children never faltered. Always pushing onward, they took turns inventing stanzas to a well-known song.

Occasionally a literary gem would emerge, and the others would chant it back with great gusto while laughing uproariously. To my astonishment, this uproar did not have the slightest effect on the birds, who kept up a constant din of squawks and squeals. Some had the most melodious voices, while others sounded like wooden cart axles in need of a good greasing.

At first, I failed to notice the subtle aroma of jungle flowers, until spotting a large clump of brightly colored blossoms, I stopped to give them a sniff. Once I had the smell, I noticed it was everywhere, surrounding us not with the mildewing scent, you would expect from a tropical rain forest, but the all-pervading fragrance of jungle flowers. It was not long before Meggi had her hair adorned in a halo of exquisite tropical blossoms.

Meggi was in her glory, scurrying from one unusual flower to the next or excitedly poking and prodding any local wildlife that might appear along our path moving slower than her. When she discovered a stand of ferns inhabited by a tribe of tiny tree frogs, none larger that the nail on your smallest finger, I thought I would never get her away. I think I spent half the day looking behind us, just to make sure she was still somewhere in sight. By the end of the morning I am certain the local birds were all making space on their branches in expectation of some new type of parrot. One that was always calling out, "Lookatthis! Lookatthis!"

Every so often, without any rhyme or reason, our entire safari, for that is how I had come to think of our little caravan, would stop. Then it was everyone into the river for a well-earned swim.

Cold from its rapid decent down the mountainside the river water was crystal clear. At the foot of picturesque waterfalls, the river formed deep pools. These refreshing oases would quickly fill with happy children all laughing, splashing, and chasing each other. It was as if the steep climb loaded with their precious cargo had not even begun to reduce their energy, although I did note several of the children who had started out carrying packages in their arms had cleverly employed local vines to create ad hoc pack packs.

Those children were so full of life and the energy of youth, I wish I could have said the same for myself. A life at sea prepares you for many things, but mountain climbing is not one of them. By the time we reached those welcome rest stops, I was gasping and wheezing like a leaky steam engine, and wondering how much further we had to climb.

What with frolicking in the cool water then drying off in the sun on one of the large smooth boulders that are such a dominant feature of the landscape, each of those well-earned breaks lasted between 15 and 20 minutes. Picturesque moments filled with the sounds of happy children hard at play cooled us off while washing away the sticky layer of dust mixed with perspiration we accumulated along the trail. Those stops also made a gruelingly endless uphill grind a lot easier to endure.

Overall, a three and a half hour expedition through the thick forests of East Timor, which bye the way was only the walking time, stretched into a daylong journey. The trek finally culminated at our long yearned for destination just as the sun became a distant glow on the horizon.

As if sunset were a cue from the director of nature's nocturnal orchestra, thousands of insects began chanting their symphony of the wild. We were soon enveloped in an all-pervading riot of sound that was exotic to our ears. What I knew to be the insect version of, "I have a great big tonker" and "come on baby how about it", in most cases sounded like the wildest combination of computer generated plings and bloings imaginable.

One little insect, although it could have been a spider as big as your hand, broadcast a constant blee-bloop, blee-bloop, blee-bloop, sounding for all the world like a French police car with its siren going. Others did successful imitations of every electronic alarm made by man. At least, we now have perfect proof that nature is copying man in her latest efforts toward evolution.

I swear there was even one creature that sounded exactly like a mobile phone ringing. The sounds were so pure they made the computer-generated versions seem a hollow, barren parody of nature's perfection, which of course they are. Besides, most of the time when my phone rings it is either someone trying to sell me something I would never dream of buying, or an SMS from the cell phone company offering me another wonderful opportunity to part with more of my money.

One insect, not to be out done for ingenuity, did a lovely job of imitating a very loud water drop falling into a still pond, which is the only way to describe the perfectly clear Plink, Poling Ki, Plink that would ring out through the forest every few seconds. When you think about all the time and energy insects spend advertising their sexual prowess, it rather makes we humans appear reticent.

Bye the time we arrived at the village, I was gasping and panting, completely exhausted, while the children who had diligently lugged all those boxes and bags up the trail seemed as fresh as when we started out. Getting old is no fun at all, the worst part being a complete lack of any future in it. Of course getting older definitely beats the alternative.

Hobbling on aching legs to the first available stool, I plonked down. I am sure they heard my sigh of relief all the way to the next village. The moon was raising, several dogs barked energetically, somewhere a cat yowled, and I began to slide into the delectable oblivion of the exhausted.

Of course, I had no sooner sat down than the welcoming reception began. Stumbling to my feet, I forced a smile to my face, and bravely shoved out my hand. The climb may have ended, but the day's activities were far from over.

While we industriously labored up the mountain, those devious mountain folk had been idly relaxing all day. Now they were well rested and ready to celebrate. All I could do, coherently, was ponder where the next uninhabited bed was - that and pray for a hand full of paracetamol.

Somehow, I made it through all the speeches, had my paw mangled by half the village, and avoided falling face first into my pudding, although I still do not remember Meggi dragging me off to bed. Without her, I most likely would have spent the night under a table somewhere.

Chapter 41
Transforming a Dream

Early the next morning, after a lifesaving cup of coffee, several paracetamol tablets, and a few delicious homemade buns, the volunteer teacher and several community notables proudly took us to visit the village school. Their school is a modest one-room building constructed from bamboo with a tin sheet roof and a dirt floor. The village children diligently trailed along behind carrying our various donated boxes and bags of school supplies.

As our modest parade progressed through the village, the entire community turned out to join in. By the time we reached the school house, I doubt if even the town drunk was missing.

Having a school is something special for that little village. Every family in the community had donated labor and materials to make it possible. The school was equipped with handmade wooden tables and benches for the children and a plywood panel painted black for a chalkboard. Although most of us would not have used the place for a goat shed, they were justifiably proud of their accomplishment.

Inside, the school building was dark and stuffy, yet brightly illuminated by the exuberance of 30 happy children all fidgeting in their seats. Each child was specially dressed in a homemade school uniform. I doubt any two of those skirts or shorts were the same shade of blue and even though clean, the shirts were far from white. On the tables, I did not see a single notebook or piece of loose paper.

Pak Hendra, the volunteer teacher, took us to the front of his class and proudly showed us "The Desk". A rickety wooden construction, that put me in mind of the kitchen table from an abandoned farmhouse. Under "The Desk" was a wooden box. Reverentially lifting it, he placed it on the desk. Inside, he solemnly informed us, were the school's educational supplies. I was not expecting much, but the contents were appalling.

At first, I thought there was nothing in the box, other than an old piece of newspaper used for the lining. That was before Hendra rummaged around a bit bringing out a small stub of white chalk, two half pencils, and a dried up ball point pen, which he proudly displayed. There was no writing paper. He explained the carefully folded newspaper provided practice at spotting letters from the alphabet, and numbers. The sad part is, Hendra's school is far from being an exception.

Little wonder he was beaming from ear to ear when he saw the boxes of school supplies his students had diligently lugged up the mountain.

Here were people so poor that basic meals are a luxury, trying their best to provide an education for their children. They gladly sacrifice what little they have so their children might aspire to a better life. Mind you, having a strong family ethic helps. After all, if little Muggins grows up to be a doctor the community wins better medical care, and old grandpa will be looked after in luxury.

After Hendra brought the students to attention, and they had sung a little song about ABC's and 123's, we brought in the boxes of school supplies. Pushing several tables together in front of the class provided a platform to exhibit the contents of those boxes, as they were unpacked.

While Meggi unpacked the boxes, I carefully positioned each item as if on display in a shop window. Soon the tables were completely covered. Meanwhile Hendra, who could not restrain himself, was constantly picking up things to uuuh and aaaah over. I thought he was going to have apoplexy when we started piling up the boxes of white chalk - that is until several boxes of colored chalk sent him into fits of ecstasy. Once we revealed all the school supplies, and shuffled our feet through the obligatory speeches, it was time for the Kits-4-Kids bags.

Chapter 42

Treasure in a Backpack

Under teacher supervision, students brought the Kits-4-Kids bags into the classroom. One by one, we removed them from their protective plastic bags, and then stacked those backpacks on the floor by the teacher's desk. When the children saw those lovely new backpacks, the room suddenly fell silent. Many of them had never seen a backpack before. None had even dreamed of owning one.

Selecting one at random, Hendra opened it. As he removed the contents, he explained each item to his students before laying it out on his desk. A wave of excitement washed over the room. When Hendra explained that these bags were for them, his message took a moment to register. When it did, pandemonium broke out. It took several minutes for Hendra to restore some semblance of order.

Starting at the back of the class, one at a time Hendra called each student up to the desk, where Meggi would shake each students hand then carefully select a suitable bag and hand it over. Backpack in hand the youngster would come outside to where I had set up my shop.

Standing them up against a wall, I photographed two students at a time, each prominently holding their new bag. Those pictures would go to the kids who donated the bags, a good way for them to see exactly where their bags went. One little boy became so excited he widdled his pants, much to the delight of the older boys.

Pictures done, the kids went back to their desks in the schoolroom. It did not take long for them to begin exploring their new treasures. Rapidly the room was filled with squeals and whoops of delight, as they discovered small stuffed animals and other toys among the school supplies in those bags. Mind you, these children had never in their lives owned a real toy.

One boy hit the jackpot. Opening his bag, he discovered a full size official FIFA football. Bubbling over with excitement every boy in the room converged on him. In their village, there were no real footballs. They played the game with a bundle of large leaves tied together with vines or string.

We intended that football for the school. In order not to leave it behind, Meggi had put it in the boy's bag, and then forgotten it was there. At that point, there was no way we could possibly have taken it back, not without breaking the little boys heart. It was all Hendra could do, getting those excited young boys back to their places.

Having always taken a backpack for granted, I was surprised to see that most of the kids had no idea how to use one. The majority thought it was meant to be worn in front rather than on their back. Once Meggi demonstrated how one works, it was comical to watch those who mastered the art of wearing a backpack industriously passing along that esoteric skill to their friends.

Memories can be funny things, yet from that day I still cherish one that stands out above the rest. In the back of the class was a young boy about 10 years old. You could tell he was excited. He spent the whole time bouncing from foot to foot, awaiting his turn. When the teacher finally did call his name, he ran to the front of the class.

As Meggi reached out to hand him a bag, he did not even slow down. Going at full speed, he grabbed his backpack and ran out the door. Puffs of dust exploded from his bare feet as he accelerated across the schoolyard. The last we saw of him, he was legging it into the forest, his new school bag tightly clutched to his chest. If you ask me, that lad was not going to hang about, risking the chance we might ask him to give it back.

Once the final Kits-4-Kids bag had a proud new owner, Hendra released the students. In a rush they noisily erupted out into the open like a cheap take-away curry. The boys racing away in the direction of the village football pitch, yelling and calling out to each other, while the girls gathered in small groups under the shade of a large tree. Squeals of delight hailed each newly discovered treasure. As they slowly dispersed, each child was elatedly carrying a backpack filled with school supplies.

More than one happy child was seen walking away holding a backpack in front of themself gazing in rapt admiration. As the excitement moved away from the school building, Hendra, Meggi, and I made our way to where the traditional village midwife lived. It was time to deliver a midwife kit.

* * *

The Kits-4-Kids bags were an idea we had been toying with for years until one day a friendly teacher ask me what the kids at his school could do to help children in the poor schools we visit. Somehow, Kits-4-Kids suddenly came to the surface and jumped out into our conversation. What would he think of having each of his pupils provide a backpack stuffed with the basics a primary school student needs for their studies?

Like all good schemes Kits-4-Kids is simplicity itself. In a flash, his eyes began to sparkle and I knew we had a new program. I could easily visualize kids who never had a pencil to call their own, opening a new back-pack, full of pencils, pens, exercise books, rulers, protractors and all the other things a kid needs for school. Mind you, the backpack alone would become a family treasure.

With a little polishing, Kits-4-Kids soon became a reality. The beauty being, the whole Kits-4-Kids concept fits perfectly with our motto of, "directly from the hand of someone who wants to help into the hand of someone who needs help in the form of the tools and supplies needed to do their job". However, this time it was being applied to schoolchildren.

A few months later, we returned to Singapore where there was a big surprise awaiting us. Kits-4-Kids were a huge success. That success grew from several very simple concepts. It was easy for kids in Singapore to understand how their bags would go directly to help kids in a poor place. The whole exercise soon became a personal interaction between two kids, providing some interesting, often amusing, results.

Unwittingly we had distilled the entire aid concept into a simple 'one on one' exercise. By stripping away all the big agencies and other peripheral paraphernalia, children could actively participate in a way that was easy for them to understand.

Here was a practical, hands on, lesson in social responsibility. From a child's point of view, they were interacting directly with other kids, without intrusive intermediaries. The result was, they not only stuffed their bags with the items on our list, but also with dolls, stuffed animals, toys, hair clasps, and many other small things that children find important. Things we adults would never think of.

We made the process more intimate by having each child write a short note explaining who they are, where they live, and the like. That personal letter went into their Kits-4-Kids bag. Not to be out done, some children included a photograph of themselves. One even included a close up picture of his pet goldfish, which later caused Meggi some consternation as she tried to explain the idea of keeping a pet fish.

These heart to heart gifts added a personal touch. One I knew would be highly valued by children who spend their days in tattered "T" shirts and ragged shorts that are often little more than a collection of holes held together by wishful thinking. Where these bags go, life is hard. Unenviable places, where even the most basic of necessities are few.

When the day for loading arrived, over 350 primary students from the German European School in Singapore delivered their Kits-4-Kids bags to *Vega*. Their visit to the boat was our way of thanking them. It was also an adventure for the children, and a chance for them to see exactly how we would deliver their Kits-4-Kids bags. We wanted them to follow the entire process, from preparing their bags to handing them over to the kids who would receive them.

Those visits were a big success, with the final group helping me to fight off a "Pirate"; who after a lot of Har-Har-Haring and cardboard sword fighting we managed to push off the bowsprit and into the water. That was the best we could do under the circumstances, seeing as how we had no "Plank" to make him walk. The kids all loved it.

When the last backpacks were safely stored away, we had over four hundred properly prepared Kits-4-Kids bags. Meggi was having fits trying to find a place to stow them all for the voyage, yet we both knew Kits-4-Kids was a wonderful idea that was going to make quite a few very poor children extremely happy.

Chapter 43
The Great Fuel Drama

"Scruples, what scruples?" I responded to Meggi's rather pointed question. "If we fail to find another 650 liters of fuel it's going to be pretty tough between here and the Banda Islands, and if you think I'm sailing this boat into the anchorage at Nila your as mad as a shop full of hatters."

You see fuel has always been one of our biggest worries, especially during our deliveries. After all, what good is it to have the boat fully loaded with the finest educational and medical supplies, if we cannot reach the islands where we deliver them? Every year I spend a great deal of my time scheming new and exciting ways to keep the fuel tanks filled. The amazing thing is some of those schemes actually work.

Arriving in Dili after a long slog against strong currents, and the southeast monsoon, our fuel tanks resembled the Sahara on a dry day. Our good friend Juan Carlos promptly chipped in 200 liters, and thanks to other friends, we amassed a total of 400 liters over two weeks. Although heartily appreciated, that was still short of what we needed for the next stage of our voyage, even with good wind.

Being close to the equator, we often have long periods of calm. Therefore, even though we prefer sailing, motoring is an important option, that is if we want to arrive before the next election but one. Considering some of those calms, perhaps that should be the second, or is it now the third, coming.

Good winds are an often wished for, but seldom conceded, blessing. One I never count on. So, after a close inspection of the central bank, which meant shifting through all our pockets, and a careful search behind the cushions, reveled the sad state of our finances, I found myself called upon to come up with yet another scheme.

You know, the type of idea where little a light bulb goes *bing* and suddenly everything seems simple? Well, I needed one of those bright flashes and soon. Otherwise, *Vega* might become a semi-permanent fixture floating peacefully in Dili harbor, without much in the way of lights.

I envy those gifted individuals who easily invent solutions to sticky problems at the drop of a hat. Me? I need to meditate on a problem, often at great length, searching for enlightenment, while fervently hoping someone else will come up with a workable solution. I say workable, as some of the wild schemes what I euphemistically call my brain comes up with would astound you.

There I was, diligently scratching various parts of my anatomy, distractedly watching the cat, with, no doubt, small puffs of steam coming out of my ears. Well, you try inventing an alternative to purchasing fuel and see how far you get. Mind you, watching the cat can be an inspiring pastime.

Where most cats are famous for their grace and agility it must be admitted Scourge, our ships cat, is a bit if a klutz. More than once, I have seen her make a leap at something and miss. It seems she cannot understand that when the boat moves the place she is aiming for also changes. It really is amusing to see her dive for the hatch entrance and miss. About halfway from launch to landing, the landing zone moves. Her paws flail in the air. Her body twists through various contortions. Then, splat goes the cat - again. It does not seem to hurt her, if you ignore the damage to her dignity, which for a cat is an item of major importance.

Twice she missed the side of the boat when jumping from the pier. Both times, she wound up in the water. Her delicate manner when leaping in and out of portholes long ago earned her the sobriquet "Feather Foot".

Returning to my fuel conundrum, I shortly considered distilling the contents of her cat box. An idea I quickly rejected. The result would have been explosive enough for sure, but the high acid content would have eaten away our fuel injectors in no time.

About then Joanne Har strolled bye with a steaming bowel of instant noodles in her hand. In one of those blindly obvious flashes of inspiration, I had a solution. This latest stroke of genius might not provide all the fuel we needed, but at least it might provide part of it.

I would have kissed that crazy Singaporean, if it were not for her famous right hook and left jab. Those Singaporean girls can be tough under their innocent looking exterior, must be all the running around shopping malls lugging heavy shopping bags that keeps them in trim.

Just before leaving Jakarta a friend gave us nine cases of IndoMie instant noodles, shrimp flavored if I remember correctly. Those noodles are nasty stuff with a whole alphabet soup of chemicals for flavoring and never a real shrimp in the whole factory, unless it snuck in with the contents of some workers lunch pail. I think Jo was the only one on the boat who ever ate them, more than once. The fact is, nasty, or not, Indonesians dote on the stuff. In certain strata of society, they consider instant noodles a luxury.

With all the small Indonesian cargo boats in port, I should easily be able to trade a few of those boxes of noodles for jerry cans of fuel. The owners of those boats are notoriously tight-fisted creatures. They easily make Scrooge look like a giddy philanthropist. That means the crew are usually surviving on rice and what fish they can catch over the side. For them a few cases of instant noodles would be a treat fit for the holidays.

All I had to do is a row over to the first cargo boat in line and convince the crew to trade some of the owner's fuel for an upgrade on their dinner vouchers. Easy enough to do in Indonesia, where the average person tends to be rather practical and, I might add, casual about these things. That is if you speak the language, which I do not.

Chapter 44

Of Charts and Counter Jumpers

Most of the stops along our route are so remote the last proper oceanographic survey was back in the Dutch colonial days. So, it comes as no surprise the charts we buy are nothing more than upgraded copies of originals from the mid 1800's. I had one chart where the latest correction date was 2012; the first printing read, "Based on an original survey from 1824".

In those days, a ship would sight an island, then send a boat ashore with sextant and clock to record the position of that island. Some might make an unenthusiastic effort to take soundings, usually only in places that might provide good anchorages. Even when an official survey vessel did go the rounds, they often managed to avoid doing a detailed set of soundings for the smaller islands.

In most cases, ships stopping at one of those islands would simply heave too offshore and send in a boat to fetch someone with knowledge of the local reefs and water depths. Then, benefiting from local knowledge, ease their way into whatever anchorage might present itself. We do that frequently in places like Nila where the reefs and channels are so twisted they would have Guru Chunkachundra chewing his beard by the time we get half way into the anchorage.

One trick that appears repeatedly in the older Admiralty Sailing Instructions is, "hang an anchor to a depth of X meters under the bow and approach with care until the anchor touches, then begin to release your cable until an appropriate scope is reached." A disclaimer inevitably follows those instructions such as, "this anchorage is not safe in all seas or rough weather and should only be used in calm conditions".

We always try to have the latest up to date paper and electronic charts on board, for what little good they do us. Having the latest paper charts is just good seamanship, after all. Although as long as they work modern electronics are very useful tools, the nice thing about paper charts is that when the power fails they continue working just fine. On the other hand, those charts do represent a major expense.

Imagine the cost of a single paper chart these days. The counter jumper at the chart shop looks you in the eye and with a perfectly straight face asks $50 for one piece of paper the size of an old Jimmy Hendrix poster. And, if you ask why government produced charts, paid for with tax dollars mind you, are so expensive he just shrugs his shoulders and goes back to reading Facebook messages on his iPad.

Oh, and did I mention they usually find some insidious way to add an exorbitant amount of tax to the already astronomical cost? Take out your ships stamp and ships papers, remind the jerk you have a right to buy ships stores and navigational materials tax free, and do you know what will happen? You are looked at funny and the fellow goes back to up loading selfies to his Face Book page. Sure, you have the right, but most chart shops cannot be bothered. Huff, huff!

If you ask me, it all hinges on the fact commercial vessels are required by law to have up to date paper charts on board at all times. So, as with any mandatory monopoly, it has become a rigged market.

The electronic charts are even worse. I should mention there exist two types of electronic charts, the ones used by commercial vessels and the ones "For Pleasure Use Only". The second are for chart plotters on yachts. They have fancy names like Gold or Max and I trust them almost as far as I would a politician or used car salesman. The real electronic charts have about 10 times the detail, and price.

I once ask the price for a set of real electronic charts for South East

Asia; without batting an eye, the man quoted me almost $2,000. Oh, and the program to run them was another $2,000. The full set of commercial grade charts for the entire world comes on a single DVD disk. The program to run them comes on a single CD disk. Little wonder there is such a thriving black market in copies of those charts, and the programs to run them.

Yet even the most accurate up to date charts are often misleading, especially in areas not frequented by commercial shipping. Those expensive sea charts often still show islands miles from where they really are.

One Island was so far off that our electronic charts showed us nicely perched on top of a volcano. There we were, our position displayed within meters, like some modern day version of the Ark, on a different island 2 miles away. In one case, a whole island was missing from the Banda archipelago. It was the island of Banda Neira, which happens to be the densely populated capital of those islands.

In the old days, sailors had few illusions about how accurate their charts were. They knew the things were missing minor details like whole continents, much less a few islands and reefs. They also knew the positions shown could be off by miles.

As a result, the old boys went through life always keeping a sharp lookout, and constantly fearing the worst. Perhaps those seamen like habits are even more important these days, than they were back then. The number of people I see out sailing, in boats loaded with fancy electronics, without the slightest idea how to navigate is appalling. And, if you ask them about reading a weather chart, they look at you as if you just admitted to having a communicable social disease.

In practical terms, those discrepancies of charted position can be dangerous when trying to negotiate a narrow entrance between jagged coral reefs to reach an island only one and a half miles wide and two miles long. Some of the channels leading to these islands are only fifty meters wide. So with that in mind, you do the math, and then calculate what my blood pressure and heart rate must be like by the time we get the anchors down and set.

Chapter 45
Goat tracks and Leaky Roofs

L ete-Foho is a remote mountain top community in East Timor that acts as the local trade and public service center. An old town, lete-Foho dates back to early Portuguese times when these rich valleys were home to extensive plantations of coffee and other cash crops.

Traditionally these high mountain valleys were the breadbasket and export stars of East Timor. Seeing the dilapidated buildings and run down appearance it is hard to imagine that these valleys once provided enough food to feed East Timor, with a very healthy amount left over for export. It says something that East Timor, once a net exporter of agricultural products, currently Imports most of the food it needs.

Arriving at Lete-Foho after a long, rather nerve racking – if not downright frightening – drive into the mountains is like emerging from the jungle into civilization. The first thing I noticed was a huge church overlooking the village. A more incongruous sight I have rarely seen. That basilica is so big it borders on being a cathedral.

The unique style of its steeple makes that church even more prominent. Try to imagine a normal church steeple. Now replace the upper part of that steeple with two huge hands positioned in the classic palms together praying position. Those hands alone must have been over twenty meters tall, and cost the village at least a year's income.

We arrived on market day. A day when people from all the outlying areas congregate to exchange the latest gossip, buy basic provisions, and sell what their farms have produced since the last market day. The whole town square fills with portable market stalls, selling everything from solar panels to one old woman with a basket full of sweat potatoes. A basket that Meggi purchased for the boats larder, after some serious bargaining that is.

Meggi was ecstatic when the sweat potatoes, including a woven basket, cost her less than half what they would cost in Dili. As for the old woman, she was grinning from ear to ear as she folded her cloth and wandered away into the crowd. She had Meggi's hand full of one-dollar bills safely stuffed into her bodice.

The distinctly rural atmosphere has a magic all its own. Wherever I looked, there was something new and exciting to observe. Most of the farmers live quite far from town. Often they arrive the day before in order to start trading and socializing early the next morning. No one wants to miss a minute of this important community cultural event.

Outside of the town, roads are almost nonexistent. Travel is by footpaths and trails. Even in our age of motorized vehicles, for the people of these mountains, horses are still the most practical mode of transportation. Squat shaggy beasts, with intelligent looking faces, those tough little horses are extremely sure footed, capable of maintaining a steady pace up hill and down for days at a time. Their clear eyes mirror the stoic nature of their owners.

Here there are no fancy leather saddles. The local saddles are hand made from bent tree branches wrapped with what appears to be a broad leaf. A leaf that once dried must be extremely robust. The brightly colored saddle blankets are all hand woven and bridles appear to be made from braded grass.

At the market, special equestrian parking lots are set aside for the horses, with stakes driven into the ground in a clear grassy area. Tethered to these stakes on long ropes made of woven grass, the horses are free to graze while their owners wander the market or imbibe vast quantities of locally distilled beverages.

The farmers all wear a smaller version of the notorious American cowboy hat. On closer inspection, I noted their hats have a slightly different shape. They are almost like a gentleman's hat from the 1920-30's bent to resemble a cowboy hat. The uniform continues with the standard farmers blue jean overall with bib and suspenders worn over a checkered woolen shirt.

I could not help but marvel at the similarity between these high mountain farmers and those I saw as a small boy in the mountains of North Carolina. There are the same weather worn nut-brown faces and wide callused hands. The only thing missing were the black 1950 vintage pick-up trucks loaded with vegetables, or more often than not tobacco.

Finding a shady place to sit, I began to study the market more carefully. Clearly, people were buying and selling, but there was another active level of social interaction as well. Young men paraded around the square, admiring the girls who aimlessly strolled around in groups of two or three, always in the opposite direction to the boys, I noted.

The girls were all trying their best to look unimpressed, even though dressed to make a good impression in their finest apparel. It was easy to see, this is an ageless traditional dance. Looking around, I wondered how many of the older couples had once done exactly the same thing, until their eyes met across a crowded market square.

Children, who always seem to inhabit a world of their own, raced around in small groups. Effortlessly dodging at full speed between market stalls and the legs of adults, squealing and laughing as they went.

On one open corner of the square, an ad hoc football game started up. As best I could make out there were five sides, all playing on the same field, with two different sets of goals. Everyone seemed to be having fun, even the goalie's, who frequently had to defend against two different attacking teams, and two different balls, at the same time.

I swear there was one team of youngsters that seemed to think any one of the four goals was ripe for attack. I also noted the ease with which players from one team would suddenly lose interest and switch to another team. Occasionally, for no apparent reason, one of the budding young football stars would run around in circles waving their arms in the air and screaming some unintelligible gibberish.

*   *   *

Having stretched our legs and admired the market it was time for our delivery. Piling back into the Toyota Hilux we headed for the local primary school, a school we had heard much about, yet never before visited.

Just a short distance from the church, our driver stopped beside a goat track that wondered off downhill at a precarious angle only to disappear behind several small buildings. To my chagrin, after a lot of backing and filling, he headed off down that track. Making a sharp turn behind the buildings, the road tilted at least fifteen degrees and pitched forward at an even more frightening angle.

Not thirty meters further along that dastardly rut, was a sharp hairpin turn where the road once again descended sharply. If you ask me, it plummeted at an angle steep enough to make mountain goats leery, before twisting abruptly to the left. By the time we reached our destination, I was in the midst of a deeply moving religious experience. I was righteously petrified, while praising the fact I was still alive.

That demonic track -some might cynically call a road - disgorged us, me with my knees knocking, in front of what at first appeared to be a series of half-abandoned colonial buildings. Later, I discovered those buildings are the Pico Ramalau Primary School.

At a guess, after being constructed in the mid-1800s, no one had cared for those buildings in any meaningful manner for at least 150 years. The roof had completely fallen in on one building, called the "Old School". I could easily imagine Noah scratching his head and counting on his fingers while attending navigation classes there. That said, the grounds were spotlessly clean, with a carefully tended row of flowers in front of each classroom.

Lete-Foho primary school has five working classrooms for 138 students. Of those five classrooms, only two are even close to what most of us would consider suitable. The rest are in various states of decay or disrepair. Two working classrooms were so unbelievable none of us even noticed them until it was time to leave. I did manage a brief peek inside one of them. After a quick glance around, it was apparent why the teachers preferred not to show them.

The school had grown over the years into a row of disparate buildings starting with the "Old School" and ending in two traditional woven bamboo walled huts each sporting a thatched roof. Both of those traditional huts stands about 1.5 meters above ground level on thick wooden pilings. I had taken those last two buildings to be a farmhouse bordering on school property, until a quick look inside showed neat rows of locally made desks and benches with a chalkboard on one wall.

The first building along from the "Old School" housed a single classroom with a dirt floor. Beams of bright sunlight streamed in through holes in the corrugated tin roof. Considering the duration and intensity of the rainy season, a dry roof would be very important.

That started me wondering about children walking to school during the rainy season, often for kilometers. It occurred to me that including a small, well made, rain slicker in every Kits-4-Kids bag would be a very useful idea. At least they schedule the long school holidays to coincide with the worst of the rainy season.

When we entered that classroom, but for the children all sitting nicely in their places reciting multiplication tables, my first impression was, they were either showing me the school storeroom, or a graveyard for ancient school furniture, rather than a working classroom. There were piles of old desks in one corner and a few abandoned wooden beams along another wall.

Shattered in several places great gaping holes rendered the floor a blend of broken cement and dirt. What with the holes in the roof, it was no great leap of imagination to picture that classroom as a muddy bog during the rainy season.

A teacher stood in front of the class at her blackboard. She was standing behind an ancient desk adorned with a few scattered papers and some fresh flowers. Although she was taping the blackboard with a well-worn stick, there was nothing written on it. The reason for this was soon apparent. There was not a single stick of chalk in the entire school.

After a short tour of the other classrooms, our guide diligently ignoring the two rustic classrooms at the end of the row, we returned to the first classroom. I felt that classroom best portrayed the general condition of Pico Ramalau Primary School. There we requisitioned several tables and began laying out our delivery of supplies and teaching aids.

As the boxes were opened and the supplies began to appear, I saw one teacher put her hands together over her mouth in that universal gesture of shocked surprise. It is a typical action that seems to come built into the female gene. In this case, a bulging of the eyes and a little gasp of astonishment accompanied her gesture.

While I was preparing a display of school supplies in front of the building, Meggi was busy with another project. Going from class to class, she passed out new toothbrushes to the students. Some years ago, we began including toothbrushes and several oral hygiene teaching posters in the supply pack for every school. Oral hygiene is an important part of community health, all too often overlooked in favor of more obvious medical needs.

As Meggi showed teachers the various posters and printed materials concerning dental care, and prepared her pile of new toothbrushes, teachers herded the children into a line in front of her. As students approached the table, Meggi gave each an appropriately sized toothbrush. Judging from the laughter and other sounds of general delight, there were some happy youngsters around where she was working.

While Meggi passed out toothbrushes, I busily arranged basic teaching aids and school supplies. Spread out on those tables was a cornucopia of carefully selected educational supplies and teaching aids, all specifically designed for primary schools. It did not take long before teachers were politely cueing up to get their hands on the materials we had brought.

Imagine those teachers congregated around where I was working, excitedly shifting from one foot to another like small children anxiously awaiting a free ice cream cone. I could see that it was difficult for them to restrain themselves, at least until we could finish making photographs for the people who had donated those supplies.

Pictures of items arriving where the need is greatest, is an important part of what we do. Those visual images are one of the few ways we have to share the experience of being there, delivering the tools teachers or health workers so desperately need to do their job. Through our pictures, the people who donate those supplies clearly see exactly where and to whom their donation goes. The woman, who donates a case of red pencils, can see her pencils clearly displayed when teachers or children receive them.

As soon as our pictures were finished the scrum began, with teachers jostling up to the tables, grabbing boxes of chalk and pencils or pens. It was all I could do to keep a straight face when the head teacher blew her whistle, just like a football referee.

A second long blast and a few briskly shouted instructions soon brought order to it all. Like naughty children, caught with their hands in the cookie jar, under the stern regard of the head teacher recently confiscated items magically returned to the table.

Our mission to Lete-Foho successfully completed, and with another wish list tucked away in my backpack, it was time to leave. The road back to our base of operations was not going to become any better, or shorter. We all wanted to arrive back at the Bakhita Center well before darkness fell. So, surrounded by happy waving children, our vehicle struggled up the hill. Grinding its way back onto a more civilized road, someone in the back of the car heaved a sigh of relief at having survived that horrible path from the school back to the main road. I was surprised to discover it was me.

Each year we visit several small schools in Ermera. The Bakhita center kindly provides us with a base of operations, and assist with transportation and their extensive local knowledge. Being an established grass roots community project they help insure our supplies reach the poorest most deserving schools. Over a period of six to seven days, our delivery team comes and goes, always reaching out to the poorest schools far up in the mountains.

Chapter 46
Noodles for Fuel

Over the years, I have traveled through some remarkably out of the way places. Settings where the local language is more akin to a throat disease than the comprehensible communications you expect from civilized people. And, before you start doubting me, you just try ordering lunch from a phrase book in Polish and see how far you get.

Those experiences taught me the value of hand gestures, facial expressions, and in general acting like the stereo type foreign prat. The locals generally find it amusing, eventually figuring out what I am after if for no other reason than to avoid sore stomach muscles from laughing so hard.

Language or no language, if I was going to trade noodles for fuel I had best get on with it. So, jumping into the dinghy, off I went to visit the nearest cargo boat, a case of shrimp flavored IndoMie noodles proudly on display while visions of fuel pouring into our tanks danced in my head.

Three boats later, vibrating like an old jig saw from enough coffee to float a barge, I stumbled on a sailor who spoke trader English. Bless that lad. He was all I needed to convert noodles into fuel. Thirty minutes later,

I had a practical solution.

The answer was an old Indonesian cargo boat with a broken engine. Practically abandoned by the owner – crew and all, I might add, it was a rather dejected old thing slowly rotting away in a corner of the port. The crew had not seen their salary in months, nor had they received any money for provisions. Reduced to begging from other ships, they were more than ready to trade the whole boat for anything they could eat, smoke, or drink.

You can see it all over the world. A ship breaks down and the owners simply act as if it no longer exists, at least as far as salaries and provisions are concerned. The crew find themselves stranded without a coin to their name, scrounging along in a strange place, surviving as best they can on the generosity of seamen from other ships. In those cases, sailors take care of each other. After all, one day it might be you stranded on an empty stomach looking for a way to survive.

Negotiations did not take long. The crew from that old boat were ecstatic at the thought of trading fuel for noodles. After all, it was not their fuel, but it was their stomachs, and they were currently rather disgruntled with the owner. Their only worry was the local constabulary. It seems the local maritime police feel any bartering done in their port should pass through their hands and be duly taxed.

We soon had a working agreement. I would bring our empty jerry cans, and some noodles of course, at about 9 PM when the local maritime cops usually went out to eat and watch football. They insisted I use a roundabout route, approaching on the side away from the cop shop. Since the outboard motor might attract unwanted attention, I should row. None of which posed a problem.

Now you know how a moonless night in Dili found me slipping away from the side of *Vega* and quietly rowing a stealthy approach to a crippled cargo boat. The dingy was loaded with several cases of instant noodles and every jerry can we owned.

Gliding up alongside the broken ship, I whispered a call. The English-speaking sailor answered it. He had come along to insure everything went according to plan. The first thing they insisted I pass up to them was a box of noodles. Something I did happily. Then to my surprise, the whole crew beat a rapid retreat to the steering house, where they set about boiling water and creating a feast of instant noodles.

There was nothing to do for the next half hour, other than watch, as they gobbled down those foul noodles and politely decline joining them. For sure, they were a happy lot that night as they burped their way to bed.

After downing the compulsory 440-volt coffee, with no sugar mind you, we finally got down to the business of filling fuel cans. I had 13 jerry cans in the dingy that well stuffed hold almost 300 liters. The question was, how many of those containers would they fill in trade?

I need not have worried, what with the crew being well satiated, and well smoked. I had brought along a carton of clove cigarettes someone gave us, knowing Indonesian sailors just love the things.

Amazing what a full belly does for one's attitude. After that big meal, generosity seemed to be the order of the day. I just kept passing up jerry cans and they kept filling them. Finally, the last jerry can was lowered into my dingy. Grinning profusely like Ali Babba after a good day chasing caravans, I untied the dingy painter and promised to return the next night with even more goodies for their enjoyment.

Chapter 41
The Doctor Dances a Jig

In the highly energetic Dr. Aida, we discovered a wealth of vital information and a dedicated partner to work with in East Timor.

Aida was born in East Timor. She speaks the local language fluently. This advantage allows her to understand the rural Timorese mentality far better than any expatriate aid worker ever will. When we first met her, Aida was finishing the initial year of a well thought out program to train rural traditional midwives at the free Bario Pite clinic in Dili.

The concept for her program came the day she noticed that rural women, being a very conservative lot, did not trust the few official midwives provided for their area by the government. They preferred to put their trust the local traditional midwife, a person who had most likely delivered them into this world and perhaps their parents as well.

Her concept is simple and effective. The community chooses a woman they trust to become their midwife. Aida then trains that woman and sends her back to the community as a properly-trained midwife. The training aspect of her program was working perfectly. Even so, she still faced a major dilemma. A problem she had been racking her brains to solve when we first met her. Where to find the supplies and equipment these newly trained midwives needed to properly do their jobs?

Training is important, but to be truly effective a midwife needs certain equipment and medical supplies. Those supplies would have to come from outside East Timor. Inside East Timor, shops offering proper midwife supplies are almost non-existent, or prohibitively expensive.

While Dr. Aida explained her problem to us, Meggi and I looked at each other, quickly exchanging thoughts through those mysterious perceptual channels two people develop after 20 years of putting up with each other. With a small mental nod of the head, I knew we both agreed. Here was a woman we could and should help. In return, we could call upon her extensive experience with isolated rural communities to design the midwife kits we were contemplating.

With enthusiastic sparks of creativity flying in every direction what followed was a very exciting morning. By the end of that first meeting, we had made a new friend and planned the contents of a fully comprehensive midwife kit.

Promises for next year are great, but what Aida needed right away were supplies to equip the midwives she was currently training. Fortunately, we had on board almost everything needed for the basic kits. Those first kits were far from complete, but they were enough to start with. As far as Aida was concerned they were manna from heaven.

As we talked and planned, Aida was often so animated I thought she would vibrate off her chair. Even though it would be a year before we could return with complete kits, and we could make no concrete promises, at least now we had a target to aim for. To me, it was another long list of items to gather from our supporters – as if the lists we already had were not enough to effectively keep us off the streets and out of the bars.

I readily admit the thought of finding all the items needed for those kits seemed an almost impossible task. Considering the other island communities we were assisting, the numbers had become truly daunting. It would no longer mean looking for a few items at a time, but hundreds of them. Each kit would easily represent several thousand dollars, and that was before the dollar started plummeting.

We would need at least 100 complete midwife kits. Each of those kits required a wide selection of supplies and equipment. How to locate all those things seemed an unachievable goal. How to find the funding to purchase them seemed even more difficult, for Meggi and I had already decided that everything going into those kits had to be new and in date. If we were going to do this, we wanted to do it right.

Looking back from the perspective of now, I know I was radically underestimating the willingness and dedication of our supporters. I was also undervaluing the effectiveness of our own dedication and our ability to animate people for such a worthy cause.

It was hard work creating those first kits, with more than one frustration along the way. But, in the end, we delivered. Even though we did our best, those midwife kits the first year were far from complete. Yet, not only was Dr. Aida over joyed, but so were all of the other midwives we were assisting. Where we saw the missing items as a failure, they saw the items we delivered as a major improvement in their ability to save lives.

The new and re-supply / upgrade kits for our second year were much closer to being complete. By the third year, we were resupplying and up grading 142 fully comprehensive kits. Each to a standard none of us would have believed possible that sunny tropical morning when we first sat together and planned them out.

The most exciting effect is to be found in the results, those kits are saving lives. Our effort is visibly starting to affect the statistics. In some areas, the maternal and natal mortality rates have fallen by over 50%. Postpartum infections have become a thing of the past.

Chapter 48
A Rocky Row Home

Ever notice how just when you think everything is progressing splendidly something always goes wrong. There I was rowing away trying to propel myself, the dingy, and about 300 kgs of fuel, through the water; and funny how you remember these things, I was softly singing the refrain from that old Beatles song, Yellow Submarine.

We all live, stroke and glide, in a yellow submarine, stroke and glide. There I was rowing along nicely over water as calm as a lake, content in the knowledge of another devious scheme well hatched, when all of a sudden there was an almighty crunch. The boat lurched to a stop, dead in the water before slowly tilting over to one side. My oar powered submarine was hard aground.

What with all my distracted exuberance, I had misjudged the passage through the reef. Of course, with so much inertia behind it the dingy slid well up into the shallows leaving half her bottom and the embarrassed expression on her oarsman's face showing.

There I was in the pitch black of night without a glimmer of moonlight to help, high and pretty well dry on a boat loaded with heavy jerry cans.

Just to keep things interesting, the tide was rapidly falling. Ah yes, blessed and many are the wonders of a life on the water.

Stepping out of a small boat onto a reef at night can be quite an adventure. That is, if like me, you have an overly active imagination populated with everything from sea urchins to stonefish and stingrays. The water being too shallow for sharks was the only advantage.

Easing one foot over the side, I gingerly explored the surroundings. Surprisingly the bottom was firm sand, not the jagged coral I had feared. Carefully studying the situation, I realized that with a bit of luck, accompanied by a lot of energetic cursing, grunting, and groaning, I might be able to shove the little monster back into deep water again. Well, I always was an optimist.

At least it seemed like a good plan; until after a few minutes of intense effort it dawned on me that the dingy is deeper aft than forward. That means the more I tried to push it back the more the keel dug into the sand; acting, for all the world, like a very efficient anchor. For my plan to work, I would need to pivot the boat around so the bow faced in the opposite direction.

I grunted. I groaned. I cursed profusely. I bent my knees and heaved until at last, a dull crepitation trumpeted my failure. I even begged and pleaded with any Gods that might currently be infesting the area. In the end, I had to admit there was no other option than to take out some of the jerry cans, swing the boat around, and then set it afloat again. Once the boat was afloat, I could reload it with jerry cans. Can you believe I wound up taking out all but two jerry cans before I got the little brute turned around?

Then came the fun part, the bit where I had to salvage of all my errant jerry cans. While I was busily cursing and shoving the dinghy back into its natural element, my jerry cans had all gone adrift. Gathering them together again proved almost as easy as herding cats. Then of course, I faced all the multifarious pleasures of hauling them back into the dingy.

It is easy to laugh at a crazy situation in retrospect. Mind you, I was not laughing at the time. Those moments stand out in memory as a series of slide show glimpses of me splashing about chasing jerry cans, soaking wet, cursing like a true sailor, and in general having a memorable time of it. Of course, some instances stand out more vividly than do others. Things like the jerry can that floated well up on the reef, giving me no end of grief to retrieve.

The dingy painter is a long one. It needs to be long for tying off on *Vega*, trees on beaches, and the like. In this case, try as I would the painter line was always about 30 cm too short for me to reach that blasted jerry can.

With the current now happily running out to sea, if I let go of the painter the dingy would quickly escape, leaving me to walk or swim home. On the other hand with the tide now falling rapidly if I grounded it enough to recover the jerry can I might not get it off again. Not that is, without taking all the other jerry cans out again. The bottom being sand, I could not even find a piece of coral to tie the painter off on while perpetrating the great jerry can rescue.

Picture me, dancing around on one foot, trying to reach the jerry can with the other foot, while bending over at the waist like some aquatic practitioner of yoga, and holding the dingy painter at full stretch in my hand. Once, I did manage to get a toe on it, mind you. That was a promising moment. Gently trying to cajole it closer seemed to be working, until my toe slipped on the fuel soaked surface.

While I watched helplessly, it wallowed away, until coming to rest just out of my reach. As if that were not enough, I lost my balance, spun around, and landed with a splash in the water. You can believe me when I say; I blessed that jerry can with every foul insult I could think of. It is a wonder the maritime cops did not hear me and come out to investigate the ruckus.

I have no idea how long I danced around muttering and cursing while desperately trying everything I could think of, all to no avail. In the end, I simply give up, tacitly accepting the loss of a jerry can and twenty-two precious liters of fuel. In a state of total frustration, I muscled the dingy toward open water and then banging a knee on the oarlock, I scrambled back onboard.

Of course, after my experience hastily unloading and then reloading, the jerry cans were stowed in a chaotic manner. Once I had squirmed into that chaos of containers there was precious little space to park myself, much less row. By the time I found a way to sit on the thwart with the oars shipped, I was not the world's happiest camper. Then just to keep things interesting on my first stroke, the portside oar hit something floating in the water.

Looking that way, what did I see? There was my errant jerry can peacefully floating along right beside the boat. Mind you, it was still just out of reach. Trust me. I rowed some impressive circles that night before finally hauling it into the boat. In the end, I was happy to have it back, but it did leave my rowing position all the worse for its presence.

The row back to *Vega* was a long one. I like rowing, as long as there is room to shift the oars. Just give me those nice long clean strokes; the kind that let you put your whole body into the effort, which is the ticket to rowing for miles without risking a heart attack. That night the short choppy strokes I was getting would not move an inflatable rubber duck through the water, much less a loaded dingy. Cramped between plastic containers of fuel, I beavered away, expending an enormous amount of effort while doing little to move the dingy.

A tired, wet, and rather frustrated skipper eventually regained *Vega*. At least I had all 300 liters of fuel intact. And people wonder why I look at them so funny when they suggest life on *Vega* must be a wonderful time blissfully relaxing, cold drink in hand, as we sail through the tropics on gentle breezes.

In case you're curious, the next night I made another clandestine trading voyage successfully winning an additional 300 liters of diesel fuel in exchange for 4 more boxes of instant noodles, 3 cans of corned beef, two bottles of imitation chili sauce, and a half bottle of Captain Morgan rum. I was also took great pain not to run aground on the return trip.

What we gained was not a surfeit of fuel. Nevertheless, with care, and the odd day of good wind, we made it safely to the Banda Islands. Mind you, I was chewing my nails the day we arrived, what with the fuel indicator pegging out around zero, and the wind looking like going sour on us.

Chapter 49

Back to the Mountains

High in the mountains of east Timor it gets pretty chilly at night, especially if you're accustomed to life in the tropics where it rarely gets cool enough for more than shorts and a T-shirt. While we loaded Kits-4-Kids bags into the back of an old Toyota Hi-Lux, for the first time in years, I was in a place so cold each breath was a brief suggestion of dense fog in the early morning air.

That day our mission would take us to a school in the subsistence farming village of Lou-mo. Lou-mo is a remote village we have been supporting for several years with school and medical supplies, as well as the odd piece of farming equipment and seeds.

The school at Lou-mo is typical of many we see along our route. The building was constructed using locally available materials and volunteer community labor, as were the wooden desks and benches for the students. Mothers carefully hand-sew the children's school uniforms – uniforms that are only worn on special occasions. They even found a piece of plywood somewhere. Once painted black, it became the teacher's chalkboard. The teachers are volunteers from the village, who each take one day off from farming every week to act as schoolteachers.

Up until that point, the community educational system worked pretty well, at least for the basics. The village is ready and willing to provide the best they can for their children, as long as it does not involve money. There simply is no money in the village to spend on school supplies or teaching aids. Almost the entirety of their economy depends on barter in one form or another. Cash is a very rare commodity, one usually reserved for such important things as farming inputs or tools.

Getting to Lou-mo is a bone rattling all-day adventure. Most of it takes place on some of the worst roads I have ever seen. Well, I have seen worse tracks in both Africa and Afghanistan, but no one had the nerve to call them roads. Our 4-wheel drive vehicle often slowed to a crawl, as the driver picked his way across or down the center of a river, or up the side of a steep embankment. The village is located only 12 kilometers from the Bakhita Center, but as Eddie is fond of saying, we could almost get there faster, and save a lot of fuel, by walking.

After bouncing around the cab of that truck all morning, I would happily have gotten out to walk. The problem is transporting the Kits-4-Kids bags, one large school resupply kit, and the various packets of seeds and farming tools we were carrying. Overall, the back of Eddies Hi Lux was rather full of useful boxes and bags, all on their way to a new home.

As soon as we arrived at Bakhita, word went out to Lou-mo and the other villages we assist that we were on our way to deliver another load of supplies. So, I was not surprised when we rounded a curve at the top of a hill and found all of the children and village elders, along with a teacher or two, lined up and waiting for us.

They could hear our 4 X 4 Hilux struggling up the mountain long before we arrived, so the welcoming committee had more than enough time to position themselves well in advance. Not surprising, when you consider our arrival is one of the biggest community events of the year, not only for the school, but also for the village in general.

Once the Hilux rumbled to a stop, I stumbled out of the cab right into the center of a small riot of laughing cheering children and most of the local dignitaries as well as anyone else who could find a reason to be there. Several noisy chickens and a rather smelly goat accompanied them.

I was still staggering around trying to get my well-shaken wits back into position and wondering if one of the near bye trees might serve to relieve my bladder, when that merry band of well-wishers accosted me. While I danced cross-legged, each of them insisted on pumping my paw while mouthing a few of the usual platitudes. I do not usually mind the inanities, much. The mangling of my mitt is what puts me off. No wonder politicians have such long thin hands, and here all this time I thought it was from stretching their fingers so they could fit them into a few more pies.

While the local authorities were diligently buttonholing me, the rest of our team was busy off-loading Kits-4-Kids Bags and the other supplies we had. Once out of the Hi Lux, those supplies made a rather impressive pile.

We dealt with the village level supplies first. Handing over bags of seeds, farming tools and the like took us all of a half hour. Most of that was due to the thank you speeches and receiving a new wish list for next year's delivery. With that accomplished, we turned to our deliveries for the school.

Before we could hand over the school supplies and Kits-4-Kids bags there were more ceremonies to perform. We all smiled through another speech from the mayor and the usual singing of the school song. At least I assume it was the school song. It could have been the latest top 40 hit in Tetun or even an ode to some tree for all I know. Another speech from the teacher and a small hand full of wildflowers for Meggi followed the song. Then some kid jumps up and starts reciting a poem about how we should be saints or some such gibberish. With the formalities concluded, we could get down to handing over supplies.

First came the boxes of supplies for the school itself. You would be amazed at all the things a school needs to function properly, everything from chalk and carbon paper to report cards and footballs. Over the years, we have pretty well standardized our school packs into those that use white board markers and those that use chalk.

Oddly, that distinction tells us more than just how a teacher writes on the board. It also gives us a good idea of how well off that school is. The poor rural schools tend to use chalk, where the schools in larger communities, the ones with "official" teachers, tend to use whiteboard markers.

Once we have opened each box and laid all of its contents out on display for everyone to see, we make a few photographs so that the people who donated those supplies can see where their donations went. That done, the teacher, then repacks it all and we move on to the next boxes.

Mind you, every village dignitary with a viable excuse is usually hovering around happily infesting the place, all of them grinning like drunks loose at night in a whiskey distillery.

School supplies are fine, but the real cheers, from both adults and kids alike, come when we bring out the sports equipment. Nothing seems to stir interest like a new regulation football, or a 2-team set of "T"-shirts, shorts, and sports socks.

Badminton is a game that always failed miserably to enthrall me, yet these villages love it, that and volleyball. It seems that having a real net for either game is a major village status symbol, having a net for both is tantamount to a town charter and their village name being marked on the map.

All of that takes time. So it was well into the lunch break before we could get down to the business of passing out Kits-4-Kids bags. To understand what one of those backpacks well stuffed with pencils, pens, notebooks, and a myriad of other educational supplies means to a child living in one of these isolated communities, let me explain a bit of the background.

When the whole family is living on less than 1 USD a day, and most of that in the form of barter trade, then $0.20 for a pencil is a major investment. $1.00 for an exercise book is a serious sacrifice. Little wonder several students often share the same pencil. That also explains why even a single exercise book is such an important commodity.

A backpack stuffed with all a kid needs for a year at school is a fortune beyond most of these children's wildest dreams. The backpack alone rapidly becomes a family treasure. Something cherished, repaired when needed, often passing from one child to the next for years to come. To make a very rough comparison, just imagine someone giving you a new 17" MacBook, or a new Ferrari, and you will have about 35% of the elation a Kits-4-Kids bag brings to a child in one of those remote rural schools.

As we brought the Kits-4-Kids bags into their classroom, every child there was imagining what it would be like to own such a luxurious status symbol. The children were so thrilled, they completely forgot about lunch. You could feel the excitement building to an almost tangible level. Wistful longing mixed with hopeful anticipation glistened in those bright young eyes.

When Meggi went to the front of the class and picked up the first backpack, a hush fell over the entire room, one that soon extended to those standing in the doorway and outside in the schoolyard. Every eye was on the bag in Meggi's hand. Every child in that room was holding their breath. Then the teacher called out the name of the first student.

A young girl sitting in the first row came forward to stand in front of Meggi. Her eyes were in constant motion between the bag in Meggi's hand and a pink Barbie bag still on the pile. Through Eddie, Meggi explained to the students that these bags were from primary school students in Singapore and a lot of other stuff about friendship and the like. While they prattled on I was busy watching the student's faces, so I did not catch most of what she said. What I did catch was Meggi putting the bag in her hand back on the pile. She then picked up the pink Barbie bag. When Meggi took that bright pink bag from the pile, the little girl's eyes almost bulged out of her head. She was so excited she was shaking. I expected any minute to see a puddle form under her.

As Meggi explained that each of the students was to receive a bag, pandemonium broke out, not only in the classroom, but outside in the schoolyard as well. All those well-behaved children suddenly went wild. It was all the teacher could do to calm them down long enough for Meggi to pass out the bags.

Throughout this explosion of exuberance, the little girl's eyes never left that pink backpack. When at last some semblance of calm returned to the classroom, Meggi started passing out bags. The first one to go was a tacky pink Barbie backpack. That bag went to a little girl who accepted it reverently. Clutching the bright pink bag to her body, she slowly returned to her seat. As she opened her new treasure and began to sort through its contents, her face was a stunned expression of joy, mixed with disbelief.

It took a good half hour to pass out all the bags, and then make a picture of each student with their new bag. It was getting late when we finally finished passing out bags, listening to the thanks of various village elders, and drinking more coffee than was good for us. Mind you, they have the best coffee in the world up in those mountains. Shame they cannot export it, for an honest price.

Piling into Eddie's 4-wheel drive Toyota, we headed back down the mountain to the Bakhita Center. In our wake, we left many very happy kids, a teacher well equipped for the next year, and a few village projects that could now advance. When we set out from the school, a Band of children ran alongside the car for almost a kilometer. Yelling and teasing each other, they took turns coming alongside Meggi's window and calling out, "Thank you Mister, Thank you Mister", before peeling off to let the next ones have a go.

The drive back from Lou-mo was torture. My poor bottom, already bruised and sore when we arrived, now faced a torturous return trip over roads that seemed even crueler the second time. Going uphill you press back into the seat, going downhill is a perpetual state of free fall and no fun at all. We arrived back at the Center an hour after sunset, sore, hungry, and exhausted.

That delivery took a full day. Most of the time we spent stuffed in a car, rattling around like peas on a drum. That is, when we were not tossing from side to side in the most brutal manner imaginable. Now, when people ask why we do it, I always remember the look on that little girls face when Meggi handed her a tasteless pink Barbie backpack.

That was only one of the many schools we help in East Timor. And people wonder why it takes us almost a month to make our deliveries there. It usually takes a day just to make one delivery, and that after a brutal day on the roads from Dili to our staging point. I for one wish they would hurry up and develop the place, if for no other reason than the roads would improve. Hopefully they will one day improve enough that I can stop arriving places feeling like my kidneys have turned to mush. I keep telling Meggi we are getting too old for this stuff, but every year sees us out there doing it again.

Chapter 50
On the Sea Again

We sailed from Dili early one sunny August morning. Our course took us east along the north coast of the island. I should say we set out motoring, since the sea was calm as a mirror and there was not a puff of wind in sight. Then again, you must admit setting sail does sound more romantic.

My plan was to avoid the strong west porting current ripping down the main channel by hugging the coast for the first few miles. That short stretch of sea can be quite vicious when the wind cuts up against the current and I had no desire to play in it that day.

My trick, if you can call it that, is to get out early and scurry as far and as fast as we can before the afternoon sea breeze sets in at about 15 knots dead against us. If we manage to get far enough before the wind picks up, I can turn and set sail close hauled for Kisar Island. A small island about 95 miles to the east from Dili.

Of course, if we do not get far enough along before the wind sets in, then it is back to a very wet uncomfortable slog dead against current and wind. A lovely time being tossed about like ping pong balls in a washing machine while burning twice as much fuel as normal.

The first few miles are always a bit slow as the current funnels around the headland where a big statue of Jesus surveys all and sundry from high up on the hill. The scenery is beautiful, even if our progress is often annoyingly slow. As we advance further along the coast, the current slowly loosens its iron grip until about the level of Cape Bundara, just beside the town of Baucau.

Right off that scenic cape, we once had a nautical escapade which added more than a few grey hairs to my poor old head. It was one of those adventures designed to remind you just how fickle the ocean can be. It also gave all of our poor bunks a right proper soaking.

The sea is always a bit choppy rounding Tanjung Liaru, a nasty place where the counter current running close along the coast meets the main current right off the headland. Of course, the wind is usually huffing and puffing at some mad sort of angle to the prevailing swell. When that happens the waves, tend to be pyramid shaped oddities that send you dancing up and down, rather than from side to side. Not at all a comfortable experience for us, or the boat.

That cape is a tricky one to get around. On the one hand, we need to stay close in shore to take advantage of the counter current. It's either that, or go out in the main current where I have more than once been pouring on enough throttle to make 6 knots and barely gaining any headway at all. A frustrating experience at the rate our engine guzzles fuel.

Talk about frustration. In that case even a saint might consider taking up the fine art of cursing, and in several different languages to boot. Nasty place really. One I would be happy to avoid, if there were only some other alternative available, which of course, there is not.

This particular bit of nastiness happened when I was on the wheel and Meggi was on the fore deck with Jo. They were preparing to set the fore stay sail. The sky was clear and the sea was choppy. It was just another ugly afternoon rounding some bothersome cape. That is, until out of the corner of my eye I saw a white line form about half a mile out on our port side. Growing vertically at an alarming rate, a rogue wave emerged out of nowhere. On it came, roaring straight toward *Vega* like the Orient Express on steroids.

I barely had enough time to turn the wheel hard into the wave and call out to Meggi and Jo. "Giant wave, hold fast", I screamed, as the boat slowly started to turn. Of course being female, both of them had to start looking around – in the wrong direction, mind you – and asking why, where, what color, and all sorts of irrelevant questions. Meanwhile, as it charged down on us, that furious piece of tortured sea was growing in direct proportion to my heart rate and blood pressure.

By then, I was gawking at a five meter vertical wall of raging water, and I swear it was still growing. With a thundering roar of foaming sea, the curling wave crest slammed into us. It washed across the decks pouring down through the skylights and in through all the open portholes. Tons of water gushed out from the relieving ports located along the sides of the boat.

Vega staggered, and then rolled hard onto her starboard side. The girls on the fore deck, still busily asking questions, were unceremoniously dumped squealing and squeaking into the lee scuppers. Thankfully, they suffered no real damage, other than wet clothes and a good fright.

Scourge, the ships cat, was not so lucky. She had been peacefully sleeping under the main skylight, enjoying the cool breeze funneling onto the salon sofa. One moment she was snoozing away, peacefully dreaming of a bowl filled with fresh tuna no doubt. The next moment she was bouncing off the cabin walls soaking wet. Fully half a ton of seawater surged in through the open skylight with a resounding crash. *Vega* shuddered, bravely shedding tons of water from her decks, before righting herself with a few indignant bobs and rolls.

There we were, with the skipper looking amazed - well, I was amazed. After all, I was not standing in a puddle that had nothing to do with seawater. There were also two rather soggy girls on the foredeck, and a well-drenched cat down below.

Lucky for us, there was only one rogue wave out and about in search of sadistic amusement. But, that single wave managed to produce havoc down below. A ton or more of seawater had poured in through every opening, creating a sodden mess that would take days to sort out. And as Sod's law would have it, the only bunk to take a direct dousing was mine. That is one of the few disadvantages of having our bunk right under the aft skylight.

It was all hands to their panic stations for those first few minutes, as I switched on the manually operated electric bilge pumps and insured the automatic pumps and engine driven pump were also going full bore.

A look over the side showed water gushing out from various places along both sides at an encouraging rate. The boat continued responding properly. Scourge the cat stood in the hatchway looking like a drowned rat. She was howling pathetically.

If you wonder why we have so many different bilge pumps, well now you know. That and the fact I was once on an old boat that sprung a leak. We were pumping by hand 24/7 for almost a week. Try that sometime and I guarantee you too will equip your next boat with pumps of every type and size.

Checking for damage below decks showed our poor bunk looking more like a swimming pool than a proper bed. The only thing missing were the goldfish and a yellow rubber ducky. How Meggi managed to get it more or less dry and useable again, is still a mystery ranking somewhere between the pyramids and calculus to me. Yet somehow, she did manage to do it, bless her little heart. I am sure her idea of having waterproof covers for all the mattresses on board also helped.

Fortunately, we had previously wrapped all our precious cargo of medical and educational supplies in copious layers of cling wrap, as a precaution against just such an event. There is one thing owning an old wooden boat teaches you. No matter how hard you try to seal things up, there will always be outside water that manages to find an insidious way of becoming inside water. So always, assume there will be leaks and protect everything accordingly.

Chapter 51
The Castaways

L ife on most of the small islands is far from easy. In many cases, there is no regular communication with the outside world, only the random interisland ferry or when the islanders mount a major expedition with one of their own small boats to the next island.

As sailors, we often look at those small local boats and wonder how anyone would ever go to sea in one, much less attempt a long voyage far from land. To give you an idea, the "new" boat on Nila has a small single cylinder diesel engine. Mind you, originally the engine had no motor mounts. When it was running, someone had to stand on top of the cooling water header so the motor would not come adrift.

Last year we took them a set of motor mounts and some long bolts so they could mount it properly. For the island youngsters, who were traditionally stuck with the job of motor mount, this was a life changing revelation in the art of modern engineering.

The fact is, these boats are not only important tools for the islanders, but they are also dangerous. The island craft are not deep-sea boats, nor are they what one would call dependable. Most do not have motors. They depend solely on a small sail for reaching or running and Armstrong driven paddles to make any head way against the prevailing monsoon. For most of the year, this area is subject to strong wind and fierce currents. The monsoon wind averages 15-20 knots and the average current is heading west at 1-2 knots.

Most of us tend to view these people as happy islanders, almost like fish when it comes to living and working around the water. Some of that image is well earned. I have often seen those strong young lads dancing around their canoes with the equilibrium of a cat. They can happily paddle all day and never break a sweat, and they know every fluke of the wind and current around their own island. But that is no guarantee of protection against disaster.

Every year through various misfortunes the wind and current sweep fishing canoes or small local ferryboats out to sea. In most cases, the lost boat reappears after a few days with the exhausted fishermen still on board. Their safe return is cause for an island wide celebration. Over the next few weeks their tales of fighting against the wind and current, their every strategy of sail and paddle, provide entertainment for the entire village. In other cases, both boat and crew are lost forever. On a small island where everyone is related, such loses are equal to a national tragedy.

On board *Vega* at sea, there is always someone on deck keeping watch, 24 hours a day, seven days a week. For one thing it is simply good seamanship. For another, it lets the rest of us get some sleep knowing a freighter on autopilot with the crew down below watching porno films will not run us over. A proper watch also prevents some uncharted bit of land that sprouted up overnight from crashing into us.

For the watch on deck life is mostly a question of fighting boredom, doing small projects when the weather allows, and the occasional excitement when a pod of dolphins or whales show up. You would be amazed at the things we have seen at sea. There was one day we counted 17 yellow inflatable children's swimming rings, complete with smiling ducky heads, as they drifted by, or the time off Surabaya, when we passed through a whole armada of colorful balloons. Add that to the giant schools of tuna, the comical antics of flying fish, and the odd huge whale jumping, and watches can be almost interesting. Well, in any case watch keeping is slightly more interesting than counting your toes or exploring your nasal cavities.

On watch, you look out for things that do not belong, shapes that are unusual, or movement that a wave would not normally make. Those are all visual clues that should automatically attract your attention. When the watch spotted a small dark shadow one morning, bobbing up and down about a mile away from our route, at first it was only a mildly interesting phenomenon, a passing point of interest to observe while waiting for the clock to tic-toc its way a bit further toward the end of the watch.

As *Vega* drew closer to that strange floating object, the binoculars came out to diligently inspect the mystery object. It soon became apparent this was not a log in the water as it resolved into what appeared to be unoccupied a dugout canoe. Such thrilling news soon had most of the crew up on deck. Here was real excitement, a high point for the day and no one wanted to miss it.

I diligently altered course for the mystery canoe while one of the lads shot up the ratlines to have a better view. None of us was prepared for what he reported from that lofty perch. "Skipper, there are people in that canoe and they look dead".

Every sailor with an IQ higher than that of a radish, fears shipwreck more than they fear the plague, a visit from their mother in law, or the tax collector. The thought of being adrift at sea without food or water and precious little chance of rescue, is the stuff of a sailor's nightmare. For that very reason, sailors throughout history have always gone to each other's assistance without hesitation or question. I did not even think about it as I reduced power and spun the wheel, altering our course to come alongside the now clearly visible canoe from the up wind side.

While the boat lost speed, we prepared fenders on the downwind side and several lines to tie off the canoe. During the approach, our man up the mast continued his running commentary. At last, we could easily see from the deck there were indeed two people lying in the bottom of a waterlogged canoe. As we watched, one of them weakly raised his hand and tried to wave. Half way through that attempted gesture, his hand collapsed limply back into the boat.

Closer now we could see two emaciated young men in an island style fishing canoe that contained some fishing gear and two paddles, one of which was broken. There was also a large white sack. The sack seemed to be full. Neither of the boys moved as we hove to alongside and made their canoe fast to *Vega's* starboard cathead using their own bowline.

While one crewmember ran below to get a water bottle, another stepped gingerly down into the canoe. Kneeling beside the first boy, he felt for a pulse in the boy's neck. He told us later that what he felt was weak, but it was there. His report of, "This one's alive", caused a long exhalation of breath none of us realized we had been holding. It did not take long to discover that the second boy, the one who had tried to wave, was also still alive.

Someone passed a water bottle into the canoe. Both boys received a few small sips of life giving water. I shall never forget the moan I distinctly heard from one boy, as water dribbled between his deeply cracked lips.

With both boys effectively incapacitated, bringing them onboard proved a difficult task. In the end, we rigged a whip from the yard and a line firmly under the armpits of each. One at a time, we struggled to get the boys out of their canoe and onto our boat. With such a small crew, it was not easy for us to haul their dead weight out of the canoe and up the side of *Vega*. Once on board we carried each of them into the shade of a small awning rigged between the masts. A few moments later, we hoisted their white sack onboard.

None of us had any experience dealing with extreme dehydration, which seemed to be the most urgent problem. I did know from my time walking across the Sahara desert that the worst thing we could do was let them drink their fill all at once. At best, that would make them sick; at worst, their systems could go into a kind of fatal convulsive shock.

Since the very name "rehydration salts" seemed to say it all, we made up another water bottle with two packets of Oralite mixed in. While part of the crew did their best to slowly rehydrate our newly rescued castaways, we tied the canoe off our stern. A canoe is a valuable thing in these islands so we would tow it behind *Vega* until we reached the next island. Getting us back up to a speed where the canoe would not tow under, I once again established the boat on our intended route. With that done, I hit the autopilot button and went forward to see what was happening.

Both of the boys were dressed in ragged shorts and old T-shirts. A wardrobe that seemed to be more a collection of holes held together by habit, than honest bits of clothing. A quick search of their pockets only turned up a small folding knife, two seashells, and an old harmonica. The knife was old. The blade sharpened so many times that only half of the original remained. The search also turned up a small pouch of leather with several tiny stones, each with a hole in it. Although interesting, none of those items helped us understand where the boys had come from, or how they came to be so far out at sea.

The white bag proved to be full of sundried cloves. The canoe itself offered even less information. Although an islander can recognize every canoe on their island and knows, exactly who made it, and who uses it, we did not have the luxury of such information. Our only hope of solving the mystery lay under an awning on top of the cabin roof in two crumpled heaps. We took turns dribbling water between their lips a few precious drops at a time, and sponging off their salt sores with fresh water.

It is not easy getting water into someone who is essentially "passed out". Unless you do it a few drops at a time, there is a very real risk of drowning the person you want to save. We noticed that dribbling a few drops right as their breathing reached its peak of inhalation seemed to work the best. I am sure a "real" paramedic would have known better ways of doing things, but we just had to do the best we could. Everything I found in our first aid books assumed the person is awake, so was of little help.

As the day wore on, our fore deck clinic improved. Sport mattresses and pillows made an appearance. Careful sponging removed more of the deeply incrusted salt that covered both boys. By early afternoon, we had managed to get a little over a liter of fresh water with rehydration salts into each of them. Both were beginning to breathe easier and occasionally move a bit. Meggi had made one of her chicken soups the day before, so in the early afternoon we began dribbling some of that into our rapidly improving patients.

Chapter 52
The Island of Teun

The small island of Teun can be located on most high detail charts of Eastern Indonesia 25 miles to the east northeast of Dammar Island. Just look for a small ink blotch. If, you are lucky there may even be a name beside it. Like all of these small islands, Teun is the tip of a semi active volcano.

On the map, Teun looks to be an almost perfect circle roughly two and a quarter miles in diameter. Its single volcanic crater reaches skyward to a little over 200 meters above sea level. Teun is an island where water depths go from several hundred meters to only 2 or 3 meters in a boat length. For a boat like *Vega*, anchoring at Teun Island in anything other than perfect weather is impossible.

People on this tiny island survive by fishing, what little they grow in their gardens, and of course, like all of these islands, the clove trade. Being their only cash crop, the annual clove harvest is an important event. Once a year during clove harvesting season many of the island residents, who have been sent away to school or to find work on other islands, return to assist with the harvest. It is normal for this island of 450 permanent inhabitants to support well over one thousand five hundred people during the harvest season.

Vega supports the communities of Teun mainly with educational and medical supplies, although we also provide vegetable seeds, fishing equipment, farming tools, and a host of other useful items that are very important for the well-being of a small community. Considering the average sea conditions during the Southeast monsoon getting those supplies ashore to the people who need them is a challenge.

Arriving off the Northwestern coast early in the morning, we heave to in the lee of the island then announce our arrival by blowing *Vega*'s antique 1940s bronze horn. This allows those who are away from the village time to get back before the excitement starts on shore. That done, we launch the dinghy and start loading it with supplies. Once loaded one team takes the dingy ashore while the remainder of the crew stay aboard slowly steering *Vega* around in circles, taking care to stay well offshore and away from the coral reefs surrounding the island.

We select these teams by the ancient tried and true system of drawing straws. Being skipper, I am always stuck with holding the straws, and staying on board to drive the boat, along with one other poor soul tasked to remain with me in case of an emergency. The rest happily rummage around for their cameras and the like, excited at the prospect of visiting an island where *Vega* is well known, one of the very few boats to stop there during the course of a year.

The landing place is a very slight indentation in the coast surrounded by coconut palms with about a hundred meters of white sandy beach. Located just behind the beach is the village of Mesa. Mesa is not the largest village on the island; that would be Layoni located more to the south on the islands western side. That village even has a modest bay, almost large enough for *Vega*. Were the bay at Layoni not open to the predominately-southeastern swell at the time of year when we visit, it would make a perfect anchorage.

Little happens around the island the whole population does not soon know about. With the arrival of a boat, especially *Vega*, half the village turns out to line the beach and help haul our dingy, supplies and all, out of the breaking waves, safely depositing it high and dry on the beach. By that time, the island drums have the other half of the population moving rapidly towards the beach. In the excitement of the moment, people quickly forget whatever work they have in hand. After all the work will still be there tomorrow, but the boat will not.

The island telegraph is not something particular to Teun. We have also seen it in use on the islands of Nila and Lesluru. The system is quite basic, yet very effective on a small island where everyone knows everyone else.

Short lengths of large diameter bamboo, with an opening cut down one side are scattered around the island at strategic points. These bamboo jungle drums hang vertically on a piece of plaited coconut fiber string from any convenient tree limb. Usually, there is a sturdy piece of wood also hanging on a piece of coconut fiber string beside each "drum".

Every person on the island has a rhythmic tap-tap that is his or her address, so if you want to get Pak Jop's attention you would go to one of these hanging drums and tap out his address a few times or until someone answers. Then you tap out your name and message. That far I could understand, but when it came to the actual message part I was completely lost, although my friend assured me that everyone on the island understood the system and that it worked just fine for most basic messages.

Once on shore a small mob of happy villagers greets our team. While children carried away with the excitement of the moment, race around screaming and laughing, the village elders insist on feeding us. That of course kicks off an endless stream of herbal teas, fresh coconuts opened for the milk, and various incarnations of banana fritters. Somehow, during all this ceremonial greeting our hard working shore team must unload the dinghy and display the latest delivery of supplies. As you can imagine, at that point the shore team has a rough life.

Meanwhile somewhere off the coast, *Vega* drifts around, aimlessly wallowing in the swells. On board, the ship's crew is hardily wishing the shore team would spread a little more canvas. Drifting around on a big open ocean might seem an easy enough task. Most people think all you need do is take the engine out of gear and grab a book, while the shore party gets on with all the work.

The reality is not so simple or comfortable. When you cut power on a boat, it will always drift around until it comes beam on to the wind and seas. With the seas coming on directly toward one side, the boat starts to roll, and roll, and roll. The only solution is to apply a little power and steer in a large circle so that the waves only come at the side for a small portion of each orbit.

While the boat and her crew wallow around in the swell getting greener and greener by the moment, on shore, a delighted teacher is receiving educational supplies and the islands health worker and midwife are receiving their re-supply kits. Of course, there are always a few tools, seeds, and other special items requested the previous year. With those items delivered, we must also gather the new list for next year.

These deliveries take time. It would be impolite, even rude, to rush the process. There is a welcoming ceremony, complete with herbal tea, and a short speech or two. By the time that is over, most of the villagers have arrived on the scene and claimed a patch of sand to sit on. With the whole village in attendance, the show can begin.

Mind you, for those people this event is a yearly highlight or at least a major diversion from the daily routine. As we open each large plastic box of items, the contents go on display for villagers to duly "uuuh" and "ahhh" over. We then photograph the items alongside their proud new owners, before stuffing them back in the watertight plastic transportation box to make room for the next part of our load. Those large waterproof plastic boxes are so highly valued we could bring them empty and still get a cheer out of the village.

In the case of reading glasses, we test each person to find the right glasses for them. All of that takes time. Little wonder we always try to reach Teun early in the morning. By doing so, there is a good chance of the shore team being finished with the delivery by sundown. Mind you, the place is lovely and the people ever so friendly. If there were a decent anchorage, we would happily spend a week there.

All of this takes place on a flat platform covered with woven palm leaf mats. That podium is the island "health post", school, and community center. The meetinghouse consists of a bamboo stage roughly five meters by six meters with no sidewalls. Suspended between several strong wooden poles, the floor is about one meter above the ground. Made from thatched palm leaves the roof slopes at a steep angle. Usually, the village elders sit in state on the platform during meetings, while the rest of the islanders select an available piece of sand to sit on.

The surroundings are what you might call tropical idyllic, with palm trees swaying in a gentle breeze and white sand under foot. Of course, there are no real roads, only sandy paths between the widely dispersed houses. They also lack electricity, cell phone coverage, or any other signs of modernity. With few exceptions, the people on these small islands are still living exactly the way their great, great, grand parents did.

Constructed from a combination of woven bamboo and palm thatch, a combination of coconut fiber twine and wooden pegs hold these houses together. Each house consists of a raised bamboo platform with woven split bamboo sidewalls and a steeply inclined roof. Most families have a fence of bamboo poles enclosing their kitchen garden and yard. A stairway consisting of several steps ingeniously fashioned from bamboo leads to a veranda running across the front of the house.

The islanders are wizards when it comes to making some of the most complicated things from bamboo. In their deft hands, a stand of bamboo becomes anything from houses and water pipes to clothing and musical instruments. One of my favorite bamboo musical instruments is a type of trombone. It consists of one hollow bamboo that the player blows into much like with a trumpet. The second part is a larger diameter bamboo that the player slides up and down over the first piece to vary the tone.

The entire village is spotlessly clean. There is not a single piece of litter to be seen anywhere. Mind you, not having any shops selling junk food or single portion laundry soap helps a lot. At least the primary source of most litter is absent right from the beginning.

For the crew who stay on board *Vega* this is an extremely uncomfortable and boring interval. Moving slowly in a large circle it is not possible to relax and read a book, nor is it possible to leave the steering unattended for more than a few minutes at a time.

With such a small island, even at our slowest speed it only takes about 45 minutes to emerge from the protected lee of the land into the wind and swell of the open ocean. Beam on to those open seas is not an experience recommended for those with weak stomachs. So, slightly green around the gills, back and forth we go. Taking 1 or 2 hour shifts, bored to distraction, and in general wishing it were all over and done with so we could get back to our normal deep sea routine, and a more relaxed work load.

Usually somewhere just around sunset, there is an intense burst of activity on the beach. Soon after, the dinghy makes its way out between waves, heading back to *Vega*. If you ask me, that lot on shore spent the whole day browsing up their jibs on local delicacies and that highly disreputable local drink called *sopi*. Meanwhile, we honest sailorly types were stuck offshore going in circles. With such a heavy roll on making a sandwich is impossible, not without chasing the bread all over the galley.

Once we have the crew back on board and our dinghy hoisted into its place on the stern davits, and believe me in a rolling seaway hoisting in that dingy is not a task for the weak hearted, we set sail for the next stop along our route.

Chapter 53

The Castaways Tale

Trying to staff an ad hoc clinic and sail the vessel with a crew of four is not an easy proposition, yet no one complained as we set up a new schedule dividing our time between ship and clinic watches.

All through the night, we hovered over those two young men trying our best to rehydrate them and feed them something at the same time. It was not until about four the next morning that they both seemed to drift into real sleep, rather than a semi coma. The difference was clear in their breathing, and the way they moved slightly to make themselves more comfortable.

I think it was about then that we all began to hold out hope for their recovery. They both slept soundly for the next 12 hours. Although we continued the soup treatment from time to time, we felt it best to simply let them rest and recover. Fortunately, the wind remained light and the seas calm.

It was late afternoon on the second day, when one of the boys regained consciousness. We soon discovered that his formal name was one of those unpronounceable alphabet soup titles the islanders love, and that his friends called him Mandi. His friend Indi took another three hours to find his way back into the land of the living. When he awoke, the first thing Indi said to his friend translates to, "This is the last time I am helping you get a wife."

At last, we could learn how they came to be so far out to sea, and so near death. The whole crew gathered around as Mandi, tried his best to narrate their great adventure. Mind you, it was a production based on hand gestures and a pocket sized Bahasa dictionary. Between the language barrier and Mandi, constantly eating anything that did not eat him first, it was a long story. We soon realized it was a love story.

The story our castaways told involved a beautiful girl whose name is Yanni, her greedy old father, and too devoted friends who set out together on a perilous adventure so that one of them could win the woman of his dreams. The two boys we now had on board *Vega* were the result of that adventure.

It seems the girl's father was not completely against the idea of having Mandi for a son-in-law, providing Mandi could meet the bride price. The bride price involved three pigs - one of which had to be a sow, a new canoe for three men, and most difficult of all, 12 pieces of cloth and two new cooking pots. All of that in addition to what Mandi and Yanni would need to set up their own house.

Somehow, the boys had managed to get the pigs by building and setting traps in the forest. Then they diligently labored for almost 6 months making a new dugout canoe. Through a stroke of luck, it even had a blue plastic sail. They had found the plastic among a pile of driftwood after a storm. The whole village agreed it was a good canoe. The real problem was the 12 pieces of cloth and of course, the metal cooking pots.

There are no shops on their island. Much less shops selling cloth or pots, and no money to buy those things even if there had been. Indi thought this was the old man's way of being tricky. Their only hope was an island with more people who might have a shop with cloth and pots. Even so, they would need something to exchange for those valuable items.

Everyone knew that the Japanese had once sent a geologist to the island exploring for gold. The old people said he found some, but it was too difficult to get at and in any case, there was not enough to make it worthwhile. But surely, there would be enough for 12 pieces of colored cloth. Based on an old tale that if you looked hard enough sometimes you would find small pieces of gold, the boys had spent weeks looking in the various streams and outfalls around the island.

Eventually, the discovery of a few tiny nuggets rewarded their effort. Unfortunately, their treasure proved to be iron pyrite, commonly called "Fools Gold". After all their work, Indi and Mandi were heartbroken. Then it occurred to them that they could gather cloves from the wild trees high up on the volcano's side and trade those.

This was something they knew how to do, even if finding trees that were unclaimed would be a tough task. It took time and a lot of effort, but at last, they had almost a full sack containing over 50 kilograms of prime cloves. That was when their real problems began.

The boys had grown up on the water. They were at home in canoes. What they lacked was the experience and knowledge of navigation between the islands. Since few canoes ever went between the islands, interisland navigation was an art few had learned. Those who did guarded their knowledge jealously. All the two boys knew was that the next island is " about two days journey 'that way' with the right winds", although no one seemed to know when or what were the right winds.

In that part of the Banda Sea, the wind and currents are seasonal. They depend on which monsoon is active at the time. Then there are the transitional months between monsoons when the currents slack to almost nothing and the wind can die out for days at a time. All this was knowledge the boys were only vaguely aware of, as they sat on the beach dreaming of the great voyage they were going to make. In fact having only ever experienced the currents inshore around their island, they were barely aware of the powerful offshore currents that can be as strong as two and a half knots.

Another problem they faced was in knowing exactly how far away the next island really was. The old people, at least the ones who would talk about it, all said it was two days away with a good wind and pointed towards the west. No one seemed to know how far away two days sailing was. To find out the boys decided to make a test with their canoe, an old half-rotten dugout that had belonged to Indi's uncle.

They sailed around the island as fast as they could from just before sunrise until just after sunset and then tried to imagine 4 times that distance. Accordingly, they calculated that the next island must be just a day's sail past the horizon.

Both boys knew that asking their fathers for permission to attempt such a perilous voyage was hopeless. So taking the same option as millions of youths before them, they made their plans and gathered their provisions in secret. When the time came, they would tell everyone they were going up the volcano to hunt wild boar for a few days and with luck, they would be back with their treasures before anyone in the village noticed their prolonged absence.

They judged a full moon to be the best time for their voyage. That way if they came to the island at night they would see it. Both boys were aware that in the immensity of the ocean on a moonless night it would be easy to pass by a small island without ever seeing it. As the moon grew fatter, their excitement mounted until at last the day chosen for their departure arrived.

Expecting their voyage to last for only two days, they loaded the canoe with water and provisions for three days. They rigged the canoe with an old mast and canvas sail, then after a small ceremony to insure a safe journey, the boys set out from the western side of their island several hours before sunrise. Their plan was to keep the morning sun at their backs and the afternoon sun in their faces during the day. At night their navigation would depend on stars they knew always came up and set in the same place as the sun.

The plan seemed logical enough, although they later discovered that on the ocean at midday all directions look the same. During those times, they soon discovered that keeping the boat on the same angle to the prevailing waves seemed to work well enough.

Throughout the first day and well into the night their canoe raced across the ocean, propelled by its ancient sail. The boys happily took turns steering. This they did by bracing a paddle against the side of the boat. They passed the time imagining a victorious return to their island, and the fame they would win from such an adventurous voyage.

It was an exciting time when the island of their dreams always seemed to be just over the next horizon. That night they kept a careful lookout, expecting at any moment to see their destination.

Up until then the wind and sea had been kind to them. About midnight their luck ran out. A dark cloud appeared on the horizon. Blocking out the stars, the cloud moved rapidly in their direction. It was a typical tropical thunderstorm. One of those one cloud storms where the wind blows for a while and the rain pours down by buckets full for about 20 minutes, before the storm wonders away to molest someone else. For most well found boats, it posed no danger at all. For an ancient open canoe with a half rotten sail, it could be deadly.

Within seconds, the wind changed from a gentle breeze into powerful gusts. One of the first gusts to hit them almost capsized the canoe, before blowing out their sail. With one of them bailing for dear life, the other struggled to keep the canoe running in front of the wind and waves. Without the sail, that was a difficult task requiring constant vigilance. Although the storm only lasted for a few minutes, the destruction it left in its wake was extensive.

When the storm passed the wind and sea calmed. The boys bailed out their boat and took stock of the damage. Not only had they lost their sail, waves lapping over the side had soaked most of their food in saltwater. Two of their precious coconut freshwater containers also fell victim to the storm. Although these things represented major setbacks, they consoled themselves with the certainty that the big island would soon heave into sight and the first part of their voyage would be over.

Sure enough, halfway through the next morning they spotted an island, it was low on the horizon almost directly in front of them. Rowing with that consistent rhythm islanders can maintain for days, the boys headed in the direction of the island, confident their difficulties would soon be over.

As the day progressed the island came steadily closer, yet it also appeared to move at a disconcerting rate from west to east. The current was sweeping them past the island faster than they could approach it. Realizing this, and with only a few miles separating them from their destination the boys began to row harder, driving their canoe through the water faster. Maintaining a slight angle to help offset the current, by the end of the first hour they could easily make out houses on the shore and even people walking along the beach. It would be a close race but it looked like they were winning.

Gathering their energy for one final effort, they began chanting an ancient war song as they dug their paddles deep into the water, thrusting with all of their youthful energy to propel the heavy canoe even faster. With their goal now clearly in sight, the two boys goaded each other to even greater displays of force. Mandi began chanting "Yan-ni, Yan-ni" with every stroke of his paddle. Digging the paddle as deep as he could, directing every ounce of his strength into rowing. The canoe surged forward. Then, half way through one of those powerful strokes, disaster struck. With a rending crack, Mandi's wooden paddle shattered.

Chapter 54

Nila's Great Sewing Machine Drama

It is almost impossible for people who live in big cities, where just about anything is available at the swipe of a credit card, to imagine how important a single treadle powered sewing machine can be on an island that has no electricity and no shops to buy things in. For an island that once boasted two of those machines, having both of them broken amounts to a major community disaster.

On our latest wish list from the Island of Nila, right at the top and underlined twice, Pa Eki wrote "Foot Sewing Machine". Fortunately, having seen the tragic state both of the existing sewing machines were in, the message was clear. I had spent quite some time that year with my trusty can of WD-40 and a few small hand tools trying my best to resuscitate at least one of those machines. My efforts were a failure.

To begin with, both machines needed a serious cleaning. When I opened them up it appeared as if someone coated the delicate internal workings with glue. A bit of forensic detective work soon discovered that palm oil was the local sewing machine lubricant of choice. Hand pressed palm oil is simply too thick for fine machinery. It also dries out rather rapidly, creating a thick coating of sticky residue.

It took me hours to clean that muck out of the gears and then came the tedious task of cleaning it out of the bearings and bushings. Even then, and with liberal applications of WD-40, both machines refused to work properly.

One of the machines water seeping in through a leak in the roof had damaged. There was serious rust on the gears and smaller moving parts. Once I removed the palm oil paste and thick layers of rust, the machine still refused to function. Well, you try playing at sewing machine mechanic with a bunch of matronly old biddies hovering over your shoulder giving advice in a language you do not understand and see how far you get.

No matter what I did, the clearances between just about every part in that machine were too sloppy for the thing to work. Either the needle missed the bobbin, or it crashed into the footplate holding the bobbin in place. And, no amount of adjustment seemed to make any difference. The other sewing machine was in much better shape, but a small metal ring that holds the bobbin in place was broken. I know it was beyond the ability of superglue to repair, because I tried it.

Mind you, I never professed myself a sewing machine repairman, but there I was, scratching my head and pondering how all my fingers had suddenly turned into thumbs. Clearly, I was a victim of my own advertising…again. Where normally I would have watched someone else do the job while merely nodding and making helpful sounds when they seemed appropriate, Meggi had to go and spout off that I was general whiz with machinery fully competent to fix just about anything. Teach me to try to show away for the girls, that will.

I guess it was really my own fault for trying so hard to impress her all those years ago with my manly mechanical skills. Even today, she still has not realized half the stuff I "fix" somehow manages to repair itself after a good taking apart and a cleanup. Most of the time I haven't the slightest idea what I did to make it work again. Maybe all those left over screws, nuts, washers, and other bits get in the way. Machines can be funny like that some times.

To be honest, sewing machines make me nervous. There are all those finely machined parts complete with little gears and oscillating bits just begging for a chance to drive me nuts. Imagine, if you take the thing apart and put just one gear back a single tooth off from where it should be, the whingie-ma-ding will miss the what-ya-macallit every time.

The result is a machine that spins around loverly like, but refuses to sew a single stitch. Oh, and we should not forget the poor slob looking a lot like me tearing out his hair and trying to figure why the thing refuses to work. Geez, the things we manly men do to look good in front of the girls.

What I did learn that year was I could not fix the one machine no matter what I did. That machine was too far gone to rescue. Maybe someone with a full micro-machine shop, and a whole lot more brains than I have, could fix it. But, there was no way I was going to fix the thing with the few tools and limited knowledge at my disposal. That machine would have to be replaced, no question about it.

The other machine was a different story altogether. It was a simple case of being well gummed up on palm oil and one small bit well and truly broken. As luck would have it that was about the only part, I could easily see how to take out and put back in again. All it needed was a replacement part. What in Singapore could be fixed with a few phone calls and an easy stroll to the shopping mall was completely unfixable on the small island of Nila where there are no shops at all.

Now the logical solution would be to take the small part from the dead machine and use it to fix the other machine. Logical, like I said, but not exactly politically correct. It seems that several years ago the owner of the one machine said something about the owner of the other machines sister in laws, cousins, sons, table manners, which of course started a feud of epic proportions between those two august matrons of island society. Enough said?

Well, one year and a month later we were back on the island of Nila. And thanks to the efforts of a friend in Singapore, we had a lovely almost new treadle powered genuine, made in China, Blue Bird imitation Singer treadle powered sewing machine on board. We also had a goodly selection of supplies for it and the almost identical other broken machine. Those supplies included several small bottles of original Singer sewing machine oil, also made in China, needles, thread, and a bunch of other bits and bobs that Meggi claimed were important for the constructive employment of any sewing machine.

Meggi and I had been transporting that machine in place of our salon table for well over 2,000 miles. Having managed its safe transportation all the way to Nila, the next trick would be getting it on shore and then up to the village undamaged. Not as straightforward a task as it might seem, considering the sewing machine was a bit bigger than our little dingy would accept as deck cargo.

In the end, the new sewing machine went ashore on board one of the island canoes. As precarious a trip as you could ever dream of. By canting the sewing machine and its table at an angle the thing fit in the canoe - more or less. It was not exactly what one would call inside the canoe; not exactly. It was more like almost somewhat perhaps on a good day balanced on the sides of the canoe looking for an excuse to escape its current confinement and go for a swim.

Those young men from Nila have a sense of balance to rival cats. They practically grow up in canoes. Even so, we did suggest they lash two of the canoes together catamaran style using bamboo poles and rope we would happily provide. Although no one openly scoffed at the idea, they did politely ignore our suggestion as being too complicated by half and a complete waste of time.

Personally, if I had been Pa Eki, knowing I was transporting Ma Lila's new sewing machine ashore, I would have used the catamaran system. That woman is always such a jolly old bird, but somehow I have a feeling trying to explain dropping her new sewing machine in the ocean might not be the healthiest or most relaxing way to pass an afternoon.

Evidently, the various island youngsters told off to do the job caught on to my logic and agreed with me. For every one person rowing the canoe there were at least two hanging onto the sewing machine. I swear there was even one lying flat on his back under it. He was hanging on for dear life to the cast iron base.

We followed along in our dingy for the whole half-mile trip ashore, while Pa Eki rowed around them in a small canoe freely imparting the benefit of his august advice and counsel. Every now and again Pa Eki must have reminded them what would happen should Ma Lila go on the rampage. That was when I saw the rowers on board the local Island style door-to-door delivery boat cringe in unison and paddle even more carefully than before.

Once safely ashore, those lads slung the machine between two long poles and manhandled it up the steep path to Ma Lila's house. Once in front of the house, with the new machine diligently in position and open for best effect, Pa Eki called Ma Lila out to have a look at her new sewing machine. Mind you, all of this was a surprise. She was not aware that new sewing machine even existed.

And surprised she was. I thought the old girl was going to widdle herself. She opened the machine and closed the machine. She pulled open the drawers sifted through the various needles and other supplies, all the time squealing like a six-year-old girl in a Barbie shop. To say Ma Lila was a happy camper would be a serious understatement.

While Ma Lila was inspecting her new sewing machine, Pa Eki diplomatically took us around to where the old rusty machine was sitting. There with great stealth and Pa Eki standing guard at the door, we dismounted the part needed to repair Ibu Rosa's machine. It was just about the only piece still useable on that poor old sewing machine.

So it was, that after the obligatory dose of herbal tea and a slice or two of Ma Lila's tasty homemade cake we set off for another village and the second part of our mission.

Less than a mile along the coast from where Ma Lila lives is the small village where Ibu Rosa lives. By land, it takes a good half hour of uphill and down to get there.

By sea, in our dingy, it was only a short cruise across a small bay. That is unless you have Meggi and Jo along who insist on stopping to ogle every new coral and stone that comes into view. On the other hand, it is still faster than going by land because the two of them would still do exactly the same thing with every new tree and shrub we passed.

Arriving at Ibu Rosa's house it only took a moment to have her machine back in service. Although being Ma Rosa she insisted on testing it on several different pieces of cloth before giving our work her final seal of approval. Her husband may be the headman of that village, but everyone there knows who really runs the shop. You should have heard her giving her daughter in law the odds while the poor girl tried her best to thread the needle with trembling hands.

As I said before, those island mamas can be tough old birds. We later saved the poor girl from at least one drama in life by giving Ma Rosa a new pair of reading glasses. Ma Rosa was as proud as a dog with two tails to be able to thread her own needle again. Turns out her eyes were so bad that without those glasses she had trouble seeing the sewing machine, much less the hole in a needle.

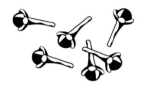

Chapter 55

Without a Paddle

In the face of disaster, Indi never missed a stroke. He paddled with all the force in his young body while Mandi leaned down to continue paddling like a surfer, with one hand on each side of the canoe. Using the power from his arms and back to propel them closer to the beach, a place of safety they could see so clearly now. Despite their best efforts, the heavy old canoe soon began to lose forward momentum, while the current close into shore grew even stronger.

With energy born of desperation, they struggled as the fierce current swept them rapidly along the beach, all the while pushing them further out to sea. They tried yelling and waving their arms to attract attention, but no one on shore noticed them.

Alternately praying and cursing, they frantically paddled toward the land. They were so close, the smell of the forest and the smoke from cooking fires drifted across the water to where they vainly fought against the unrelenting current. The smell of cooking was a torture.

By late afternoon, having drifted past the island, disappointment and exhaustion overtook them. Just after sunset, they both fell into a deeply troubled sleep.

The following morning, they awoke to clear skies without the slightest sign of land. Taking stock of their meagre provisions, they found two coconuts filled with fresh water, some dried fish, and a piece of cake. Saltwater had only slightly spoiled the cake.

Thirst tormented them, both wished nothing more than to grab one of those coconuts and drain it to the last drop. Instead, they settled on a system of rationing. They limited themselves to a few small sips of precious water at a time. Breakfast that morning consisted of half a small dried fish between the two of them and one sip of fresh water each. That single mouthful of stale fresh water was the finest drink either of the boys had ever tasted. They spent the rest of the morning huddled under a scrap remaining from their sail.

Neither boy was under any illusions. Their situation was grave. The possibility of rescue, or reaching another island was poor. The fact is, although they knew of other islands and even continents somewhere out there, they had not the slightest idea where those lands might be, or how far away.

Four days later, they were near the end. The freshwater was gone, and although they had watched several tropical thunderstorms pass close by, not a drop of rain fell on their boat. Drifting in and out of consciousness both boys could only lay in the bottom of their boat awaiting death. When the shadow of *Vega* fell across their canoe, Indi was certain it was just another hallucination; even so, he tried to wave his hand.

We picked the boys up roughly seventy miles downwind from the nearest island. As it turned out, they came from an island where we stop to deliver medical and educational supplies every year. After a bit of confusion it turned out the boys knew about us also.

We had one delivery stop to make and then we would take them home. It took several days for their story to come out in bits and pieces. As it did Meggi and I decided to play Cupid, in exchange for the bag of cloves we would provide the cloth and cooking pots so that Mandi and Yanni could be married. We also gave both boys a heavy stainless steel bush knife with a sharpening stone and a well-made scabbard. Other crewmembers chipped in several T-shirts and a few short pants to improve their wardrobe. Someone had even found rubber sandals for them. All of this they kept in two brightly colored backpacks we had left over from Kits-4-Kids.

A week later, we arrived and anchored off their island. The first thing we noticed was the somber atmosphere, no happy groups of people formed on the beach, and only a few canoes came out to greet us. The people in those canoes looked miserable, that is until Mandi and Indi appeared on deck and started jabbering away in the local dialect.

Both of the boys were dressed in their finest new clothes, with the new bush knives, dangling from a piece of rope tied around their waist. Mandi had even found a pair of gaudy plastic sunglasses somewhere, which he wore with great pride at every opportunity.

Suddenly it was huge smiles and laughing all round. There was yelling back and forth to the shore where the happiness quickly spread like oil on water. The village had been in deep mourning for two of their young men presumed lost at sea. It turned out the boys were not as sneaky as they thought. A fisherman had spotted their sail, the morning they left. Naturally, the villagers assumed the wind and current had carried them away. The day we arrived, they were preparing a memorial service in the village church.

One of the first to arrive in the second batch of canoes was a very attractive young woman. Jumping onto *Vega*, she ran to Mandi and threw herself into his arms. Well to be precise, she threw her arms around his neck and wrapped her legs tightly around his waist. She was crying and laughing at the same time, while Mandi staggered around under her weight, trying not to fall over. One of our friends provided us with a rough translation of her first words to Mandi, "You great idiot, if you ever do something like that again I will un-marry you that same day, and make you sleep with the pigs."

At last count, Mandi and Yanni had two lovely children. They named their oldest girl, *Vega*. Indi also married his childhood sweetheart. Several years ago, he asked us to bring him a selection of vegetable seeds. Having vowed never to set foot on a boat again, he is now the island's most successful vegetable farmer.

Chapter 56
The Original Spice Islands

The 135 mile sail to the Banda Islands is usually one of high seas and strong winds, both coming from the South East. For the first time in months, *Vega* is truly in her element. She loves those long slow swells and enough wind to drive her along nicely under plain working sail. Even though we often meet 5-6 meter swells, the fact they are so far apart means the boat rises in a stately manner for several seconds then slowly slides down into the next valley between waves. On the wave tops, her sails fill completely with 20 to 25 knots of steady breeze. The deep troughs rob her sails of wind.

In a completely natural rhyme *Vega* rolls into each wave, roaring white water cascades over her windward rail flooding across the deck, her relieving ports open as water gushes freely from her downwind side on the rise, then thump closed as she rolls back again. This is true blue water sailing at its best, even if some of our volunteer crewmembers find it an awe inspiring, even overwhelming, experience.

As she rises on the waves, one side is even with sea level while the other looks down into what seems to be an enormous gulf, five to six meters deep. It is an awe-inspiring experience, for those who have never seen it before. For Meggi and me, it is just another day at sea.

That trip usually averages a little over twenty-four hours of magnificent sailing far from shipping routes, reefs, and islands. A wonderful sojourn at sea all too soon cut short by our arrival in the glorious Banda Islands so rich in history and natural beauty.

The search for these islands by European powers in 15th century led to the fall of ancient South American Empires, the conquest of India, and the eventual domination of China by the British. These tiny islands, that enticed a Spanish queen to gamble her crown jewels, were at the heart of several vicious European wars.

Once considered among the most valuable real estate in the world, the Banda islands are now a forgotten backwater, rich in historical reminders from a time of brutal war, greed, and genocide. Yet before the arrival of Europeans, life on these islands was different.

For thousands of years Arabian, Indian, and Chinese merchants journeyed with regularity to these Islands, peacefully engaging in trade. They exchanged ceramics, metal implements, rice, and cloth, primarily for nutmeg, mace, and cloves.

Spices acquired on these trading missions often journeyed to China on junk rigged sailing ships then onwards by camel along the famous Silk Routes, or on swift sailing Arab trading dhows to the Persian Gulf. There merchants transferred the spices to caravans for the journey onward to the Mediterranean. Thus, an ever-growing demand by Asian, Middle Eastern, and European nations for the spices of South East Asia was satisfied.

Some years ago, archeologists working in the ruins of the ancient Iraqi city of Terqa on the banks of the Euphrates River, unearthed in a sealed ceramic vessel dated at 1750 BC. It contained clove buds that could only have come from the Maluku Islands, thousands of sea miles away. This important find clearly indicates the extent of the spice trade from these small islands over 3,000 years before the first Europeans arrived.

The first Europeans to arrive in, the Banda Islands discovered an important international and regional trading center. In addition to items from India, Arabia, and China other goods moving through Banda included cloves from Ternate and Tidore in the north, bird of paradise feathers from the Aru Islands and western New Guinea, along with massoi bark for traditional medicines, and slaves. Ikat cloth from the Lesser Sundas traded for sago from the Kei Islands, Aru, and Seram. Highly capable local trading vessels called Belang or Orambai, carried most of these cargos.

In his 1515 AD book *Suma Oriental*, the Portuguese apothecary Tomé Pires reported the Bandanese as being part of an Indonesia-wide trading network and the only native Malukuan long-range traders taking cargo to Malacca, although some shipments from Banda were also being made by Javanese traders.

There just under the horizon six small islands were calling out to us with their thousands of years of history. Soon we would be exploring them first hand. A prospect I always find exhilarating.

Chapter 57
The Heart of History

As the stars slowly faded into the early light of dawn, a dark gray smudge on the horizon rapidly resolved into a verdant green island lost in the middle of Indonesia's Banda Sea. We were sailing along nicely at a steady 7 knots, reaching across the southeast monsoon 4 and 1/2 degrees south of the equator. Our next destination, a small group of islands that changed the world.

Ahead of us lay a modest archipelago consisting of 10 islands with a total land area of less than 40 square miles. These islands, once considered so important by the European powers, inadvertently caused the fall of several ancient South American Empires, the conquest of India, and the eventual domination of China by the British.

These are the Banda Islands, for thousands of years the only source for two of the most sought after spices on earth – nutmeg and mace. They are an important stop on our yearly humanitarian delivery route.

These tiny islands, that enticed a Spanish queen to gamble her crown jewels, were at the heart of several vicious European wars. Once considered some of the most valuable real estate in the world, these islands are now a long forgotten backwater located far out in the Banda Sea. With a population of roughly 17,000 warm friendly people spread over six islands, the Banda Islanders are always ready to assist visitors and very proud of their archipelago's long colorful history, a history that is as rich as it is fascinating.

I find the pre-European history of the Banda islands intriguing, yet quite difficult to come by. It seems there was a conscious effort on the part of the Dutch to destroy or suppress any mention of pre European Bandanese history. Then again, few people want to teach their children a history full of blatant greed and bloody genocide. Even the British, who have always seemed rather proud of their piratical heritage, avoid the topic completely. For the Bandanese, those memories are far from forgotten.

Convincing people back home that a bunch of half-naked savages need civilizing for their own good was always an easier sell than admitting that greed and colonialism were out to destroy a long established way of life that had peacefully supplied the world's demand for cloves, nutmeg, and mace for several millennium. By the time Christianizing the poor misguided heathens went into the mix, the good people of Holland soon believed they were doing the Bandanese a favor.

By the time Europeans arrived in force, what started as random cargo moving from island to island on small local boats had developed into an important flow of international commerce. That trade moved along routes well known to many of the Eastern seafaring nations. Without knowledgeable local pilots to guide them, the first Europeans would most likely still be wandering lost around South East Asia, having never found the Banda islands.

Some of the ships employed by those early Asian traders were much larger, and better made, than the ones utilized by Europeans. Long before the Europeans arrived in South East Asia, the Chinese were building the largest wooden sailing ships ever known. Not only did China have better ships, as inventors of the magnetic compass, and celestial navigation, they benefited from a more advanced system of navigation and chart making.

Nutmeg and cloves native to the Banda Islands arrived in China at an early date. A reliable tradition holds that Chinese courtiers in the third century BC were required to carry cloves in their mouths to sweeten their breath when addressing the emperor.

While Og and Zog were still running around the forests of Northern Europe wearing animal skins and wishing that some Greek lad would hurry up and steal fire from the gods, so they could pinch it from him, the Egyptians accomplished a massive public works feat rivaling their construction of the great pyramids.

Opposite Luxor in southern Egypt, wall paintings from the tomb of Queen Hatshepsut provide details of the ships and cargo from one of history's first documented spice trading missions. That mission occurred in 1493 BC. Ironically, Columbus, whose real name was Cristobal Colon, set out in 1492 AD. Although coming to the game almost three thousand years late, he was also searching for the fabled Spice Islands.

The trade in far Eastern commodities was so important to the Egyptian economy they dug a shipping channel from the river Nile to the Red Sea, almost 3,000 years before the Suez Canal. Granted it took them until the days of Ptolemy II before they finally figured out the system of locks necessary to open that canal to the Red Sea, but they got there in the end.

The Egyptians undertook that colossal engineering project in order to facilitate the flow of spices and other rare commodities from the Far East into the Mediterranean.

This spice trade became so extensive Pliny feared the annual export of hard currency in the form of gold and silver to import spices from the East would bankrupt the Roman Empire. To quote Pliny, "by the lowest reckoning India, China, and the Arabian states take from our empire over 100 million sesterces a year (for spices)."

In an effort to break the Arab monopoly on cinnamon, cloves, nutmeg, and mace, in 100 AD, the Romans improved the Egyptian canal. They then began sending impressive fleets of trading ships as far as India and Thailand. Many of the spices they were searching for originated from the Spice Islands in what is now Indonesia. The Romans were not the first, nor would they be the last Europeans to expend vast fortunes searching for these little islands.

The objective of their search, were two rare spices that grew only on six tiny islands. Those spices brought about the accumulation of vast riches for some, and ultimately the brutal exploitation and almost complete annihilation of the native population by the Dutch.

In 1667, the British traded one of these islands to the Dutch for another small island in North America called Manhattan. That trade also included all of New York, Connecticut, New Jersey, and Long Island just to sweeten the deal. At a time when one kilo of nutmeg was valued on a par with gold, that deal was not as disproportionate as it seems today.

Controlling the sole source of nutmeg was a monopoly well worth a king's ransom, and more. Little wonder the Dutch were so adamant, and brutal, in their efforts to dominate these small islands, then to maintain that monopoly, even at the cost of committing genocide against the native population.

Like so many sailors before us, we were happy to see those fabled islands coming closer with every hour. Soon we would moor *Vega* in our usual place, greet our friends, catch up on all the local gossip, and then start our delivery of school and medical supplies.

Chapter 58

Pirates, Patrons, and Thieves

If anything indicates the importance these small islands once had for their European masters, it is the vast expenditure of treasure and effort invested in a plethora of fortifications built to enforce and defend that monopoly. Everywhere you look, there are watchtowers and fortifications designed with one thing in mind; to keep the other greedy European nations from making off with what the current band of interlopers with a royal commission were busy stealing.

That may sound rather crude considering all the time and effort European governments spent convincing their populations that their real reason for dominating these islands was to bring civilization to the naked savage inhabitants. Not forgetting the angle so often chanted to the masses that those poor lost souls needed Christianizing, by force of arms if necessary.

The truth was much simpler. The spices grown on these islands were worth their weight in gold, literally. The country that controlled those spices could reap a fortune re-selling them to other Asian and European nations. It was all about greed and merciless exploitation. Little wonder that the nation with the best and most dynamic merchants wound up colonizing the place.

Those were the halcyon days of Europe's piratical conquests. It was a time when anyone with a royal letter of marque could fill their pockets by stealing riches beyond their wildest dreams. Those letters usually read a bit like "I King Dogfish the Grasper here bye license my loyal servant Muggins the Younger and his band of merry men to steal whatever they can get their hands on from anyone far enough away that they can't cause me any trouble, as long as I get my cut". Laugh all you want, but that is exactly what was happening. Of course if you take a squint around the same thing is still going on today.

The up-shot of all this was that whoever happened to be industriously exploiting some distant land had to diligently defend themselves from others of their ilk who also wanted to get rich quick on someone else's account. Ah, the glory days of European expansion when all a lad needed was a stout ship, an eye patch, and a Letter of Marque to have it almost as good as modern day bankers.

In case you're interested here is the current definition of Letter of Marque: "a license to fit out an armed vessel and use it in the capture of enemy merchant shipping and to commit acts that would otherwise have constituted piracy".

*　*　*

Banda Niera is the capital of the Banda Islands. The island atmosphere is easy going and friendly with a strong colonial flavor. The Portuguese chose this convenient site to establish themselves when they first arrived in the early 1500's. It was not long after that, in 1516, they started building the poorly sited Fort Nassau. The Dutch finished that fort in 1609.

Fort Belgica quickly followed Fort Nassau. Sitting atop a small hill overlooking both the northern and southern anchorages, Fort Belgica enjoys a position that was much easier to defend. The Dutch began construction of Fort Belgica in 1611. Both of those old forts make wonderful destinations for an evening stroll through the town.

At one time Niera town was famous for its many "perkenier mansions", opulent houses built during the golden age of the Dutch "Nutmeg Barons", a title applied to the wealthy nutmeg plantation owners.

At the height of the nutmeg boom, the barons squandered immense fortunes in a vain attempt to replicate the lavish life style their wealth would have purchased in Holland. Judging from the number of ancient gin bottles regularly washed ashore in front of the old governor's mansion, they also spent a great deal of their time completely intoxicated.

Half a world away from their home country, Dutch perkeniers existed like feudal lords surrounding themselves in arrogant luxury, pampered by a small army of local servants and of course slaves. They were rich, yet they could not fully enjoy the benefits of that wealth. Little wonder, between the depressing weather these islands are subject to for most of the year and the enforced isolation so far from home, many of the European community ended their days by committing suicide.

Although shorn of their sumptuous luxuries, many of those once impressive colonial residences, with their stately columns and imported marble floors are still standing. Strolling through those lovely small provincial palaces it takes little effort to envisage the frustration of those displaced plantation owners. Although wealthy beyond their wildest dreams, they could only retain that wealth through self-imposed exile on these remote eastern islands where most of the year it rains. Of course for the Dutch that might have made the place seem more like home.

Chapter 59
What is it Like Out There

I always said, one day I was going to write a book about all the dumb questions people ask me concerning life at sea. Things like "what do you do at night, do you put down the anchor and go to sleep?" Or "where do you do your shopping when you are out there?" "Aren't you afraid of the dark at night?" Many of those questions are enough to make you wonder if computers, hand phones, and television really are causing serious brain rot these days.

I once read where some Swedish kids did a science fair project subjecting alfalfa seeds to hand phone microwave emissions while they were sprouting. The seeds not exposed to microwave emissions, sprouted nicely and grew normally. The seeds exposed to hand phone microwaves refused to grow at all. Maybe that is the problem with young people today; their seeds never sprout properly.

I know most kids in modern cities lack the slightest idea of what the real world is like. They think milk grows on trees in little cartons, and meat or chicken comes in plastic packages from a factory somewhere. At least they are mostly right about the meat and chicken.

One frequently asked question is, "what do you do when the weather is bad and the seas get really rough?" Now that question makes sense, at least to me. What I do when the weather is bad and the seas are rough enough to make a whale puke is wish with all my heart that I could be somewhere else. A log cabin on some pleasant mountainside would be my first choice.

Anyone who tells you they enjoy being at sea when the weather is acting up belongs in a padded room, preferably under restraint for their own protection.

When the gales are howling, let no one tell you its fun, because bad weather at sea really is no fun at all. The way I see it, any well-designed boat, and fish for that matter, are perfectly designed for a life at sea, even when the weather goes wild. People on the other hand are land dwellers. For us aspirations to a life at sea, are like fish wanting to be farmers. We adapt ourselves the best we can. And, insure our boats have a plethora of carefully placed handholds.

What is it like to be on watch when a real screaming stinker is blowing? Ah yes, welcome to the joy of a life at sea. Try to imagine sitting out in the open with the wind howling a wholie and the rain blowing horizontally like some demented creature emerging from a fire hose. Then, add seas crashing against the hull tossing great buckets of salt water into your face every few seconds. To that lovely image, add the boat violently pitching and rolling making it hard to avoid hurling bodily out of your place at the wheel.

Once you have all of those cozy conditions clear in your mind, blend them all together and you have a relatively good idea of what it is like being at sea when the weather acts up.

If you ask me, one of the most fundamental inventions the first sailors made was the foul weather jacket. Of course, the art of producing foul weather gear has progressed dramatically since those early days when Og and Zog sported their first designer animal skin ponchos. Maybe one day I should put together one of those slick glossy coffee table books full of pictures and illustrations on foul weather gear through the ages. I could call it, "A Leak in Time."

I based that title on a fact; every single foul weather jacket made will always start leaking more or less exactly three quarters of the way through a watch. The precision with which this happens has often set me speculating, might there be engineers who dedicate themselves solely to designing those insidious leaks.

This being the age of highly targeted specialization, I can easily imagine engineers with a long string of letters behind their names all slaving away in some obscure R&D lab. There must be those who specialize in sleeves, others doing hoods, and of course all of them wanting to reach the pinnacle of their profession and design leaks for the back of the neck. Those insidious little infiltrations carefully engineered to send an annoying trickle of cold water down the center of your back, at precisely the moment when it seems you might make it through a watch without getting too wet.

That may not be as dumb as it sounds. After all, there are highly paid engineers who spend their whole lives designing things to break after a very precise amount of time. Some bright lad designs something to do a job properly, then along come these people to make sure it will need replacing precisely when the next model is about to be released, or the day after the warrantee expires. Just try to imagine one of that lot in a singles bar trying to explain the joys of his profession to a delectable young woman with a knicker drawer full of failed vibrators.

Chapter 60

Thousands of Miles From Home

High on a hill overlooking the wide sheltered bay formed by the islands of Gunung Api, Banda Niera, and Banda Besar stands ancient Fort Belgica. Built by the Dutch in 1616 this typical five-sided fortification was intended to protect Dutch colonialists from invasion by other greedy European powers. It also allowed the colonialists to fend off the native islanders, who were down right irate when the Dutch forcibly insisted on a monopoly over their long established spice trade.

Those tensions lasted until 1621 when Dutch East India Company (VOC) soldiers and hired Japanese mercenaries, under the command of Governor General Jan Peiterszoon Coen, seized complete control of the islands, killing, enslaving, or forcing over 90% of the indigenous population to flee for their lives. From an estimated indigenous population of roughly 15,000 only about 1,500 survived the carefully orchestrated genocide instigated by Coen.

From high on its hill top prominence fort Belgica enjoys a splendid view of both navigable entrances between the islands, with Gunung Api's lush tropical green standing proud over all. What must it have been like for a Dutch soldier, standing on those battlements in the 1600's with Gunung Api belching sulfurous smoke and fire into the air as it violently erupted less than a mile away, I can only imagine.

Approaching Fort Belgica from the town side, there is a path leading to the curved archway of the main portal. Climbing that path, I tried to imagine what it must have been like for native warriors charging up hill in a desperate attempt to regain control of their native land. Attacking those high stone walls, from where the thunderous boom of heavy cannon loaded with grape shot and the pop-pop of muskets showered down a leaden storm of sudden death, would have taken unwavering courage. The gripping fear as those terrible lead balls ripped into flesh with a dull smacking noise, would have tested any man's courage to its very limits.

Today, that hill is a pleasant park with flowerbeds and a few scattered shade trees. On one side, local farmers have appropriated modest plots of land to grow vegetables. Gardening plots are at a premium on Banda Niera, so any space where vegetables can grow soon becomes someone's garden.

Just inside Fort Belgica's impressive grey stone gate is a guardroom. There local youngsters studying to be official tour guides collect a modest entrance fee and volunteer to conduct a tour of the fort. The tour they give is quite knowledgeable, even if their stories can become a bit fanciful should the mood strike them.

That day I wished to wander through this imaginatively restored historic monument without distraction. I preferred to let my mind drift, searching for that déjà vu impression I often find in such places. I have always felt something deeply quixotic every time I see one of these old forts, perched high on some remote hillside. Sadly, that impression rarely survives once inside those massive walls, where the ambiance is stark and utilitarian.

From the dimly lit guard chamber, a second set of massive stone arches lead into the glaring tropical sunlight of an inner courtyard. Once inside, the pentagonal design of this classic European fortification is easy to discern from the crenulated towers located at each corner. Each tower served as an elevated defensive position and a protected passageway for the stairways leading up to the ramparts.

There is something magical about being inside one of these old five-sided forts. Accustomed to spending our lives in buildings and rooms with four walls, when we confront a building with five sides, something disorienting happens to the way the mind interprets reality. Even consciously trying to count the walls can easily become a difficult task fraught with frustration.

As with most fortifications from this period, accommodation, and storage spaces existed under the massive crenellated ramparts between towers. A well stands in the center of the courtyard giving access to the cisterns. An intricate system of drains once collected fresh water from Banda's copious rains for storage. Inside the rooms, the ceilings are high pointed arches designed to support the ramparts above.

The rooms are cool, even though the sparse unglazed windows only grudgingly allow entrance to a negligible amount of light and even less ventilation. At each of the five corners, almost directly under the towers, a modest suite of rooms existed for the grandees of the fort. Those would have included the commander and his officers or perhaps even the governor and his crew in times of conflict.

Those special rooms under the base of each tower were far from what I would call elegant accommodation. They struck me as cheerless caverns with nothing other than a safe refuge from the enraged local chamber of commerce to recommend them as living spaces.

On a more pragmatic note, even though Meggi and I searched every available nook and cranny, there was no indication the fort had ever sported toilet or bathing facilities. With several hundred men in residence, one can only assume strolling under those great walls at night was an undertaking fraught with more than one unpleasant risk. We also failed to discover a kitchen.

Within each tower, the steep half twist of a narrow stairway leads to the wide ramparts above. Emerging from the claustrophobic darkness below into the open air and bright sunshine makes for a very a pleasant change. Crenelated openings in the walls clearly mark positions from which cannon could dominate both the bay and the hill leading up to the fort.

Today a few corroded old cannon mounted in cement protrude from the walls, while even more lie slowly rusting away from neglect in the high grass surrounding the fort. If you ask the islanders, they claim there is a plan to "one day" hoist up and mount those old cannon along the walls. We have been going there for years now and so far, "one day" has yet to arrive.

Emerging into the sunlight, Meggi and I explored the southernmost rampart, admiring the spectacular panorama of Banda Besar and Gunung Api. Arriving at the western tower, we ascended even higher. Climbing the narrow ladder that leads to the roof above was an adventure in itself.

There is a small square entrance hatch at the top of the iron ladder. It passes through 50 cm of solid masonry. The hatch is so narrow that only after much twisting and painful contorting did I finally arrive on the roof. At one point, I was sure my knee and backpack were jammed so hard against the side that Meggi might have to call for a crane to extricate me.

How a man in full armor carrying an antique musket and long fighting sword could have made it up there in a rush is a complete mystery to me, although Meggi did kindly remind me that solders of those times were not quite as tall, nor as well fed as I am.

If you ask me, it was the vegetable shopping she insisted on stuffing into my backpack. Well, you try wiggling through those narrow openings with a load of cabbage, potatoes, and onions on your back and see how far you get. You would be amazed how bulky a few veggies can be when you find yourself in a tight spot. Good thing I went first. At least that way Meggi missed me floundering onto the roof then blundering to my feet in such an undignified manner.

As I looked out over the crenellated bulwark, it was easy to imagine being a soldier 400 years ago. My mind conjured up images of living in remote isolation half a world away from country, friends, and family. A small troop of poorly equipped soldiers, surrounded by thousands of people who would far prefer to see my friends and me rotting in hell than infesting their islands.

I could almost feel the weight of a heavy metal helmet on my head, hot from the sun beating down on this beautiful tropical bay. I sensed in my bones the boredom from constant weeks and months of watching an eternally empty sea, hoping, dreaming, and praying for a ship from home.

Chapter 61

Lost but not Forgotten

From my elevated position, I had an unprecedented view far out across the endless sea. Long days would pass staring at the same constantly blue horizon, wishing, hoping, praying, yet never sighting the elusive ship from home. Try to imagine the excitement when after months or even years of complete isolation and utter boredom, a sail appeared far out on the horizon.

Frantic signals flashed between those garrisoning the Fort high above the village of Lonthor on Banda Besar to where I stood on Banda Niera. Perhaps from my very position the watch saw those signals. Turning to call down into the courtyard the signalman would have been full of excitement. A call to alert his companions an unknown European ship was approaching. A throng of excited men swarmed onto the walls, all intently observing as slowly a ship emerged, steering for the entrance to the bay.

There would have been much more than the potential joy of seeing a ship from home in those men's minds. These were hotly contested islands. Several times English and even Spanish ships had attacked with an eye to capturing them for their own merchants to exploit or at the very least making off with a ship load of nutmeg and mace. A jolly mornings work with cannon and sword leading to a treasure that might set a captain and his crew up nicely with a life time supply of country houses, pubs, and other sailorly fantasies..

Could the approaching ship be hostile? Might it be a warship full of powerful artillery and heavily armed men intent on an attack? Even a successful pirate attack, something the English were not at all adverse to having a go at, might fill a ship with nutmeg, cinnamon, and mace. A cargo so profitable the captain and crew might retire back to their home country in luxurious comfort for the rest of their lives.

With this in mind, the men of fort Belgica would have titillated their cannon and double checked the priming of pistols and muskets, and then eased swords in their scabbards. The islands they guarded were a treasure trove whose vast riches stood coveted by every scoundrel on the seas and every monarch in Europe.

As the ship slowly approached, apprehension liberally mixed with exhilaration would have been rife. Imagine the joy when the fort commander saw through his telescope the brightly colored Dutch flag they were all praying for. Sailors would look closely to insure the ship was truly Dutch built, for it could well be an enemy ship flying the Dutch flag.

Flying the enemy's flag was an age-old deception used by many sea going scoundrels in the hope of approaching closer to an enemy unhindered. Arriving within cannon range uncontested, the attackers would haul down the false colors and hoist their real national flag as they fired the first devastating broadside into their unsuspecting victim. Even a ship clearly built in Holland would have been no guarantee. Pirates could easily be employing a captured Dutch ship to facilitate a surprise attack.

Meanwhile down in the town excitement spread through the community like wild fire. A ship! A ship has arrived! The whole town would turn out, calling and cheering as the ship glided through the narrow reef fringed entrance between Gunung Api and Banda Besar. If peaceful the ship would turn head to the wind before dropping anchor in front of the governor's mansion. As the critical moment approached, more than one would be holding their breath.

Slow match burned in tubs beside carefully loaded cannon, wafting its special scent along the battlements as gunners tended their pieces, all the time watching for any indication of aggression. Swept up in the turbulence of their times those brave adventurers were alone, far from their home, with little hope of any assistance should hostilities break out.

The tension during those final moments as the ship rounded up into the wind and came to anchor must have been unbearable. As the anchor splashed down into crystal clear water, a universal sigh of relief might have been heard. Yet only when the ship began firing a salute to the fort using blank charges would the tension finally begin to ease. The long wait was at last over. They had not been forgotten or even worse abandoned to their fate by the mother country.

Excitement ran high. For many there would be mail from home, along with everything from cheese to gin and even such items as sewing needles, thread, and shovels carefully stowed away in the ships hold. The company vessels that touched here to load nutmeg and mace also provided luxury items craved by the small Dutch population.

Thanks to the highly lucrative nutmeg trade, the affluent Dutch perkeniers could afford to import a cornucopia of luxuries all the way from Holland. Ship owners and captains were more than happy to supply that demand, at exorbitant profit for themselves. The benefits a ship captain might realize on his personal private venture trade goods were almost on a par with what could be earned as his share for successfully transporting a full cargo of nutmeg and mace safely back to Holland.

While the Dutch cavorted with joy at the prospect of gin and cheese from home, many of the people watching would not have been happy to see another European ship arrive. They were descendants of the original inhabitants. The scant few who miraculously survived the genocide. Somber faced people who still remembered the legends of when they had not been slaves and their islands had been a thriving regional center for trade. For them there was only sadness at their great loss.

* * *

The majority of historical research plays down or completely ignores the scope and volume of precolonial trade centered on these islands. Even so, all the evidence suggests that regional and even international trade was central to Banda's pre-European economy.

For thousands of years ships from Arabia, China, and India regularly called in at the Banda Islands to trade goods from their own countries for nutmeg and cloves. Before the arrival of Europeans, the Banda Islands were a central hub for an extensive sea born trade. Locally built sail powered trading vessels ranged far and wide, trading throughout the region. Ceramics, metal, and other trade goods from China, India, and Arabia were traded onward to New Guinea, Kai, Aru, Timor, and some believe as far as Australia and Malacca.

Early chroniclers describe how forest products, such as shipbuilding wood, aromatic tree bark, bird feathers, and the staple food sago, were brought from Aru, Kai and New Guinea in exchange for cloth, rice, metal utensils, and glazed ceramics from China, India, and Arabia. Thus, Banda served not only as a spice producer, but also as an important transshipment depot, between the trading world and the eastern regions.

Various villages specialized in trade with a certain regions and in some cases specific islands or villages. Communities carefully guarded the navigational secrets as well as bits of the local language required for those voyages, passing that secret knowledge down through generations. Some villages sent trading ships out to islands in the eastern regions such as Seram, Kai, Aru, and New Guinea, while other villages traded with Timor and further afield.

For more than three thousand years before the European invasion brought that long rich history and its culture to a bloody end, native Banda Islanders actively exploited their knowledge and those trade routes.

Whereas the Portuguese adhered to the traditional method of trading for spices, often-employing resident Chinese, Indian, or Arabic traders for the purpose, the Dutch had other plans. They wanted nothing less than complete domination of the global spice trade.

In 1621, Dutch East India Company (VOC) soldiers and hired Japanese mercenaries, under the command of Governor General Jan Peiterszoon Coen, invaded the islands. In a carefully engineered scheme, they murdered or enslaved up to 90% of the original population. Many survivors fled to the Kai Islands, where small pockets of original Bandanese society still remain. Others villages sent filled what boats they had with survivors dispatching them to the distant island communities of their trading partners.

Where for thousands of years peaceful trade had provided the Banda islanders with a rich market for their spices and a source of goods that allowed them to build their own extensive trading network. Now, all trade was fiercely controlled. The Dutch became the only ones permitted to extract profit from these islands. Draconian measures were put into place. Locally owned vessels were forbidden to have sails or venture away from their home island without special permission. The important trade in food stuff such as sago, which many communities depended upon, collapsed.

* * *

While I was busy daydreaming, the sun slowly slipped behind Gunung Api, casting the village below in shadow. First one then another of the mosques began their timeless ritual calling the faithful to prayer. The smell of cooking fires and spices hung in the air. Slowly I turned, strolling over to the ladder that, with some effort and luck, would take me back to 21st century Banda Niera. A sleepy island where motorbikes coexist alongside bicycle-powered rickshaws called Bajacks and friendly children call out "Hello Mister" to every passing stranger.

Taking my leave through the massive entry portal, I noticed another great cannon lying abandoned in the grass beside the wall. I could not help thinking of European occupation in these islands as the poignantly moving account of a viciously brutal domination driven by greed.

Fortunately, this has not left the islanders in a chronic state of melancholic depression. In fact, to have suffered so much in their history these islanders seem to be some of the happiest people I have ever met. Then again, few of the islanders you meet today are direct descendants of the original inhabitants.

* * *

Banda Besar is the largest of the Banda Islands. It is the home of Banda's oldest and most celebrated nutmeg plantations along with the remains of Fort Lontar (1624) and Fort Concordia (1630). This long thin crescent shaped chain of mountains about one kilometer to the south of Banda Niera provides the southern anchorage with superb protection from the occasional strong wind and heavy seas.

The island's name means "Big Banda" and this is where the majority of the nutmeg plantations are still located. Once this island was a source of fabulous wealth. An island where Dutch plantation owners, called Perkeniers, ruled their plantations like feudal lords. Vast fortunes were spent in a vain attempt to reproduce an elegant European lifestyle thousands of miles from their native land.

Meggi and I wanted to visit the island again to continue exploring the many historical remains. Fortunately we could combine a trip to historic Banda Besar with our delivery of medical and educational supplies to the community of Waer and the island of Hatta.

* * *

Waer is a small community located on the southern side of Banda Besar. It is a friendly community we have been assisting for the past several years. A historically interesting community, Waer is one of the oldest continuously populated settlements in the archipelago. It first appears on the "Jansonnius map" from 1620, although the community existed as a base for inter-island traders long before being recorded by the Europeans. As one of the archipelagos oldest and more remote settlements Waer has its own special magic.

It was early morning when a roughly built local island boat negotiated its way alongside *Vega*. Its peeling pastel blue paint was highlighted with a strip of intense red along the rub strake. At the helm, which is painted a garishly bright yellow, the oldest son of our friend Ishmael stood proudly steering his small cargo come ferry boat.

With a small crunch of wood against wood the two boats joined. Standing beside me, and a large pile of boxes, I heard Meggi mutter a most unladylike expression. The scowl I saw her directing at the boat's cheerful young driver spoke volumes about her opinion of his seamanship. It seems no matter how much she fusses with our fenders, those local boats always manage to find a way through her defenses. Several deep scratches in *Vega*'s well cared for paint bare silent testimony to the fact.

After a bit of fender juggling, we soon had his boat safely tied up alongside. With the welcome assistance of our fellow passengers, Doctor Ruth, Meggi, and I began passing down the many boxes and bags of supplies destined for the clinic, midwife, and school of Waer community and Hatta Island. The majority of those fellow travelers, being from the town of Waer, knew of *Vega* and our mission.

The cheerful way they all pitched in to help and the many "thank yous" we received were encouraging. With our precious stores all loaded and safely protected from saltwater spray by a blue waterproof plastic tarp, Ishmaels son energetically cranked life into his single cylinder inboard engine. I noticed Meggi and Ruth in the bow carefully fending off his boat from ours as the two slowly separated. With no neutral or reverse gears, maneuvering one of those local boats in a tight space is always an adventure.

If there is a special sound I associate with the local island boats, it is the Pop-pop-pop of their single cylinder inboard diesel engines. None of which sport the slightest pretense to an exhaust silencer. Some of those rough and rugged 'Made in China' diesel engines can be heard for miles. It always amazes me the drivers have not all gone deaf. Yet noise or not they are dependable hard working little engines, which are easily repaired and consume only a modest amount of fuel.

The boats themselves are long and narrow with no decking to speak of. Their only condescension to luxury is a small aft cabin where lucky passengers can duck in out of the hot sun or rain and the splashing waves. The inside of that cabin is no luxury. Primarily designed to house the boats engine the cabin has a single long wooden bench along each side and tends to be rather hot and noisy.

On the other hand the open cargo bay can be even more uncomfortable. As the boat splashes its way through the long swells of the Banda Sea the passengers huddled under a blue plastic awning. For the following hour and a half trying to keep the cargo and themselves as dry as possible became a serious challenge.

To reach our destination the boat must forge its way against the monsoon wind and waves. Of course, the drivers want to go fast, so they can make as many trips as possible in a day. That means the boat is constantly splashing into the waves. This slamming throws up thick spray which the strong wind blows back across the boat. The ferry boat drivers have either become extremely agile at ducking behind the cabin, or completely inured to being soaked to the bone for hours at a time. The unfortunate guys who drive the regular run, must be as wrinkled as prunes by the end of a rough day,

Lacking their hardened attitude to flying salt water, and having all our boxes and bags of supplies to protect, Meggi and I spend most of that voyage huddled together trying to maintain a pretense of dryness. Ruth, who is as curious as a kitten, kept sticking her head out from under the tarp for a look see. Each time she did, her effort was rewarded with a splash of saltwater in the face. As we thumped and slammed our way around Banda Besar I couldn't help smiling at the thought, 'at least there are still a few experiences you won't find in the lonely planet guide'.

You may wonder why we choose to endure such an uncomfortable boat ride rather than make the short 4 km journey across the island by road. The reason is simple. The roads are in such poor condition only the hardiest motorbikes can safely negotiate the mountain crossing from north to south. With no 4 wheel drive vehicles on the island, and even if they had I doubt I would risk my life in a car on those crumbling roads, motorbikes or local boats are the only available form of transport.

A charming little town, Waer straddles a modest normally placid river, which during the rainy season becomes a raging torrent. As ancient as it is, and although the place has a well preserved fort, the town of Waer still does not have a port. There is only an open stretch of slightly sheltered beach where boats can come close enough for their passengers to hop over the side and wade ashore. Whatever loads arrive are passed from hand to hand, or balanced precariously on someone's head for the trip ashore.

Often for days at a time when the weather is rough, or the seas from the south run dangerously high it becomes impossible for boats to land. Especially in the rainy monsoon season when it is not at all unusual for a boat to be turned back by high waves breaking on the beach. During those times when the rains render their tenuous mountain road impassable, the village is completely cut off from the outside world. Fortunately for Ruth, Meggi, and I, the seas were relatively calm that day when our boat arrived.

With a crunch our boat grounded on the beach. After hours cooped up under the blue plastic tarpaulin we were all looking forward to stretching our legs. Or in my case, discovering where the local dogs hiked their legs. But, relief was not to be. There on the beach our good friend Doctor Hendra was patiently waiting for us.

Since he was expecting us, Hendra had a contingent of local fishermen drafted into service. They were standing around shuffling their feet all ready and waiting to help off load the supplies we had brought. Having years of experience at it, they made short work of getting everything ashore, and considerably to both Ruth and Hendra's relief, all of those supplies arrived completely dry. One man even offered to carry Meggi ashore on his back, an offer he did not bother extending to me.

Our first stop was the Waer community clinic, which Doctor Hendra heads. Much to the delight of the village gossips, we formed a small procession through the town. An impromptu parade composed of villagers of all ages, may of the participants loaded down with boxes and bags, all on their way to the community clinic. Once you factor in the children running along beside us and the older folk coming up to ask what was afoot, there must have been a hundred people who eventually arrived at the clinic. The last fifty meters or so the whole cavalcade slowed the pace a bit, so Doctor Hendra could run ahead and position himself to officially greet us.

Personally, I find Doctor Hendra an amazing person. Of unpretentious average height for an Indonesian, he has black hair that he wears trimmed short and twinkling brown eyes. When he discusses his medical problems, those eyes take on an intensely serious cast and his long delicate hands become animated. Even his normally cheerful voice takes on a different tone. A soft spoken energetic young man, Hendra first came to this isolated posting fresh from his internship in Jakarta. The assignment was part of his official Ministry of Health national service.

No sooner had he arrived, than Hendra fell in love with the place and its slow easy paced way of life. A lifestyle that must have seemed like a complete turnaround from the hustle and bustle of life in the over populated hugely polluted mega city of Jakarta.

Having very little calling him back to Jakarta, when his term of national service was over Hendra volunteered to stay on. Two years later he met and married a local girl from Banda Niera who had just finished her medical studies. Now, with his experience Hendra could have almost any posting available. Yet year after year he stays on at Waer.

Perhaps his lovely new wife Oki, who is also a doctor and was born on the islands, has something to do with the adoption of his new home. In any case the people of Waer love the man, and hold him in the highest esteem. I have rarely met a more content person, even if he does face constant frustration caused by a shortage of supplies and equipment.

From his unexceptional community clinic Hendra struggles to provide medical services for the southern side of Banda Besar and the nearby island of Hatta. Not at all an easy task, when you consider the island of Hatta and the southern side of Banda Besar spend almost half of every year completely cut off from the outside world. Even though he has a rather nice Ministry of Health water ambulance at his disposal, for emergency cases and visits to the island of Hatta, there is constantly something wrong with the motor, and even when the motor is working, there is rarely any money for fuel or oil.

Although the clinic building is still in an unfortunate state, it is much better than the first time Meggi and I saw it. Somewhere Meggi still has the pictures from that first visit. The clinic roof was falling in, the doors and windows were eaten away by termites, and the whole place desperately needed of a coat of paint. Of the eight rooms available, only two were serviceable. In one of those two rooms the roof leaked so badly Hendra had to construct a tent over the examination table too protect his patients.

Thanks to several of our friends who provided for the materials, and the local community who donated the labor, at least now the roof doesn't leak anymore. The entire building has been freshly painted and the doctor's living quarters restored. There have also been a few other important improvements we were able to assist with.

Over the years Meggi and I have provided doctor Hendra with equipment and supplies for his remote clinic. The first time we saw his place, it was only from a since of politeness and a wish not to injure his feelings, that we managed to call it a clinic. He really had almost nothing at all to work with, no drugs, no bandages, not even a laboratory microscope. The microscope he was using at the time came from a child's introductory biology set. It was all we could do not to laugh, when he showed it to us.

Well somewhere in the boxes we had just landed was a complete professional binocular laboratory microscope set as well as a portable ultra sound scanner, a multi check blood analyzer, and several other important pieces of equipment. There was also a stock of expendables and drugs for his clinic. While Hendra sent word for the local midwife to come meet with Doctor Ruth and pick up her re-supply kit, together we sorted through what we had brought for him.

As he unpacked box after box the radiant smile on his face said it all. When we unpacked the laboratory microscope and assembled it, I thought the man was going start giggling. The new portable ultra sound scanner, a completely unexpected addition to the clinic, had him dancing around like a kid at Christmas.

Since we had almost everything he requested the year before, the expression on his face was one of unmitigated pleasure. Dr. Hendra has that ingrained dignity one rarely finds these days. He is a proud man who tries to maintain a tight control on his emotions. Yet as he sorted through the equipment and supplies we delivered, more than once a smile curled his lips and a twinkle lit up his eyes. Being a man of few words his comment was simple, "With this I can save lives. Thank you".

Coming from Doctor Hendra that simple statement was an accolade equal to a seven-course knife and fork sit down dinner at the town hall complete with fireworks, speeches, and champagne toasts. Of course later we had to stand in front of the clinic while Hendra made a blessedly short speech. By then we had several hundred people out front, all excitedly milling around, gawking, and in general looking happy. Several hawkers roamed the crowd, possibly trying to sell popcorn or sausages in a bun.

Just about the time Hendra finished his say and I thought we might get off lightly, up pops the town mayor to put his oar in. Being a good politician, he rambled on interminably while I stood there trying to look pleased with it all, Ruth tried to look intent, and Meggi shuffled from foot to foot. By the time the two speakers wound down, the good folks of Waer were looking pretty content. If you think about it, they had good reason to be so pleased.

Judging by the number that came up later to mangle my paw or pat me on the back, if it had been Election Day I might have become the new lord mayor. Meggi, who usually shuns public appearances like the plague, put on her best face for a deputation of the local ladies, while Doctor Ruth wisely managed to slip off looking for a toilet.

* * *

Next it was the turn of Waer's midwife, a dignified elderly woman with years of experience safely bringing babes into this world. She learned midwifery from her mother who had learned from her mother going back so many generations no one was quite sure when her family first became the village midwives. Although deeply traditional she was also intensely interested in learning as much about her profession as possible.

Several years ago we gave her one of our first basic midwife kits. She was very happy to receive it. Over the following years we upgraded and re-supplied her kit. This year we had another re-supply and some serious upgrades for her as well as Doctor Ruth who instantly took her aside and started Doctor Ruth's Mini-Workshop on how to use some of the new equipment and drugs. The next thing I knew, the midwife and Doctor Ruth were headed off into the village, deep in an animated conversation which for sure included bottoms, babies, and the next cup of tea with biscuits.

On arrival at the clinic, I noticed more than a few people lounging about under the giant trees that surround it. After all the excitement and speech making subsided, and Dr. Hendra unpacked the boxes and sorted their contents onto tables. Whenever he came to a box with pharmaceuticals he would sort through them until he found the one he was looking for. Then taking a dose in his hand, Hendra went to the door and called to someone waiting under the trees. That person would then receive their medication along with whatever instructions Hendra felt necessary. Then after thanking Doctor Hendra, and often times us also, those patients would wander off back into the village.

Later Hendra explained to me he had been out of most important medications for the past several months. In fact things had gotten so bad, he was spending most of his modest salary to purchase drugs for his patients at the retail pharmacy on Banda Niera. Knowing we would be arriving that day, he had put all of his more urgent ambulatory patients on notice to be ready and waiting at the clinic when we arrived.

The more critical cases he would personally pay a quick visit, delivering their medication while we visited the school. The less urgent patients he would see after we returned from the small island of Hatta, or over the following days. While Hendra packed his carry out bag with an assortment of medications we turned to the other reason for our visit to Waer.

Before continuing with our deliveries for Hatta, Meggi and I wanted to make a delivery of educational supplies to the Waer village school. We had a selection of large boxes and bags all prepared for them containing basic educational supplies, teaching aids, and sports equipment. Several young boys were already sitting beside the box containing sports equipment. I could see them surreptitiously eyeing up the new footballs and team shirts.

Out of the corner of my eye I saw the head teacher standing under a tree beside the clinic surrounded by more students. The kids were shifting from foot to foot with excitement and most likely wishing with all their heart we would get on with it. It must have seemed an eternity before at last Doctor Hendra called them over to where we stood surrounded by boxes and bags of school supplies.

Leaving the clinic and a happy Doctor Hendra behind, we set out for the school. Our porters consisted of school students drafted into a little extracurricular activity by their teachers. Advance rumors of official regulation footballs and team uniforms insured a surplus of volunteers. When we set out for the school, a line of children snaked out behind us. Many with a box or bag balanced on their head or in the case of the heavier boxes, slung between two or more likely looking young lads.

As our line of cheerful porters wound their way through Waer village toward the school, it wasn't long before we gathered a large following of inquisitive kids and interested parents. Although most tagged along to see what the excitement was about, many were intensely interested in what we had brought for the school. More than one parent came along side to shake my hand and say thanks.

Waer's school is government sponsored. That means, being out of sight and out of mind, they are provided with a building and a few teachers paid for by the Ministry of Education, and exactly the kind of material support you might expect a place located far from any major population center to receive. Yet for the parents of Waer, procuring the very best education possible for their children is important. Teachers had freely discussed the importance of our past contributions at community meetings, so many parents were excited to see what this year's donation consisted of. They were not disappointed.

The school building had just been refurbished. It looked almost new under a coat of bright paint and its recently repaired windows. Once inside the story changed a bit. Several of the classrooms had no tables or chairs for the pupils. Young students sat on the floor in organized rows to take their classes.

Even after five years of consistent support from our side, everywhere we looked there was still a dire shortage of the most basic school supplies.

We also noticed that many of the books, posters, and other teaching aids brought in previous years were prominently displayed and clearly well used.

While the students were diligently standing around in lines, singing songs to welcome us, and reciting little speeches, it didn't take me long to unpack the supplies we had and range them on display. My display was on the floor. I wanted to make a few photographs for the people who donated the materials.

Whenever we make a delivery, we always take photographs. And I for one think it is important. Someone once said it was a way of showing off. They felt our way of laying out everything so that each donation can be easily seen was akin to blatant advertising.

Well, I disagree. Those pictures are our way of showing the people who donated those supplies exactly where their donation went, who received them. And how happy they made those kids and teachers. It also gives us a chance to document the state of a place for future reference. As far as the comments from NGOs we meet along the way, I figure, it's just a case of sour grapes. Since what we do with almost nothing, makes what they accomplish with their huge budgets look bad.

With those school supplies safely delivered, and a new wish list of items for next year safely tucked away, Meggi and I returned to the clinic where we met up with Doctor Ruth. In our wake we left several very happy teachers busily sorting books, posters, pencils, and pens. The kids had already discovered the new footballs and other sports equipment. Those supplies they were busily sorting through bye themselves. Judging by the happy sounds coming from the playing field, at least one of those new footballs was currently being put to the test.

Back at the clinic Doctor Hendra had finished sorting, distributing, and storing his medical supplies and was ready to accompany us to the tiny island of Hatta. Since the government water ambulance was broken again, he wanted to take advantage of our chartered boat to make the visit. Once there he and Doctor Ruth would conduct clinic. Employing some of the small disposable syringes we delivered, a child immunization program he had been putting off due to a shortage of syringes could now continue. When we arrived he had two of the black ballistic nylon traveling supply bags we brought him two years before, all packed and ready to go. The rest of his team was waiting for us on the beach.

Chapter 62
The Hatta Break

Hatta Island is a remote place located south east of Banda Niera and Banda Besar. It was once famous for its teak forests, long ago decimated by the Dutch. At one time, those forests provided wood for local boat building. There is currently a locally inspired project afoot to replant teak trees on the island. A project we gladly support.

Today Hatta has little of economic interest, other than some of the finest underwater panoramas in the world. Which easily explains why every time we go there Meggi always brings her diving mask and snorkel along. The unspoiled reefs are stunningly beautiful no matter where you look. Long white beaches, swaying palms, and superb diving make Hatta one of our favorite small island escapes.

Historically, Hatta has had only one major military incident, at least that we know of. That was when an English warship's captain fired his cannon in a noisy yet harmless manner and caused the British flag to be planted on several places around the island. He had no intent of taking possession of the island, he simply did it to enrage the Dutch colonists on Banda Niera and Banda Besar. It worked.

The Dutch were convinced the English had landed in force intent on occupying Hatta Island. Taking several days they mounted a major armed expedition to oust the supposed British interlopers. Arriving some days later in full force, with cannon and all, they soon discovered that the Britt's, after having purchased all of the available vegetables on the island and then – being Britt's - indulging themselves in a bit of petty looting, were long gone. Only their flags remained behind. One unconfirmed rumor has it there was also an empty brandy bottle at the base of the main flagpole with a note inside. The note read, "Happy April Fool's Day".

Hatta Island is like a lost a backwater for the back of beyond. It is one of the most isolated places you could ever imagine. For several months out of every year this island's small population is completely cut off from the other islands by a heavy swell and rough seas that make landing a small boat an all but impossible feat. Fortunately, for us the day we chose to visit Hatta Island the seas were calm and our small local boat had no problem at all approaching close enough for us to disembark safely along with the many boxes of supplies we had brought for the midwife and the village school.

While Doctor Hendra was busy with vaccinations and general clinic, and Doctor Ruth was deep in conversation with the local midwife, Meggi and I slipped off to make our delivery to the school. With that mission accomplished, we located a likely stretch of beach. While Meggi amused herself snorkeling, I curled up in the shade to finish a book I was reading. The place was so peaceful I soon dozed off for a siesta.

The next thing I knew a young boy was speaking to me. The little pest clearly wanted my attention. Opening my eyes, I squinted in the bright sun. I could see Meggi walking down the beach toward where I sat. One hand full of snorkeling kit and the other trying to balance a large collection of lose seashells. The grin on her face said it all.

Well the boy was on a mission of his own, Hendra had sent him to locate and retrieve Meggi and me. The clinic was over, the last child vaccinated, and the boat was waiting to take us back. Our short spell in paradise had ended.

Getting to my feet, I dusted the sand off and waited for Meggi. Soon the three of us were strolling down the beach toward where our boat waited. Two hours later, having dropped Hendra and his team off at Waer, we were back on board *Vega*. The last of our yearly deliveries successfully accomplished.

Chapter 63
The Mystery of the Missing Forts

Gunung Api is the volcano that frequently appears in all those old paintings and drawings you see of the Banda Islands. For 400 years, every painting or illustration of Gunung Api showed it erupting. On almost all of the old maps, the volcano is shown erupting, a sign it could be used as a navigational aid. For sure, erupting volcanoes make great landmarks. On a clear day their plume is visible for twenty or thirty miles, long before the mountain or the actual island becomes visible.

Old references indicate a 660-meter high volcano belching a column of fire and smoke easily seen from far out at sea. In the days when navigation was more a case of semi educated guess work than an art form, ships arriving from ports half a world away employed that pillar of smoke by day and the volcanic fire by night to help locate these tiny islands.

After a long and often difficult ocean voyage, this was the first visible sign of land for many ships arriving fresh from Europe. It would also be the first accurate position many of them would have had for weeks. Whether it actually did erupt or not for the old navigators, we do know for a fact it last erupted in 1988 destroying three villages. That eruption created several massive lava flows still visible as huge black scars on the island landscape.

If you have never seen a volcano up close and personal as it spouts and fumes take my word for it, the experience is awe-inspiring. Most of us are accustomed to seeing nature, at least geological nature, as something rather placid. That is until you see a huge mountain blow over 500 meters off its top while enthusiastically spewing ash and lava to the four winds. An occurrence that happens all too frequently in Indonesia.

Today Gunung Api still smokes, occasionally. But most people know it for the view from its peak and its century old cinnamon plantations. Getting to the summit is a tough climb. But, providing you manage it without suffering a heart attack on the way up, the view is an unsurpassed panorama of the islands.

From high on Gunung Api, it is easy to make out the rim of an ancient volcanic crater that once exploded leaving these few islands as the remains of its rim. Before it went bang, that mountain was one of the tallest in the world. Pretty impressive, considering its base starts some 5,000 meters under the surface of the Banda Sea and the actual mountain top extends under water for miles in every direction.

Chapter 64
Old Stones and Older Boats

Meggi and I are both fascinated by ancient ruins, old boats, and maritime history. We often joke that searching out "old stones" is one of our preferred pastimes. There is something about old ruins, long ago abandoned by the people who gave them life, that attracts us like two iron nails to a magnet.

Even though the old ruins we visit often enthrall me, the ships have always been what attract me the most. Little wonder wherever we go I am always giving the local merchant craft a squint. I enjoy studying their often-curious shapes and trying to understand how those shapes must have evolved to suit the local sea conditions.

Traditional sailing rigs can be even more interesting. I enjoy following the evolutionary thread where local materials and skills played such an important part in their development from woven palm fronds and rope made from coconut fiber to canvas and more recently plastic awnings with polypropylene cordage.

Seen against that background you can imagine our delight when a few years ago we arrived in The Banda Islands just in time for the traditional

Kora-Kora races. For over a week before those hotly contested races began teams could be seen out training in their long sleek 50 man canoes. Meggi and I spent hours sitting on *Vega's* bow watching as boat after boat raced up or down the bay often at fifteen knots or more.

After that, the races were almost anti-climactic. For me Kora-Kora will always be hundreds of men all dressed in their everyday kanga and head cloth paddling those long thin canoes in almost perfect harmony. Once the ceremonial dress came out for the real races, something magical seemed to evaporate from the scene. I could no longer imagine them setting out to greet and perhaps help tow in a newly arrived trading ship, or armed with their traditional weapons slipping away at night to raid another island.

The actual races were too modern, too artificial for my taste. Mind you the tourists ate it up with a big spoon. And who am I to say what is authentic and what is not? When you delve into the frequently tortured history of these islands and their culture, it is amazing they managed to maintain as much as they have.

Those Kora-Kora were the archetypical Bandanese war canoes. The originals carried well over one hundred rower/warriors and were often arranged like catamaran, with a house suspended between two hulls. The long thin canoes seen today only hold from thirty to fifty rowers. The rest of the crew consists of a captain, two or more bailers to toss out any water that comes in, several musicians playing drums and gongs, and a helmsman who sits at the stern and steers with a large paddle.

Mind you, with such a mob of people all busily going at it, there may well be a goat, two chickens, and a cat on board as well. I am always amazed when they get all that lot into the canoe without tipping it over. Averaging twenty two meters in length with a beam of only one and a quarter meters, these boats are modeled on the once dreaded war canoes of the Moluccas.

Today, these impressive craft are only used on special ceremonial occasions, and for the highly contested inter-island Kora-Kora races. The races are regional events with boats and teams coming from several districts to participate. Winning those races is considered an important feat, bringing prestige to the community that fields the successful team, as well as to the individual crewmembers.

Each boat is brightly painted in its team colors. The teams themselves all dress to match in bright turbans and sarongs. Powering their way through the water at up to 15 knots the visual effect is stunning. In perfect time, the rowers deliver two power strokes followed by a rest stroke, with their paddles raised in perfect unison. When racing, they often strike a rhythm that closely resembles the movement of a centipede's feet, an esthetically pleasing and impressive feat to watch.

The cargo version was quite a bit wider and more full bodied. Called Belang or orambai, those trading boats carried rectangular sails made from platted palm fronds closely resembling square sails. The local cargo boats had one or two masts. They were steered by a large paddle hung from the stern. With their high curving bow and stern, slightly reduced in modern imitations, those cargo vessels were strongly reminiscent of a Viking long boat. Many of them made very impressive voyages, maintaining an extensive regional network of trade routes for thousands of years before the Europeans arrived.

In one local legend, a Bandanese orambai sailed on a spice trading mission to Malacca, where the crew first came in contact with Islam. Excited by their new discovery they continued the voyage, eventually arriving in Mecca. Upon their return, they brought Islam back to the islands. Pushing the historical frontiers back even further, there are several cave paintings in East Timor dated roughly 18,000 BC clearly depicting sailing vessels similar to the traditional Belang and Orambai. That would have been at the height of the last Ice Age when two gigantic continents called Sundaland and Sahul were the big thing in South East Asia.

Chapter 65
The Lost Forts of Gunung Api

Like many an adventure this one began innocently enough. It all started over dinner, when our friend Abba Rizal commented on an ancient map of the islands that had recently come into his possession. I should mention that, like us, Abba is a fanatic on old stones and historical mysteries. Although, being a native born Banda islander he tends to confine his historical studies to the islands. "The old chronicles clearly state that at various times there were no less than three fortified emplacements on Gunung Api," he said lightly slapping his hand against the table for emphasis.

He glanced around the table then shook his index finger in the air. "Three stone built fortifications on an island the size of Api and no one can find them." He shook his head in disgust and continued, "I have asked all of the old people, the hunters, and even the palm wine tappers on that island. They all know the stories, yet none of them has the slightest idea where even one of those forts might be." Mind you, coming from a man like Abba, this was equal to a highly vocal tirade delivered in the House of Commons.

More to prevent him knocking over my drink than for any other reason, I off handedly suggested that if Abba felt it so important why not mount an expedition to go out and find the lost forts of Gunung Api. Then of course, Meggi jumped in with what a wonderful idea that was and the next thing I knew we were all having coffee out on the terrace and pouring over the old maps. Which by the way were useless.

Even though we were due to leave in a few days, for inveterate "old stone" lovers like Abba, Meggi, and I, this was a challenge we could not ignore. Aside from the fact it would be great good fun and a bit of innocent adventure, those old forts are an important part of the Banda heritage. They needed rediscovering, if for no other reason than to provide an interesting place on Gunung Api for tourist excursions.

Here was a chance for Meggi and me to make a useful contribution, while indulging our love of exploration and old ruins. Our friend Abba, who among other things is the elected president of the Banda Island Tourist Association, was constantly bemoaning the lack of interesting places for tourists to visit on Gunung Api. An old fort might be just the ticket for an afternoon of snorkeling mixed with ancient ruins.

Having reviewed all the available information, the three of us agreed to mount an expedition the following morning in search of the three lost forts. We would start the search by circumnavigating Gunung Api in our dingy. That would give us a good indication of possible locations for the forts, while at the same time allowing us to make a general survey of likely new snorkeling site. The logic being that any defensive fortification would face the sea. From the water, we would have the best chance of spotting any telltale signs of ancient human activity.

If we could find even one of those lost forts and should that fort be in reasonable condition, it would not be long before the locals cleared away paths and created open spaces where visitors could wonder about gawking and taking pictures of themselves. We could only hope that excavations and academic research would out pace touristic development. Which of course, it rarely does.

You might think that finding at least one out of three large forts on a small island would be an easy task. Well I am here to tell you, it isn't. Especially when the entire island is shrouded in densely packed undergrowth, with the exception of those few places covered by the latest lava flows. Searching for anything on an island that sports few if any trails or even goat tacks worth following, is not an easy task. Then again, if there were paths leading to any one of those forts, the people living on Gunung Api would know about them by now. From personal experience I can assure you, children get into everything.

Here is the background for our search. Gunung Api is about four kilometers from north to south and one and a half kilometers from east to west. The volcano ascends to a height of slightly over 660 meters. Most of that is mountain, with only a few flat places along the coast.

The volcano last erupted in 1988 spewing ash all over the neighborhood and creating two major lava flows. Both are still clearly visible as enormous black scars along the flanks of the island. This volcano has three craters; two on its sides, that disgorged rivers of lava during the last eruption, and the main one on top that amused itself by ejecting copious amounts of smoke and ash.

Before starting out we reviewed what little material is available concerning each of the forts we were searching for. There was not much information available, other than a few references in old manuscripts and the single reference we had from an 1800s era Dutch sea chart. Abba was a great help, had spent hours struggling through old books and other local sources. Meanwhile I was hot on the internet and of course, we downloaded the latest Google Earth satellite photographs. There were no references posted, which is not surprising, and the Google images were useless due to dense vegetation covering the island.

We knew that hidden somewhere along that rugged coastline were the remains of three Portuguese and or Dutch-era fortifications. All the available evidence agreed at one time they were there, although none of our references had bothered to document their positions. No one currently living on the island was certain where they were located, or even if they still existed. More than one person informed us they had been destroyed by volcanic eruptions, either in the last century or in 1988. This advice seemed to have some credence in that two of them did not appear on our navigation chart. Then again, those forts were also absent from the older charts dating from the early days of the Dutch until roughly the mid eighteen hundreds. Perhaps the Dutch had purposely omitted those locations for military reasons.

We decided to search for the fort indicated on our chart first. Should that prove fruitless we would continue with our circumnavigation of the island. From that starting position, we could expand our search area looking for additional clues that might lead us to the other lost forts. Of course there was a problem searching for the one indicated on our chart. The indicated position was so vague, as to be almost useless. Again, we suspected the Dutch of purposely confusing the charted position for military reasons. We also faced another problem, the shape of the island had changed several times since the chart was created.

To make life even more complex our reference books gave four different names for the three fortifications we were searching for. Those names are Kota, Batavia, Orange, and Columbia. Even though this posed a problem when asking people living on the island about those ancient ruins, we treated it was another important clue. Perhaps one of those forts had started life as Portuguese before being taken over and renamed by the Dutch.

* * *

It was early afternoon when Meggi, Abba, and I set out in *Vega*'s dingy on our mission of discovery. Thanks to Abba's wife Dila, we had with us a well-stocked picnic hamper of snacks and several large bottles of drinking water. A pile of snorkeling gear occupied one corner of the dingy. We knew these were not big forts like Belgica or Nassau. They would be smaller coastal fortifications which we estimated to be no more than fifty meters on a side, with walls of roughly five or six meters in height.

Gunung Api is made of volcanic stone and so were the ancient walls we sought. Moss and jungle growth might further disguise the remains we were seeking. Under those daunting conditions, we could pass within meters of an important clue and never notice it. Seen from that perspective, the odds of finding anything in that maze were pretty well stacked against us.

Finding those forts, if they still existed, in the thick tropical foliage of Gunung Api would pose a considerable problem. By now, the walls could very well be no more than piles of rubble, or thickly covered with jungle vines and brush effectively acting as camouflage. Our big hope lay in discovering indications of a manmade landing once used to supply a fort. From there an overgrown path might well lead us directly to one of our lost fortresses.

Even though we were in high spirits and hoping for at least one discovery, we also knew such a find would depend on luck as much as any skill we might bring to the search. The densely forested coast when seen from our small boat could easily hide such remains, especially walls damaged by past volcanic eruptions or simply from age and neglect.

As our five hp outboard puttered along across a bay with water as smooth as a lake, I began to realize what a difficult task we had taken on. And, how little time we could dedicate to our investigation. Meggi on the other hand was perched in the bow enjoying the vast multicolored coral gardens as they passed beneath our keel.

More than once our expedition sidetracked, slowly circling over one of the more spectacular brightly colored maritime spectacles. With Meggi hopping from one side of the boat to the other, chanting a constant litany of, "look at that, look at this, did you see the…" we made our way toward the southern coast of Gunung Api. The search was on.

Navigating a small dingy in such clear water can be a daunting proposition. Although our dingy only draws about 40 cm, the water is so transparent judging the actual water depth becomes difficult. It was Meggi's job to keep watch in front of us and warn me of rocks or coral heads in our path.

Of course, Meggi soon became so engrossed in the scenic beauty passing beneath us, she frequently ignored her other mission. We cruised along with Meggi gleefully squealing at each new coral head, and my concentration divided between cautiously eyeing the bottom and scanning the coast for signs of human activity. Since we were still on the side facing Banda Naira, Abba pointed out the various sites and gave us a running commentary.

You see, there are many ruins on the island of Gunung Api. Not the least of which is an entire village abandoned during the last volcanic eruption and never repopulated. An eerie place that one is, with houses and shops still standing intact, yet completely devoid of people.

Let me tell you, water so clear it seems to disappear is not easy to navigate in. Thoughts of hitting a submerged rock with the propeller of your outboard and having to row home are even worse. Amazing how the mere thought of a long row back concentrates the attention. On the other hand, Meggi was like a kid at the circus, dancing with delight as each new reef or coral garden slid beneath our keel. The way she was constantly pointing and gesticulating anyone seeing us from a distance might think we had a snake loose in the boat.

What appeared as a rather small island on the chart, quickly became a lengthy convoluted coastline slightly more than eight nautical miles long. It is a rugged coast, where any one of the many small coves and bays might hide some clue to the object of our expedition. Abba and I took turns scanning the coast with our binoculars. Several times a natural rock formation appeared to be manmade. Each time we diligently investigated.

Have I mentioned Meggi is one of those people who is constantly exploring her surroundings and easily distracted by a beautiful coral reef passing under the boat, or a strange bird hovering overhead? She loves exploring new places. That woman can spend hours happily looking for sea shells or fragments of old ceramic on beaches, ambling among ancient remains, or simply wandering aimlessly taking in the sights and sounds of a new place.

That day she was in her element as we cruised through flawless water with pristine coral reefs only a meter or so below us. The water was so clear even at depths of 10 meters or more no detail was hidden. It was this water clarity, and her incessant bottom gawking, that led us to our first discoveries.

We went all the way around the southern end of Gunung Api and about half way along its western coast discovering only dense scrub forest accented by the impressive lava field left over from the volcano's latest eruption. That lava forms a massive black scar where the separation between the verdant green of plants growing in the pre-existing rich volcanic soil and the newly minted black stone of the lava flow are as distinct as if cut with a knife. A raw awesome beauty, that left us feeling humble in its shadow.

The shear massive bulk of lava that had flowed out of the volcano's side and down into the sea is breath taking. It was easy to see where the whole island had grown in size during the last eruption. If one of our lost forts had been located in the path of that flowing lava, it was lost forever under a million of tons of rugged volcanic rubble.

Chapter 66

Of Broken Bottles and a Sunken Ship

L ate in the afternoon, we decided to turn back. Although we had explored many lovely inlets and coves, including several caves well worth exploring with mask and snorkel, as an excited Meggi was constantly certifying. During that time, we saw nothing to indicate the existence of fortifications. Although, the diversion of snorkeling in one of the world's most pristine marine environments, was more than enough to compensate us for our efforts, it would have been nice to see at least some sign of an ancient fortress.

On the return trip, we retraced our steps. Following the coastline much closer than before, Abba and I carefully scrutinized the shore searching for the slightest indication of human works. This time we explored every nook and small bay. That way Abba and I could look for clues to the fort, while Meggi, effervescent as always, continued to enjoy cruising over the brightly colored coral gardens.

Most of that shoreline consists of near vertical walls made from weather-sculpted stone and topped by dense tropical foliage. Twice we spotted likely places. But approaching closer, we discovered they were not manmade constructions, but mere quirks of nature and the light. New snorkeling sites aside, up until then our expedition appeared to be a failure.

Turning into the southernmost bay on Gunung Api, Meggi spotted the long abandoned skeletons of two old traditional Bandanese sailing ships. They were both firmly aground, at the bottom of the bay. With her squealing, squeaking, and pointing, there was nothing else for it, but to investigate them. So, having more or less already given up our search for the day, I turned the dingy into the bay. I steered for the two derelict hulls.

That bay is basically a mangrove inlet and very shallow. Arriving at low tide, it took patience for me to discover a way through the coral heads and jagged black stones from the last eruption littering the bottom. My roundabout route eventually took us to where those two skeletal wrecks lay rotting in the mangrove mud. Both hulls had clearly been reposing there for many years.

One was all that remained of a traditional Bandanese sailing prahau. A type that was once the favored long distance trading vessel from these islands. The other was a disintegrating built up dugout canoe. The type of local fishing boat where planks added to the sides employ only pencil sized dowels for fastenings. A practical system employed by the local boat builders to fashion a canoe larger than permitted by the available trees.

As we approached the shore, Meggi began yelping, hopping up and down, and frantically gesticulating from the bow. I thought she was warning me of something on the bottom, which in her own way she was. Being the cautious type, I took the engine out of gear. As we began to drift, I could see why Meggi was so excited. Scattered on the sea floor were broken pieces of Old Dutch gin bottles.

These glass and ceramic bottles come in two types, each with a very distinctive shape and color. The ones she saw were fired earthen ware, beige and light brown in color. The other type are made of glass that has turned almost black over the centuries. Those are extremely rare.

In a flash, she was over the side wading along beside the boat in search of an unbroken bottle. You see, Meggi is a true collector. And one of her dreams is to find an unspoiled example from each of those bottle types for her collection. Several times in the past, she came close to realizing that ambition, only to find a piece missing when she dug her prospective treasure free from the sand or mud. From what I could see as we approached the two derelict hulls, there were only broken pieces littering the bottom. But she was not to be deterred from searching.

While we waited for Meggi to scour the bottom in search of bottles, Abba, and I drove the dingy ashore, pulling it up onto a sandy patch between the two rotting hulks. It was a pretty little spot, consisting of a small sand and mud beach tucked under several large overhanging trees. Once we had the boat safely secured to a tree limb, we both turned our attention to more pressing matters.

As any man will do after spending hours cooped up in a small boat, we each went in search of an appropriate tree to relieve ourselves. An old ships rib provided the perfect setting for my immediate purpose. Happily putting it to a use its builder never intended, I began to reflect on shipwrecks and the many abandoned ships and boats I have visited over the years.

There is something mystical about an abandoned wooden sailing vessel that calls out, begging to be explored. Or perhaps those pleas stem from loneliness and a desire to once again feel the tread of bare feet on her decks, and the voices of those who gave her life.

Sadness and mystique seem to permeate the air around such ships, conveying ghostly reminders of each vessels past. One can almost sense the halcyon days of fair wind and distant voyages intermingling with the dreams and aspirations of those who once brought her to life. Those who once cared for her, spreading her sails to the wind, or steering her by a convenient star through the long hours of a tropical night, a steady flow of glowing phosphorescence streaming away in her wake.

Once fresh from the builder's yard with her paint gleaming in the bright sunlight this abandoned wreck would have been someone's pride and joy. And once she innocently made this final voyage to where driven far up onto a tiny beach on the highest of tides, she came to rest, abandoned to the depredation of neglect, wood worm, and rot.

I wonder if her owner felt the sadness that such forsaken vessels evoke. Did she call out to him in unspoken words that with a few repairs and some new paint she would happily carry cargo to distant ports? Her death knoll was easy to see in her un-pierced stern deadwood. That vessel had never been fitted with an engine. Sail alone and the winds of fortune powered the boat, for her entire life. The things that pass through one's mind while busily watering the local vegetation must amaze you.

Chapter 67

Meggi Discovers a Treasure

Abba and I finished our project then met back at the beach to stretch our legs and gawk at the scenery. Meggi soon waded ashore grinning from ear to ear and sporting a hand full of broken ceramic pieces she promptly stowed in the dingy. Then gave another of her famous chirps of excitement at finding more shards spread all along the beach. Having been rather distracted by other things, neither Abba nor I had even noticed them.

Within moments, she was following a trail of broken bottle shards that led her straight into the bushes like breadcrumbs in a fairy tale. No sooner had she disappeared into the underbrush; presumably, to do what Abba and I had just finished doing, than we heard her calling us in a loud excited voice. Uncertain if she was under attack by a heard of sex-crazed baboons or had simply stubbed her toe on a rock, with Meggi you can never be certain we rushed in her direction. I distinctly remember snatching up a large stick as we raced toward the sound of her voice wondering what could have befallen her – and being Meggi it could be almost anything.

We almost collided, when she burst out of the underbrush excitedly telling us she had found a flight of what looked like colonial era stone steps. They were leading from nowhere off into the dense jungle. Then she launched off into something about purple flowers and huge spiders, which neither Abba nor I understood a word of.

With Meggi calmed down we eagerly followed her back through the thick undergrowth to the stairway she had discovered. They were definitely stone stairs constructed to the standard double arm span width popular with the European military of the epoch. A bit more poking about showed the stairs as part of an early colonial era road that eventually disappeared into the dense jungle.

Following the remains of that wide path once crudely paved with stone flags, we forged our way through giant spider webs and dense foliage. Fortunately, stout sticks soon did for the spider webs while a sharp bush knife made short work of the hanging vines, snakes, and creepers. Between dodging spiders, vines, and other assorted flora and fauna, we almost missed what we were looking for. Abba was the first to spot it. About ten meters off of to the side of our path, looking like something straight out of Indiana Jones, was an old stonewall roughly five meters in height. It was partly covered with vines and moss.

Excitedly forcing our way through the thick brush we realized the wall continued both to the left and right of where we stood. Following the wall, we slowly circumnavigated the outer perimeter of an enclosure. On the side facing away from the ocean we discovered where the main gate had once stood. Slots in the outer wall showed where wooden roofing beams had once been lodged. Clearly, this was one of our lost forts.

Passing through the ruined gate, we found the interior to be in surprisingly good condition. Even though over grown with scrub brush and a few trees, it was easy to make out the roofless rooms that still occupied each corner of the walls. On closer inspection, we discovered half-buried portals leading into large underground spaces hidden below the wide ramparts. Ramparts where the forts cannon would have stood.

Having no portable lights, and with spiders as big as your hand swarming around the place, not to mention the assortment of resident snakes, we decided to put off exploring such mysterious chambers for another day. Those well protected spaces would have been for the storage of gunpowder and other important supplies.

Wandering around what had once been the court yard, I was fascinated by what we had found. Here was a long abandoned fortification that to our delight was in much better condition than many of the others we had seen, such as fort Lonthor, on Banda Besar. It was also some distance away from where the nautical chart had positioned it.

Abba was in a transport of ecstasy. He kept saying that all his life he had lived on the islands yet never knew this fort existed. Of course being Abba, he quickly began planning a modest pier to bring visitors ashore in the little cove and how to clear away a path around the walls. He also quickly agreed that we needed to report this find as soon as possible to the proper archeaological authorities, so they might instigate plans for its excavation and perhaps even basic restoration.

Not being able to resist the temptation, we randomly chose a likely spot and with the help of a sharp stick dug a small hole. Only centimeters below ground level, we found shards of Chinese porcelain and pieces of what Abba identified as copper nuggets once used for trade. The urge to continue digging for new discoveries was hard to resist, but resist it we did. After carefully replacing the pieces we had uncovered we refilled the hole. Our superficial finds strongly suggested the site was undisturbed. That will be good news for the archeological team we hope one day pitches up to properly excavate and document the site.

By counting the gun embrasures, we established that in its halcyon days our fort proudly mounted fifteen large cannon. Although the three of us performed a perfunctory search of the surrounding jungle, we failed to discover any cast off cannon. That does not mean there are none still waiting to be discovered. They could easily be hiden under the thick layer of decomposed vegetation. After all, our exploration was only superficial. We purposely avoided digging or any other actions that might disturb an apparently undisturbed archeological site.

Having successfully rediscovered one of the lost forts, we were a happy crew full of speculations as our little outboard diligently transported us back to *Vega*. What with Meggi rambling on about seashells, spiders, and broken bottles, and Abba happily planning how to have the fort cleared and cleaned up for tourists, and me trying my best not to crash into anything, the return trip went quickly. Later that evening, the three of us sat around the dinner table recounting our adventure to all who would listen.

The next morning we were too busy preparing for our departure to worry about lost forts. Getting *Vega* ready for the sea again is nothing at all like on a small sailing yacht where basically all you need to do is pull up the hook, then hoist the sails, to be off and gone. We have awnings to take down, sheets to be re-run, engine and electronic checks, a whole list of preparations to be done before we finally cast of our lines and go.

Take the engine for example; I always check the oil, coolant, gearbox oil, and prop oil as soon as we arrive at a new place, just in case of an emergency where we might need to shove of quickly. But, I also like to re-check those things before we leave –"in case of a case" as the Germans like to say.

Chapter 68
Goodwill for All

As we were busily preparing *Vega* for imminent departure we received a deputation of Bandanese community leaders. Arriving un-announced they ask to come on board in order to speak with Meggi and I before we left. Of course we were happy to meet with our friends, even if we were a bit flustered at having to delay our preparation for departure in order to receive them.

Once we had them all safely on board and after the obligatory greetings followed by coffee, observations on the weather, and exciting news about who had won the latest football match somewhere, they sprung a big surprise on us. Mind you, these were some of the most important civic and political leaders on the islands who had not come that sunny morning in their usual capacity as good and welcome friends. Unknown to us they had come in their more formal capacity as important island officials.

Together, grinning like Cheshire cats, they presented us with a lovely certificate signed and sealed by all of Banda's most important dignitaries. That certificate appointed and confirmed us as official "Good Will Ambassadors at Large for The Banda Islands". I must admit that little ceremony took me right aback.

Meggi was stunned speechless. Mind you that is in itself made the occasion worthy of a red tick mark on the calendar. Somehow we muttered and mumbled our heartfelt thanks as we accepted the certificate, along with a few thankfully short speeches.

It was quite an honor for us to have our efforts on behalf of the island communities recognized in this manner. On the other hand that recognition now gives us an "official standing" as we attempt to gather the materials and other forms of assistance needed by our friends on the islands.

That Honor adds to what Pa Eki said to us a few years ago, 'you are our voice to the outside world. They may have forgotten us, but you remind them we are still here'. When I think about the huge differences between the Banda Islands where the government is trying to make improvements and the tiny island of Nila where that same government pulled out in 1978 abandoning the islanders to their own devices, the contrasts are stunningly different.

Chapter 69

Good bye Banda

Leaving the Banda Islands is a sad time for us. We have so many good friends there and always manage to accomplish so much during our visits. I shall never forget the first time we were departing those islands after a few highly memorable weeks.

We bid all our friend's farewell and good-bye, waved until our arms hurt, and all the rest of that stuff you do at those times. Then finally, we hauled up the anchors and headed for the open sea. Passing between Karaka Island and Banda Naira, I couldn't help remembering the first time we visited these islands.

When we departed, Meggi and Jo both got all choked up. As we passed the northern tip of Gunung Api, Meggi looked at me with tears in her eyes, 'Banda is so perfect, I don't want to go'.

Jo was just as bad. There they were busy blubbering away about how beautiful the place is. Try to imagine the pair of them standing on the aft deck sniffling and honking into their hankies while going on about how much they enjoyed the Banda Islands. Well, I can't really blame them, much. After all, I also enjoy visiting the islands and seeing the friends we have there, more than I generally like to admit.

Even now, after all these years I still get the same feeling she so aptly expressed on that first of many eventful voyages to the original spice islands. There is simply something magical about those tiny little islands lost in the middle of nowhere that seems to permeate every stone, cave, and crevasse. It does help that we always time our arrival for the peak of the short dry season, something not to ignore with islands that regularly receive over 160 cm of rain every year.

For me going around the top of Gunung Api is where our old delivery year ends and the new year begins. It is the moment when we stop delivering and start collecting again. Before us are thousands of sea miles and all the hard work of once again filling the boat.

It would be one thousand five hundred miles before our next stop. Our longest sail of the year, and usually the most enjoyable. With the wind either slightly before the beam or pouring over the stern quarter, *Vega* glides along happily logging between one hundred and twenty and one hundred and fifty sea miles every day. Those are exhilarating days at sea, with perfect weather and reliable sea conditions. The stuff our dreams consist of.

With *Vega*'s square sail filling nicely we turned south southwest on the port tack, gliding along at a stately pace between Gunung Api on one side and the islands of Rhun and Ai on the other. Watching those two islands so steeped in history pass down our starboard side, I reflected on what we had accomplished that year.

We had achieved a lot for schools and medical services all along our route. But there was still, a great deal left undone. The lists we carried for next year's deliveries were not long ones, but every item was important. Behind us there was someone waiting and hoping that next year we would pitch up with at least a part of his or her "wish list".

Thinking of places like Singapore, Kuala Lumpur, or Jakarta – just to name a few – and all the useful items shuffled from one place to another like rubbish, it is enough to make you cry. Looking at our lists for next year, some of the items seemed meaningless, yet for the teacher with no chalk or the midwife with no bandages every item on those lists, each box of paper clips, push pins, or rubber bands is a treasure.

I have often reflected on how to make people living in the luxury, one might even say the decadent splendor, of a modern city aware of the vast disparities that exist between their way of life and that of someone living isolated and forgotten hundreds of sea miles from the nearest small town. Try as I will, I always seem to fail.

Being able to run down to the corner pharmacy and buy drugs or hop over to the next shopping mall to see a properly trained, well equipped, doctor is a given for some people. For the people we assist, the ones who fantasize over a simple list of exercise books, pencils, and pens, such luxury is only imaginary. An aspiration to strive for, yet one so far out of their reach it is difficult for most of the people we work with to even imagine it.

As the hours slipped by like water under the keel, we quickly fell back into the easy rhythm of watches at sea. That night my watch was under a cloudless sky with the stars so close it seemed I could reach out and touch them. We had the big square running sail out and were making between two and three knots on a breeze that barely managed to fill it, or carry away the smell of cooking from down below. I remember the smell of onions frying that wafted up from the galley, an aroma that always sets my mouth to watering, and my firmly rooted hope that Meggi was making one of her famous sweet and sour tuna sauces.

Going below for a cup of coffee, the boat seemed enormous and strangely empty. All of the boxes and bags that accompanied us for the past several months had found homes. In our wake, the lives of thousands of people had slightly improved. With luck, we even saved a few lives. Once again, the cabins are spacious and comfortable rather than cramped and cluttered with boxes or bags. Yet somehow, even though I know that within the next few months the boat will start filling up again with tons of school supplies, Kits-4-Kids bag, and medical supplies, she still seemed empty.

Perhaps our year is like the way they teach breathing in yoga. We inhale by loading, then there is a pause while we move to our first delivery stop. When the deliveries begin it is like exhaling, and then there is another pause while we return to the north and the whole cycle begins again.

Chapter 10
That Magic Hour

It was that magic hour when dawn is near yet night still shrouds the world. I was alone at the helm as the last of the stars faded, the sea a profound indigo grey in the half-light of morning. Long deep-sea waves rolled in a stately procession along our ship's sides. Through my unfocused thoughts an old sea ditty surfaced:

> *Evening red and morning gray are certain signs of a very fine day;*
> *But evening gray and morning red, Make a sailor shake his head.*

Have you ever noticed how each morning just before dawn the sea and sky take on a dark and sinister gray appearance as if to remind us that although today might be fine weather, just below the horizon another aspect still looms, an aspect of raging storms and howling gales that only fools disregard at their peril.

In the growing light, I toured the deck. I was checking sheets and halyards, taking in all the hundreds of things that can come adrift in the night. I stopped at the main mast to snug up a loose topping lift, then coil the fall back on its belaying pin. Looking out along the bowsprit, I walked forward taking the forestay in my hand. Bracing against the rise and fall of the bow, I noted the set of the headsails, there was a slight sag in the forestay. It would need tightening soon.

Vega was vibrantly alive with the sounds of a sailing ship reaching across the spice island sea on a steady South East monsoon. The foam racing back from her bow told me we were sailing at about 6 knots. A slight vibration in the forestay reminded me that today the starboard cap shroud would need setting up again.

Looking up along the great curving belly of our main square sail I checked its set, then gave the port tack a slight heave, taking up slack from the nights run. I always find it amazing how much brute power that square sail generates, yet how easy it is to manage.

Glancing aft to where the sun would soon raise, I noted we were still right on coarse. Not, that I expected anything else. A good sailing ship with properly trimmed sails all but steers herself. She may drift a few degrees to one side or the other of her course, but at the end of the day makes good a relatively straight route.

That seems to be something forgotten by most modern sailors. For them, it is all about driving a boat. Bending her to their will, while they chase computer-generated images across cyber world screens between precise waypoints. They prefer to click buttons rather than feel their boat – rather than working together with her to achieve the best results.

Boats will talk to you if you let them, telling you exactly what they need to get on with their job of sailing the seas safely. All you have to do is pay attention, feel, and sense that marvelous interplay between wind, sails, water, and hull. If you must constantly be fighting her with rudder, then something is amiss with the trim of your sails or the design of your boat, or perhaps the guy sailing that boat.

* * *

It was three AM, our last plotted position put us 283 miles south-southeast of the nearest land. This is our second day running under square sail alone. It seems like only minutes since I stood in the bow watching fiery green phosphorescence erupt around us as *Vega* cleaved the sea throwing spray out to her sides in sheets of glowing luminosity so bright I am sure I could read medium sized print by its light. Occasionally a dolphin comes racing along the side, its form outlined in the ghostly liquid green of tropical phosphorescence.

That was then, only moments ago it seems. Now, it is raining. The squall driven wind is blowing a deluge of cold rain horizontally across where I sit at the steering. Having changed to fore and aft sails, *Vega* is close reaching across a boisterous sea.

The boat is rolling and pitching hard as she slams into the choppy head sea making it difficult to read the compass through the rain on the dome and the salt in my eyes. As if that were not enough, every fifth or sixth wave hits the bow splashing upward, where the wind flings it straight back into my face. When I am lucky I manage to close my eyes and turn my head away before the deluge arrives.

I have the hood up my foul weather jacket. Part of the hood is a special flap to cover my mouth and nose. Between the wind and blowing rain, without that protection it would be difficult to breath. I have a good foul weather jacket, but the water still finds its way in through the seams, suddenly appearing at the back of my neck to drip down my back.

If you imagine sitting in a thunderstorm with someone throwing a bucket of seawater at you every few seconds, that lovely image will be close. Ah, the myriad joys of sailing. To be honest this is not fun, not exciting, and not at all adventurous, it is pure cold wet misery – and I still have three more hours until the end of my watch. Two hours and forty-eight minutes remaining, if you want to be precise.

The only highlight on our horizon is tomorrow's landfall. Providing this line of thunderstorms really does move on as predicted somewhere in the middle of her next watch Meggi should start seeing a reddish glow reflected from the clouds hovering over an active volcano.

Chapter 11
A Promise Made Good

Meggi first spotted the tiny island of Komba at four in the morning. Even though the island was still below the horizon, she could see the volcano erupting. Glowing fireworks spewed up into the night sky every few minutes, and a deep red glow reflected in the clouds hovering over its active crater. Lucky girl, she had an impressive fireworks display to amuse herself with for the whole of her night watch.

Komba volcano erupts roughly once every 12 minutes, belching a billowing column of steam and ash into the otherwise clear air. Each convulsion spews out enormous red-hot stones that cascade down the scree flow then crash into the sea. Many of those stones are half the size of *Vega*.

The deep throated boom and the hissing roar of escaping steam, combine with the almost subsonic rumble to form an experience none of us will ever forget. The sea around the island quivers with each eruption. Something I could easily see reflected in my coffee. We spent the better part of a morning drifting around oohing and ahing in front of that island, often as close as a few hundred meters from the scree flow where huge stones were crashing into the sea. The experience was fascinating.

Meggi had just finished reading Patrick O'Brian's wonderful book *The Wine Dark Sea*, for about the fifth time. O'Brian vividly describes an undersea volcanic eruption throwing stones like mortar bombs. In that story, red hot flying stones caused great damage to the hero's ship. So Meggi was often heard muttering we were too close and what if one of those stones crashed down on us.

Still in all, I bet she would not have traded that experience for anything, except maybe another volcano, with big glowing lava flows added. There are some moments in life that you simply cherish, and if you ask her now she will tell you that was one of them.

Later in the morning, we slowly circumnavigated the island accompanied by large schools of dolphins and a pod of friendly whales. They frequently came within meters of us, closely inspecting *Vega*. All the time I was busy taking careful bearings and noting the wind drift. Coming around to the western side of the island put us downwind of the eruption plume. Within minutes the decks were covered in a thin layer of fine volcanic ash. Feeling that ash grit between my teeth was unpleasant.

The western side of Komba Island is quite different from the eastern part. Where the eastern landscape is stark and lunar like, the western side is green and lush with the typical vegetation you would expect on a small tropical island. There is even what appears to be a temporary fishing camp tucked back into the corner of a small bay where an interesting shelf of shallower water was just begging us to come in and anchor for a few days.

Nothing gives you the sensation of really living like standing on a tiny island in the middle of nowhere that is an erupting volcano. The ground is shaking, there is a veil of ash falling from the air, the slight smell of rotten eggs and a constant background of roaring rumbling volcano permeates everything. And you can trust me that when the whole place gives an unexpected violent shake followed by one almighty thundering roar, you suddenly realize exactly how puny we humans really are. In any case that is another story.

Girls being what they are, I was soon besieged with a hundred reasons why they should go for an exploratory snorkel along the peaceful southern shore. Both Meggi and Ruth had convinced themselves there were multitudinous wonders that deserved staring at and most likely ancient pirate ships filled with chests of gold, for all I remember. The upshot is, while I watched the boat, read drifted around in circles, they took the dingy and went off snorkeling. An hour or so later, they returned to the boat bubbling over with excitement at what they had seen.

You see, thanks to that volcano the bottom around Komba consists of course sand that is pitch black in color. Go snorkeling there and you get all the vibrant colors of a pristine marine environment highlighted against a black velvety backdrop. Judging by how the girls were excitedly hopping from foot to foot, that effect must be spectacular. It seems that the occasional earthquake even helps preserve the local corals by shaking off any accumulated layers of silt.

Immediately Meggi decided, and I agreed, that next year we would stop and go ashore on this strange little island lost in the middle of nowhere. That visit to Komba Island also confirmed us in our desire to visit another isolated volcanic island indicated on our charts. That island is a newly emerging and still very actively erupting.

Next year, with a few minor tweaks our route will take us right by it. Perhaps we can stop for a closer look. After all, it is not every day you get to see an island emerging from the depths of such a deep ocean as the Banda Sea. That volcano had to grow more than 4,000 meters, just to reach the surface. What emerged is only the tiny tip of a gigantic undersea mountain that must have been erupting for ages, before it finally broke the surface.

Just after lunchtime, with our decks covered in a thin layer of volcanic ash and the volcano giving us another impressive belch of roaring smoke and steam, we turned away from Komba Island. Once again, striking out on our original route we headed west, through a peaceful sea under a sky so blue that even our red sails, filling to a gentle breeze, seemed to take on a purplish tint.

It is not every day one feels deeply impressed with how lucky you are to be where you are, doing exactly what you are doing. For me that visit to the Island of Komba will always remain deeply etched in my memory as one of life's more interesting moments.

* * *

There is something magical about the swish and glide of a boat under sail. Hurling along at 6 knots, our vessel bravely shouldered aside the waves, advancing through the water with an effervescent flow. Suspended from tall wooden masts, red sails effortlessly harvested the power of an unwavering monsoon wind. Her stem perpetually sunders the present, as our little ship bravely sails into the future.

A frigate bird soars above our mainsail, hovering motionless on invisible currents of raising air. Whoosh, splash, sparkle, miniature rainbows peel away from the bow, announcing a rush of spray that soon races down our ships side. Streaming out into the past, a foaming wake reveals the gradually dispersing shadow of our existence. As the boat rolls away from the wind, out of habit I tighten my grip on the main shrouds.

From my position half way up the windward ratlines the rhythmic creak and groan of lines working through wooden blocks provides a counterpoint to the whistle and moan of wind in the rigging, a musical sound, constantly changing pitch in phase with the roll of the boat. Everyone on board, including the cat, is enjoying another beautiful day at sea.

Speaking of the cat, for Scourge the most fascinating part of life at sea are the flying fish occasionally landing on her deck. Fluttering and flapping they provide great good fun for a prowling cat, and a rather decent little snack, all delivered within an easy paws reach. The best part being, that flying fish do not fight back. Scourge is a small cat with delusions of being a full size Bengal Tiger.

She will viciously attack without mercy absolutely anything, as long as the intended victim is much smaller than she is. Watching Scourge stalk the decks intently menacing her rubber ball with the bell inside, or a fluffy rope end, is almost as much fun as watching her scamper back to the boat and dive behind one of us at the mere sight of another cat. Being an inveterate wimp, she never hesitates to run at the first whiff of trouble. When frightened, she suddenly becomes the most snugglesum animal imaginable.

Typical of many Asian cats, Scourge has a kink right at the end of her tail. Most of the cats you find in south East Asia have distorted tails. Some have no tail at all. Clearly, this is not a natural state of affairs, so I decided to investigate. Being such a deep-rooted part of the local tradition, it took me a while to discover why. Everyone seemed to think it so obvious they could not be bothered to explain. In the end I did manage to worm it out of someone at the Royal Langkawi Yacht Club.

It all started with the way a cat will occasionally stroll around holding its tail straight up and vibrating it. Well, back in the long forgotten past, some bright cat hater with nothing better to do than smoke the local mushrooms and guzzle palm wine, decided cats do that to attract and capture a chunk of someone's soul. Exactly why they would capture souls, or once captured what they did with them, remained a rather nebulous mystery. Seeing the world through delirium and the herd of gossamer winged pink elephants flying around his head, he decided a cat with a distorted tail would be unable to steal souls.

This earth-shattering discovery soon spread throughout Asia condemning any kitten with a normal tail to extinction. When only cats with crooked tails survive to breed, well you get the idea. Not only does our cat have a contorted tail, she likewise sports several different colors, ranging from black to white through various shades of brown, with both long and short fur. Darwin would have loved the furry little dear.

Chapter 12

The Skipper Gets Worried

With Komba Island several days in our past, *Vega* was once again running along at five knots under her main square sail and mizzen staysail. The weather was idyllic. A gentle following breeze carried us along over calm seas. Considering all the excitement we could have been facing, everything seemed to be going along just fine. To me that was a warning signal I have learned the hard way not to ignore. When everything seems to be going along just fine, that is when I began to worry.

If there is one thing I have learned about boats and the ocean it's that as soon as you think everything is going along the way it should, something is going wrong that you haven't noticed yet, and most likely it will not become apparent until around three in the morning. Or just at the end of your next night watch, whichever comes first.

How I see it, the only logical way to deal with the ocean is to employ a healthy dose of paranoia. It also helps if you have a strong streak of cowardice in your general make up, as both of those rather useful traits tend to make you think twice before setting out when the weather forecast is a bit dodgy.

As a general observer of life, I am totally convinced paranoia is a major survival trait, one that allowed our far distant ancestors to make it down from the trees and stay alive long enough to spread out and prosper.

You try existing in an environment ripe with stealthy fast moving long teeth and sharp claws that just love the taste of raw human flesh and see what happens to your stress levels. The result of all this is that I am rather proud of being more than just a little paranoid. You see after all these years at sea, I do not believe the ocean is out to get me. I know for a proven fact it is. Never forget that old sailor's proverb stating that, anything which can go wrong at sea will go wrong, and at the worst possible moment.

There must be a reason why in every language Nature is female. I can just imagine two of my ancient ancestors fresh from the trees huddling in what little shelter they could find looking around apprehensively when one whispers out of the corner of his mouth to the other:

"Hey Og, I been thinking about this nature stuff. Must be a woman nature, because for sure she's a real Mother", at which Og nodded knowingly, then went back to watching the dark lurking shadows around their small island of humanity. "Yeah mate, I just wish someone would hurry up and discover that fire stuff. Old Zog says we have to invent Gods first, so one of us can slip round and steal it from them."

Those people had it tough. Little wonder it took thousands of years for them to start living in caves. After all, bigger and stronger things than our quivering ancestors already had all the better caves occupied. "Hey, I have it!" says Og. "Let's go live in that cave up there". "Right mate", says the other one, "and who's going to evict the saber-toothed tiger that currently holds the lease?"

Meggi says I worry too much. But, I doubt if you can to worry too much at sea. I even worry about the things I am forgetting to worry about. Then again an old mentor of mine once said, "It's never the emergency you prepare for that happens," which is not much help, because the ones you do not prepare for are always bigger than the ones you do prepare for. If I followed that line of thinking any further, I would sell the boat and buy a cactus farm.

Fast forward, enough to make a Hollywood special effects man dizzy, and you have the likes of me sitting my midnight until 3 am watch at the wheel of an old wooden sail boat on its way across the Banda Sea. I am busy deliberating on what is about to break now that everything is going along so smoothly.

And people wonder why I have so many gray hairs in my mustache when I live in the tropics on a sailboat. Most of them imagine my daily fare consists of blue skies, white palm fringed beaches, and pretty girls in grass skirts with no knickers on. I would be more than happy with two out of three; after all, I never was very big on beaches and come to think about it who really needs grass skirts in the tropics anyway?

Chapter 13
The Cat and the Milk Sea

Some of the seas we sail have the largest concentration of healthy photo plankton on earth. The Banda Sea is notorious for its "Milk Sea", where huge carpets of phosphorescence turn the entire ocean a glowing white, or greenish blue when something disturbs them, giving the sea an aspect of glowing milk. Being so far from light pollution, the effect is spectacular.

For some bizarre reason when people think of the sea, they imagine an endless procession of raging storms and huge waves. The truth of it is, most of the time the sea is rather calm, and I might add boring. Mind you, the alternatives being what they are, I never complain about being bored at sea. Those periods of calm are when we see some of the most amazing things.

Like the night, we were drifting along on the Banda Sea with a light wind and the water so calm, you could see the stars reflected in it, and there were stars by the billions that night. It was one of those pure crystalline evenings when the Milky Way really does look like a pool of spilt milk pouring across the sky, leaving behind a trail of errant stars perched somewhere just above the light on our masthead.

Well maties, on a night like that there is precious little to do other than stare at the stars, read a book, or rummage your mind for something worth deliberating. In the middle of the Banda Sea, spotting another ship, even hull down on the horizon is a rare event. I was just settling in with a hot chocolate and a good book – all prepared to enjoy four lovely hours of boredom, you will note- when out of the corner of my eye I saw a flash of light.

Eyeing the general direction of that mysterious flash, I waited for it to repeat itself. I did not need to wait long before the whole sea along our starboard side erupted in a ghostly flash of greenish white, and when I say the whole sea, I mean the entire bloody shop from boat to horizon was suddenly aglow. This lasted for about ten seconds before settling back into the usual dark water one expects at night. I have seen just about everything you can imagine at sea, especially at night, but this was an exceptional event.

Calling down the hatch that there was something strange to see, I went back to staring in the general direction of the original flash. Just about then, a rocket exploded out of the water leaving a shining trail of ghostly light. Around where it surfaced, I noticed a ring of glowing water spreading out from the center. No sooner had it erupted than there was a slight splash accompanied by another display of light. About that time, the wind began to pick up and so did our boat speed.

It took me a few seconds to realize that I was seeing a band of dolphins out to enjoy a midnight snack. I love watching dolphins. Say what you will, they seem to be the happiest creatures at sea. And more than smart enough not to let on how smart they really are.

This might be a good time to impart a bit of nautical esoterica concerning phosphorescent plant life. I spent many an enjoyable moment laying with my head protruding over the stern of an old sailing boat as we ghosted along through a sea teeming with tiny luminescent critters. Looking down into that swirling mass of light I felt like a god looking down on the universe. There were swirling constellations of every size and type trailing away in the wake.

You see those little critters never phosphoresce when the moon is out. They only turn on the lights when there is no moon. Long ago, I concluded that photo plankton do this as a defensive mechanism, one that completely confuses any predators lurking in the area to the point they lose their appetite and wander off in search of an easier meal.

The logic is simple, since the stars look like tiny spots of light, by imitating the stars luminescent plankton create a state of mental confusion where any fish out to eat them begins to believe it has somehow emerged from the water into the air. The buggers promptly get so confused; they forget about dinner and concentrate instead on getting back into the water about which time the plankton switch off the lights and slink away on the nearest available current.

Chapter 14
Pilot Whales and Sunsets

Just off the northern coast of Flores we hove to in the midst of a large pod of black and white pilot whales. There must have been a hundred of those delightful small whales all around the boat. I never did figure out if they were feeding or simply enjoying a rest from their migration, but whatever the reason that hour we spent among them was magical.

They seemed to be formed into small groups, perhaps families. Occasionally a group would approach the boat and forming a circle of heads poking out of the water hold a conversation among themselves, clearly commenting on how the neighborhood was going downhill or perhaps blaming us for the paucity of small fish these days. Trying to explain how one would nod its head up and down addressing the group, then another would take up the thread, and how funny they looked from where I sat while doing so is beyond me. You simply have to try and imagine it for yourself.

With their heads held well out of the water they would give us the once over nodding their heads up and down in our direction to have a better view, then turn back to their circle and chatter away with each other for a bit, before turning to give us another eyeballing.

When I say they chatter it is a fact, heads bobbing up and down they really do chatter away among themselves. Something we could clearly hear from the closer groups. Mind you when they were not busy inspecting the new neighbors, roughly half of a circle would remain on the surface intently watching us, while the other half went down for a seafood snack. Then there was a shift change, so the other half could saunter out on the sly for a quick meal.

With hundreds of them surrounding the boat as we drifted along peacefully, they made quite a spectacle. Meggi of course was ecstatic, racing from one side of the boat to the other squealing every time something new occurred. She wound up on the fore main top, a privileged position giving her an exceptional view down through the crystalline water.

Not to be out done, Ruth who was every bit as excited as Meggi, finally found a perch out on the end of the bowsprit. Another position giving the widest possible field of view. Once established there, if you ignore the animated arm waving and excited yells, she more or less settled in to follow the action. Jo contented herself with going from side to side to watch the show. A show that lasted until the sun had almost set. Then as if alerted by some mystical signal, all of those whales slipped below the surface at the same time. Although we waited for another fifteen minutes, we never saw them again.

While Jo and Meggi hoisted *Vega*'s tanbark red sails, I went back to my place at the helm. As the fore staysail filled on the starboard tack, I steered us back to our original heading. By then, we were well into the Flores Sea on a course taking us almost due west, directly into the gradient orange of the setting sun.

I confirmed the set of our sails, then checked the horizon for any sign of other ships or thunderstorms. The sea and sky were empty. Meggi sat beside me taking my hand in hers. She leaned against me and mumbled something I failed to catch. Looking around taking in my surroundings, I knew there was not a single place I would rather be.

Scourge appeared from down below. Without as much as a bye your leave, she took up her position wedged between me and the steering box. I scratched her head and she purred her satisfaction. Then like a gentle mist rich with the aroma of night flowers, it came to me. After all my years of searching, at last I had found my place in life. Hugging Meggi while *Vega* glided along her route, I realized there was nothing else in this world, I would rather be doing.

Epilogue

Soft morning sunlight illuminated where I sat with the golden hues of a Malaysian island morning. The air has a silky feeling, deeply scented with the dusty savor of land and the sharp tang of salt from the open Sea. Sitting by the steering station with a fresh brewed cup of coffee in hand I savored such a rare morning.

Mosques provided the background music, each calling their faithful to the second Morning Prayer. What began with a single clear strong voice, quickly became a discordant cacophony of amplified sound as every mosque in town proudly joined in. Each with its own powerful loud speakers. All have the volume tuned as high as it will go.

Over the years while living and traveling in some of the world's most exotic places, I grew to treasure the call to prayer as both a great way to keep track of the time and a marvelous background accompaniment for the symphony of my daily life. That all pervading music, ritually repeated five times a day, is for me a distant echo from Samarkand and the mysterious splendor of *A Thousand and One Arabian Nights*. Although I doubt if these days Scheherazade's wardrobe would pass muster.

Depending on which direction I let my gaze wander this lovely morning presents either an idyllic island setting or something completely different. Just to the west, a few hundred meters off the stern of our 120 year old sailing vessel, is an uninhabited island. Golden brown in the morning light the island is alive with the sound of tropical birds and a million insects. There is only the hint of a green tree here and there to break its dry season monotony.

Such a peaceful setting, invites exploration. An invitation readily accepted by Meggi who took a cup of coffee, along with her mask and snorkel, and our dingy for an early morning investigation of this new anchorage. I can just see the tip of her snorkel as she happily delves into every cove and inlet.

Undoubtedly she will return later with another beachcomber's collection of shells and driftwood, her face beaming with the honest pleasure of her latest discoveries. I can easily picture her, bubbling over with tales of brightly colored coral gardens and strange colorful fish.

We just came out of the boat yard three days ago, with *Vega* freshly painted and a few minor repairs all neatly done. These days of peace and tranquility are a way of rewarding ourselves for once again surviving the boat yard. In the morning our short break comes to an end. Bright and early we will haul up the anchor and set sail, beginning another year of collecting and delivering. *Vega* will sail over seven thousand miles before we see this snug little anchorage again.

For the next three months we will be constantly on display, selling our T-shirts and spice packages, blatantly mooching and begging for the items needed to full fill our humanitarian commitments. Tons of school supplies and hundreds of Kits-4-Kids bags will flow into *Vega*. In Jakarta we will load even more school bags and all of the remaining medical supplies on our lists. By the time we began our deliveries, *Vega* will be so full we start sleeping out on deck.

Those deliveries will take us a little over five months and many thousands of sea miles to complete. Five months of reaching out to some of the most remote island communities on our planet. We make the deliveries, but the real heroes are our friends who provide the items we deliver.

Only the Beginning

If you enjoyed *The Vega Adventures* then read on for a sneak peek into *The Windsong Adventures*, another true story of adventure, romance, and the madness of a young man with a whole lot of "I want a boat" and no money who salvages an abandoned sailing boat hull from a beach in West Africa only to wind up crossing the Atlantic alone on a leaky old boat with rags for sails and a broken rudder.

"One of the most amazing true sea adventures I have ever read...skillfully spiced with a wonderfully naughty sense of humor."
Scott Murray, *SEA Yachting Magazine*

SHANE GRANGER

The Windsong Adventures

1976 - 1979

A Reef in Time

Another wave exploded with a thunderous roar against black jagged rocks not ten meters from our port side hurling tons of tortured white water high into the air. Within seconds, a sheet of angry spray slammed across where I perched precariously out on the end of Windsongs bowsprit. Distilled through the retort of fear, a raging torrent of raw adrenaline surged through my body. I was alternately cursing Fate, a woman with the sickest sense of humor since Torquemada developed his fully automatic laugh a minute fingernail extractor, and praying to any God who might be listening for deliverance from the nightmare of potential death and destruction surrounding me.

Franticly blinking the saltwater from my eyes, I desperately scanned the turbulent sea, anxiously searching for any path to salvation. Of one thing I was certain, we were trapped in every sailor's worst nightmare come true. The strong tidal currents that sweep unpredictably along West Africa's Gambian coast had drawn *Windsong* into the infamous Bijol rocks.

Only minutes before Abduli's frantic cries, "Rocks, Rocks, Mr. Shane! Save us! There be rocks everywhere!" had startled me from a deep dreamless sleep. Half naked I raced up on deck where it took me only a moment to realize not only was he right, but also thanks to the light of a full moon I could clearly see where getting out of such an ungodly mess alive and in one piece would require some sort of major miracle.

You see, Cape Bijol is a gigantic labyrinth of ship killing rocks and coral reefs extending almost 20 miles along the southern side of the Gambian coast and only God knows how many miles out to sea. The place is notorious for powerful currents and countercurrents, a rather convoluted section of seafloor that to this day remains uncharted.

Without hesitation, I turned *Windsong* hard on the wind in the direction of the open sea. The last thing I wanted to do was take the boat deeper into that maze of jagged rocks and coral flats. How we managed to deviate more than 20 degrees from our intended course and be thirty miles further south than I calculated, posed a mystery that could wait for later.

While Serge took the wheel, I headed for the bow sprite to have the best view forward. From there I would send steering instructions back to Serge via hand signals. Peggy and Abduli meanwhile busied themselves trimming the sails to compensate for my sudden course change. We had been sailing along peacefully almost dead downwind, now the boat would be close hauled, as tight on the wind as our ragged old collection of sails would allow.

Funny how some things stick in your memory, I raced out onto the bowsprit praying fervently for salvation. I have repented more times in my life than I can remember. Usually it's me gibbering like a gerbil, vehemently promising to be good and never again put buttons in the collection plate, while facing yet another dastardly experience with my knees knocking and heart pounding to beat the band. But I was never foolish enough to think it might make some sort of difference in the celestial scheme of things. I figure it as one of those things to do when there is no place left to run and you are fresh out of places to hide.

I seriously doubt there is a god around with nothing better, or more amusing, to do than follow my peccadillos with any interest. So it's not very surprising when I beg for salvation, my idea of salvation being that whatever it is scaring the bejesus out of me at the moment, should go play somewhere else and leave me alone in peace, I receive very little in the form of heavenly intervention, or even an anomalous guardian angel.

Then again, you never know, so best show willing, which of course I did, 'Oh dear God if you can see fit to bring us through this one safely I shall give up strong drink and promiscuous fornication forever. Well at least the strong drink, and that's a promise.' I most likely muttered a lot more gibberish along those lines, because from my new position out on the bowsprit I began to fully comprehend the ghastliness of our situation.

You see, we had inadvertently sailed into a small cove formed by the reef. I could easily see the cursed thing had us surrounded on three sides with vicious saw toothed rocks. The only sure way back to the safety of deep water would be to retrace our route. A course that would take *Windsong* right into the eye of the wind, something no sailing boat can do without tacking, and room to tack up wind was a luxury we did not have.

That left only one option, I must find a different escape route by picking our way between those hair-raising rocks and shoals. That would not be an easy task, especially at night with no depth sounder to help guide me. All I had to go on was the look of the water swirling around those malicious rocks, standing out black and jagged like an ageing sugar addicts teeth.

Frightened? Of course, I was afraid. I was scared half out of my wits by then. Not only did I stand to lose my boat on the second night after launching her, but also there was every possibility that none of us would survive the long swim to shore through all those jagged reefs and the pounding surf. If you think that's not enough to set a man poised out on the end of a bow sprit surrounded by horrors and dressed only in his knickers to trembling, well best think again.

With eyes burning from flying salt spray, I carefully studied the water ahead for any hint of where a deep channel might be hiding. Spotting a stretch of calm water between two out cropping's of rock, I waved my hand to the right, signaling Serge to turn a bit more to starboard. We would be sailing right at the limits of *Windsong*'s windward abilities, but it might just be possible. Slowly approaching what I devoutly prayed was the entrance to a channel, a confluence of moonlight, shadows, and rock gave the impression of a giant sharks maw filled with ragged teeth, one we were sailing right into.

The opening between those jagged killer rocks could not have been more than 50 meters wide, although from where I stood, with my knees knocking away in twelve-part harmony, it looked more like five meters. Once between the rocks there would be precious little room for error, reversing our route would be impossible.

From his place at the wheel, I could hear Serge yelling to me, asking if I was certain that was the best way to go. Well, I was not at all sure, because nothing gets a brain working faster than an honest dose of fear, although I have never been certain if those thoughts are the clearest or not, because fear also makes you see what you want to see, and then dive head long in that direction. But, be damned if I could see any other route open for us to take, So, once again I signaled a turn to the right. Within minutes, we were fully committed.

By the time our bowsprit slowly passed through what I hoped was an opening, I could hear my heart pounding, twenty to the dozen and I must have been a dull shade of blue from tightly tensing my stomach muscles and holding my breath, both at the same time. With the wind beginning to drop, we were moving along slowly, so slowly in fact I swear there were times we appeared to be going backwards. Once through the opening, the channel twisted slightly to port before running straight toward the open sea. I signaled this to Serge. The new course brought us several degrees off the wind, which I knew would reduce our leeway and perhaps even increase our speed.

Passing the first large rock down our port side, I could indeed see a passage through the rocks, even if it did look like the devils cauldron at teatime. We would be navigating down the center of a channel between two ragged lines of rock. From where I stood, that passage appeared to go on forever, although I doubt if it was more than 75 meters long. Between flying sheets of spray, I could just make out what appeared to be the end of it, and the blessed open sea beyond.

Waves were furiously crashing against the line of rocks I devoutly prayed would continue passing down our port side, sending explosive fountains of angry water thundering into the air, while above us the sky was clear and calm with only a few scattered trade wind clouds slowly drifting in the moonlight.

As we cleared the shelter of the entrance, the first blinding sheet of spray swept over where I stood. Within seconds, I was completely drenched. Squinting and blinking I strained my eyes to make out the channel ahead of us. Another wave thundered against the rocks on my left. Clinching my stomach muscles hard, I willed *Windsong* forward. At least for the moment, we were still floating and still sailing.

My heart skipped several beats as our keel briefly touched the bottom, slewing the boat several degrees to port. My throat was dry and my hands sweating as I quickly signaled Serge to adjust our course to starboard. Thankfully, the boat responded, returning to her route without touching again. We were sailing at a walking pace hard on the wind, as close as the boat and our ragbag of sails would allow. Up ahead I could see my chosen channel narrowing to about 20 meters wide. With waves, pounding against the rocks on both sides of us, the noise was deafening, while our passage to freedom seemed tighter than the knot in a misers purse strings.

I began to make out the signs of a wave driven current sloshing back and forth between the two lines of rock. As each new wave crashed against the rocks on our left water pouring over those rocks would set up a momentary flux that pushed us straight toward the rocks on our right, then as it drained away, the current would pull us back again to port. During the calm between waves, *Windsong* would bravely ease back into her position, dutifully maintaining the delicate balance we desperately needed to clear that hell bound passage and gain our freedom.

How long we glided along that nightmarish channel, I have no idea. It seemed like ages, but could just as well have been only moments. Having only a light breeze to work with the boat responded slowly, inching along at two or three knots. I waved my hand to the left, guiding Serge back into the center of the channel. Gradually the boat responded.

Without preamble, the channel began to widen, opening out into what appeared to be clear deep water. Advancing at the speed of a racing snail on Valium first the rocks on my left slid behind me, then the rocks on my right. *Windsong* began emerging into what looked to be safe water. Holding my breath, I watched as those cursed rocks slid further astern. When the rocks on our port side cleared the stern, someone on the aft deck began to cheer. Exclaiming in blasphemous amazement, I began to breathe again. Perhaps that was my mistake.

I had just begun to wonder if it might be safe to fall off the wind a bit more to port when I noticed the boat drifting too far to starboard. I signaled Serge to turn even further to port. With only meters separating us from deep water and freedom, our keel touched again with a resounding thud that echoed throughout the hull. I hastily signaled Serge to turn more to port. The response seemed to take forever. With the wind failing the boat reacted even more slowly than before.

Free now of the rocks along our port side, there was nothing to break the force of the waves as they rushed towards us beam on. The balance had been broken. As each wave rushed across our path, it relentlessly pushed *Windsong* toward the rocks on our starboard side. Taking a deep breath, I signaled Serge to turn hard a port and yelled for Abduli and Peggy to let out the sails. That would bring the boat onto a beam reach, which is her best point of sailing. It would also gain us separation from those cursed rocks on our starboard side.

While I waited for the result of that turn, I saw one of those sights alarming enough to freeze the blood of an Eskimo. A wave much larger than the others appeared out of the night, mercilessly boring down on us. Without the rocks on our port side to break its thrust, that wave would pick us up and fling the boat sideways like a rubber ducky in a bath tub. Screaming a string of curses in every language, I could think of, I grabbed the outer jib stay and hung on for dear life as that monster from the deep began to curl over at the top. And people wonder why I have so many gray hairs.

The stern of our boat was still clearing the rocks when the damn thing hit. The results were instantaneous and catastrophic. Mercilessly driven sideways, the aft portion of *Windsong*'s keel grounded with an all mighty grinding crunch. Within seconds, spun away from her route to safety, *Windsong* slammed broadside onto the waiting reef.

Another breaking wave smashed across her pushing us further onto the reef, where the boat solidly grounded on her starboard side. Waves from the open ocean were crashing against her, hurtling unfettered sheets of spray across the decks. The force behind that spray effortlessly ripped one of our sails to shreds. The scene came straight from Dante at his best, as each new wave pushed us further onto the reef with a thunderous crash followed by a bone-jarring crunch.

To find out more about
THE WINDSONG ADVENTURES follow us on
Facebook at "Historic Vessel Vega"

About the Author

SHANE GRANGER (1948- until his luck runs out) has been in love with the sea since he was seven years old. Having worked as a radio DJ, advertising photographer, boat builder, director of museum ship restoration, and bush pilot, he has always come back to the sea. Shane has sailed thousands of miles solo, most of that on a square-rigged brigantine he salvaged from a beach in West Africa – a vessel he once single-handedly sailed across the Atlantic without a functioning rudder.

After walking across the Sahara Desert, and being kidnapped by bandits in Afghanistan, his greatest ambition in life is to find a comfortable niche where he can enjoy the healthy benefits of monotony and boredom. He currently lives on an ancient wooden sailing boat with his partner Meggi Macoun and their cat Scourge.

Lightning Source UK Ltd.
Milton Keynes UK
UKOW04f1916070915

258236UK00001B/94/P